Collins | English for Exams

Practice Tests for
IELTS

T0340420

3

Published by Collins
An imprint of HarperCollins Publishers
Westerhill Road
Bishopbriggs
Glasgow
G64 2QT

HarperCollins Publishers
1st Floor, Watermarque Building, Ringsend Road,
Dublin 4, Ireland

First edition 2021

10 9 8 7 6 5 4 3 2

ISBN 978-0-00-845322-0

Collins® and COBUILD® are registered trademarks of
HarperCollins Publishers Limited

www.collins.co.uk/elt

A catalogue record for this book is available from the
British Library.

MIX
Paper from
responsible sources
FSC www.fsc.org **FSC™ C007454**

If you would like to comment on any aspect of this book,
please contact us at the given address or online.
E-mail: dictionaries@harpercollins.co.uk

 facebook.com/collinselt

 @CollinsELT

Authors: Louis Harrison, Rhona Snelling and Peter Travis
Editor: Celia Wigley
For the Publisher: Gillian Bowman and Kerry Ferguson
Typesetter: Jouve, India
Printed and bound in the UK using 100% Renewable Electricity at CPI
Group (UK) Ltd
Audio recorded and produced by ID Audio, London

Acknowledgements
P41 wastewater reuse system diagram adapted from ©
Commonwealth of Australia 2020 (CC BY 4.0); p50 table
adapted from 'Growth of global trade-related freight and
emissions to 2050' table, International Transport Forum
at the OECD; p71 graphs reproduced from Labour Force
Survey Household datasets, ONS (Open Government
Licence v3.0); p105 'Groynes' photo © CarlsPix/
Shutterstock; p127 diagram adapted from 'Life circle of
eel' drawing by Salvor Gissurardottir, August 2006
(CC BY-SA 2.5); pp175–7 IELTS Sample Answer Sheets
reproduced with permission of Cambridge Assessment
English © UCLES 2021.

The Publishers gratefully acknowledge the permission
granted to reproduce the copyright material in this book.
Whilst every effort has been made to trace the copyright
holders, in cases where this has been unsuccessful, or if
any have inadvertently been overlooked, the Publishers
would gladly receive any information enabling them to
rectify any error or omission at the first opportunity.

All exam-style questions and sample answers in this title
were written by the authors.

Contents

Introduction

Who is this book for?

Collins Practice Tests for IELTS 3 will prepare you for the IELTS test whether you are taking the test for the first time or re-sitting it. It has been written for learners with band score 5–5.5 who are trying to achieve band score 6 or higher. The book, with its answer key and model answers, has been designed so that you can use the materials to study on your own. However, the book can also be used as part of IELTS preparation classes.

Content

Practice Tests for IELTS 3 is divided into three sections. The first section contains an introduction, an overview of the IELTS test, and strategies for success in the test. The second section contains four complete Academic tests and two General Training tests for Reading and Writing. The third section contains a mini-dictionary, a full audio script, sample answer sheets, answer keys for the Listening and Reading components, and model answers for the Writing and Speaking questions.

Specifically, the book contains:

- Tips for success – essential advice for success in the test
- Overview of the IELTS test – a quick reference to IELTS whenever you need to remind yourself of what to expect on exam day
- Strategies for success – advice about how to tackle each of the components in the test
- Practice tests – four complete Academic tests and two General Training tests for Reading and Writing
- Mini-dictionary – definitions and examples of the most important high-level vocabulary from *Practice Tests for IELTS 3* (definitions are from Collins COBUILD dictionaries)
- Audio script – the full texts of what you will hear in the Listening and Speaking components
- Sample answer sheets – familiarise yourself with the answer sheets used in the Listening, Reading and Writing components of the IELTS test
- Answer keys – the answers for all the questions in the Listening and Reading components
- Model answers – example answers for the Writing and Speaking components, all of which would achieve the highest marks in the IELTS test

Recordings of the Listening passages, questions from the Speaking components and the model answers for the Speaking components can be found online at **www.collins.co.uk/eltresources**.

Other IELTS resources

This is the third book of practice tests. If you would like more practice tests, there are four more practice tests in *Collins Practice Tests for IELTS* (ISBN 978-0-00-749969-4) and *Collins Practice Tests for IELTS 2* (ISBN 978-0-00-759813-7).

Collins also offers a wide range of exam preparation books, including our Skills for IELTS series (*Reading for IELTS, Writing for IELTS, Listening for IELTS* and *Speaking for IELTS*) and our *IELTS Dictionary*. Please go to www.collins.co.uk/elt to find these and other resources.

Tips for success

Make a plan to succeed and start by following these tips.

- Register for the test early. If you are applying for university, check the application deadlines.
- Make sure that you register to take the test well before the deadline to ensure that your scores arrive on time.
- Find out the score requirements for the universities you want to apply for. Degree programmes that have minimum-score requirements typically post them on their admissions websites.
- Start to study early. The more you practise, the more you will improve your skills. Give yourself at least one month to complete all of the practice tests in this book. Spend at least one hour a day studying and don't give up. Remember, by using this book, you are on your way to high scores in the IELTS test!
- Time yourself when you complete the practice tests.
- Don't be afraid to make your own notes on the book. For example, writing down the definitions of words you don't know will help you remember them later on.
- Read or listen to the model answers as many times as you need to.
- In the Writing component, return to the questions and try to come up with new responses. Keep practising until creating responses within the time limits becomes easy for you.

Using the book for self-study

Having access to someone who can provide informed feedback on your answers to the Writing and Speaking questions is an advantage. However, you can still learn a lot working on your own or with a study partner who is willing to give and receive feedback.

Ideally, you should begin by working through the *Strategies for success* for each part of the test. Reading this section will help you know what skills are needed when doing the practice tests.

When you are ready to try the practice tests, make sure you attempt the Writing and Speaking tasks. These are skills that can only be improved through extensive practice. At the same time, you should aim to become well informed about a wide variety of subjects, not just those covered in the book. The IELTS Writing and Speaking components can cover almost any topic considered to be within the grasp of a well-educated person.

Practise writing to a time limit. If you find this difficult at first, you could focus first on writing a high-quality response of the correct length. Then you could start to reduce the time you take gradually until you are able to write an acceptable answer within the time limit. You should become familiar enough with your own handwriting to be able to accurately estimate the number of words you have written at a glance.

Model answers should be studied to identify the underlying approach and effect on the reader. Don't memorise essays or letters or attempt to fit a pre-existing response around another test question. By working through the practice tests in the book, you should develop the skills and language to effectively express your own responses to unseen test questions on the day.

Overview of the IELTS examination

The International English Language Testing System (IELTS) is jointly managed by the British Council, Cambridge ESOL Examinations and IDP Education, Australia.

There are two versions of the test:
- Academic
- General Training.

The Academic test is for students wishing to study at undergraduate or postgraduate level in an English-medium environment.

The General Training test is for people who wish to migrate to an English-speaking country.

The General Training test has two components, Reading and Writing, which are different from those in the Academic test.

The test
There are four components in the Academic test.

Listening	30 minutes, plus 10 minutes for transferring answers to the answer sheet. There are 4 sections in this part of the test.
Reading	60 minutes. There are 3 texts in this component, with 40 questions to answer.
Writing	60 minutes. There are 2 writing tasks. Your answer for Task 1 should have a minimum of 150 words. Your answer for Task 2 should have a minimum of 250 words.
Speaking	11–14 minutes. There are 3 parts in this component. This part of the test will be recorded.

Timetabling – Listening, Reading and Writing must be taken on the same day, and in the order listed above. Speaking can be taken up to seven days before or after the other components.

Scoring – Each component of the test is given a band score. The average of the four scores produces the Overall Band Score. You don't pass or fail IELTS; you receive a score.

IELTS and the Common European Framework of Reference
The CEFR shows the level of the learner and is used for many English as a Foreign Language examinations. The table below shows the approximate CEFR level and the equivalent IELTS Overall Band Score.

CEFR description	CEFR level	IELTS Band Score
Proficient user (Advanced)	C2	9
	C1	7–8
Independent user (Intermediate – Upper Intermediate)	B2	5–6.5
	B1	4–5

This table contains the general descriptors for the band scores 1–9.

IELTS Band Scores		
9	Expert user	Has fully operational command of the language: appropriate, accurate and fluent, with complete understanding
8	Very good user	Has fully operational command of the language, with only occasional unsystematic inaccuracies and inappropriacies. Misunderstandings may occur in unfamiliar situations. Handles complex detailed argumentation well
7	Good user	Has operational command of the language, though with occasional inaccuracies, inappropriacies and misunderstandings in some situations. Generally handles complex language well and understands detailed reasoning
6	Competent user	Has generally effective command of the language despite some inaccuracies, inappropriacies and misunderstandings. Can use and understand fairly complex language, particularly in familiar situations
5	Modest user	Has partial command of the language, coping with overall meaning in most situations, though is likely to make many mistakes. Should be able to handle basic communication in own field
4	Limited user	Basic competence is limited to familiar situations. Has frequent problems in understanding and expression. Is not able to use complex language
3	Extremely limited user	Conveys and understands only general meaning in very familiar situations. Frequent breakdowns in communication occur
2	Intermittent user	No real communication is possible except for the most basic information using isolated words or short formulae in familiar situations and to meet immediate needs. Has great difficulty understanding spoken and written English
1	Non user	Essentially has no ability to use the language beyond possibly a few isolated words
0	Did not attempt the test	No assessable information provided

Marking

The Listening and Reading components have 40 items, each worth one mark if correctly answered. Here are some examples of how marks are translated into band scores.

Listening   16 out of 40 correct answers: band score 5
23 out of 40 correct answers: band score 6
30 out of 40 correct answers: band score 7
Reading   15 out of 40 correct answers: band score 5
23 out of 40 correct answers: band score 6
30 out of 40 correct answers: band score 7

The Writing and Speaking components are marked according to performance descriptors.

Writing – Examiners award a band score for each of four areas with equal weighting:

- Task achievement (Task 1)
- Task response (Task 2)
- Coherence and cohesion
- Lexical resource and grammatical range and accuracy

Speaking – Examiners award a band score for each of four areas with equal weighting:

- Fluency and coherence
- Lexical resource
- Grammatical range
- Accuracy and pronunciation

For full details of how the examination is scored and marked, go to: **www.ielts.org**.

Strategies for success

Listening

This table shows the format of the Listening section of the IELTS Test.

	Number of questions	Number of marks	Number of speakers	Context	Timing	Write answers
Part 1	10	10	2	everyday social interaction	Approx. 30 minutes	on the question paper
Part 2	10	10	1			
Part 3	10	10	2–4	educational or training situation		
Part 4	10	10	1	academic topic		
Transfer of answers					10 minutes	on the answer sheet

You will receive one mark for each correct answer. Scores are then translated into the IELTS 9-band scale and can be whole bands (e.g. 6) or half bands (e.g. 6.5).

You will hear a range of accents from countries where English is the first language. Therefore, you will hear speakers from the USA, Australia, Canada and Great Britain.

The questions follow the order of the conversation or talk, so make sure you move through the questions in 'real time' as the recording continues.

Questions and required skills

The questions are presented through one of six task types. The six task types are:

1 Multiple choice (A, B or C)

What do you have to do?

Choose one* correct answer or one correct sentence ending for each question.
(*Sometimes you may need to choose more than one correct answer, but this will be specified in the test instruction if so.)

What language skills will you need?

1. Understand information about an everyday topic.

   You could listen to authentic English-language conversations in podcasts or on radio shows, but try to select shorter conversations rather than longer or more complicated ones. Listen and identify the topic, sub-topics and any general points of information. Make notes and then listen for a second time to check your ideas.

   You can also prepare for this task type by having as many conversations as you can in English. Choose five everyday topics, e.g. a course or subject, transport in your city, jobs that are suitable for students, health and fitness, a new hobby, and have a conversation with one person or two people, giving your thoughts on this topic. For example, why you want/don't want a new hobby, which hobbies might be interesting and what you would need for them, which hobbies you have tried and enjoyed/not enjoyed, which hobbies you would/ wouldn't recommend to your friends. Try to have as broad a conversation as possible and listen carefully to the other speakers. This will help you become familiar with the range of a topic, its typical sub-topics and the general points of information that are discussed between speakers.

2. Identify and use important information from the questions.

   Before the recording begins, you will have time to read the questions on the test paper. You can approach this in a similar way to questions on the Reading test. First, quickly skim read the questions (including the A/B/C options) to find out what the topic is, e.g. a new club or a customer order. Then scan the questions and look for important information about the context. For example, is someone complaining about an order they have placed or do they want to find out how to return an item? Underline the words and phrases that provide this information. The words you underline will likely be nouns, verbs or adjectives – words that carry meaning. You don't need to focus on grammatical words, such as articles or prepositions, as these offer less information about the topic or context.

When you listen to the recording, follow the order of the questions on the test paper and use the words and phrases you underlined to focus your attention. The speakers may use these words or other words that express the same meaning. Make a decision about which option best answers the question and choose your answer. Try to decide promptly as the conversation will be continuing whilst you choose your answers – it is important not to miss the next question and lose a mark. Repeat the process with each question.

3. Recognise the difference between general information and specific points.

You can practise this skill by listening to any English conversation (e.g. from a course book, a podcast, an online video) twice – the first time to practise listening for gist or general information only, and the second time to listen for specific information.

The first time you listen, make notes on gist information such as:

- How many speakers are there?
- What is their relationship? e.g. friends, colleagues, teacher and student
- Where are they? e.g. at home, at work, in a shop, in college
- What are they talking about? e.g. a subject they are studying, travel arrangements
- What is the purpose of their conversation? e.g. to make a decision, to discuss a problem

Before you listen a second time, imagine you are going to retell the conversation to someone. What additional information do you need to retell it?

Then listen a second time and make notes on specific information such as:

- How do the speakers feel and why? e.g. excited about their plans, dissatisfied about an experience at a restaurant
- What key words and phrases do the speakers use to express their feelings or give descriptions? e.g. a stressful journey, a peaceful location
- How does the conversation conclude? e.g. the speakers decide to take a new subject

As you practise this two-step approach and improve, try listening and carrying out both steps in one listening, not two. This will help you develop the listening skills required for the IELTS test.

4. Locate and understand specific information.

If the question asks about a *market*, think about language related to this topic (e.g. fruit, vegetables, stall holder, stall, haggle) and listen carefully for these words. You may or may not hear these *exact* words on the recording, but the important point is to start focusing your attention on the specific information that you need. It will prepare you to listen effectively. You can even jot down relevant words whilst listening and use these to help answer the question and/or check your answer.

Be aware that there may be information in the recording that is there to deliberately distract you from the correct answer. This is another skill that you will need to demonstrate – locating the relevant information and therefore the correct answer, and dismissing the irrelevant information and the incorrect answer. Careful reading of the question will allow you to choose between relevant and irrelevant detail. For example, the recording may describe the location of student accommodation, but if the question is about the student's opinion of the accommodation, then the location is not relevant to the question.

2 Matching

What do you have to do?

Match a set of numbered items to a set of options.

What language skills will you need?

1. Understand information about an everyday topic.

See *Listening 1 Multiple choice (A, B or C)*, point 1.

2. Locate and understand specific information.

> See *Listening 1 Multiple choice (A, B or C)*, point 4.

3. Recognise the relationship between two speakers and the context.

When listening for gist, one of the points to focus on is the relationship between speakers. You can assess the relationship in many ways, such as context, formality, expressions and intonation. Context is probably the easiest way to assess this relationship. Where are the speakers? What are they talking about? Do they know each other? You will hear a range of everyday topics and these could range from a conversation between close friends to an exchange between a hotel receptionist and a guest.

Formality can be assessed by how the speakers refer to each other (do they use first names or 'Mr/Mrs'?) as well as the expressions used. In informal conversations, speakers will use less formal language, like 'See you later', not 'I look forward to seeing you later'. In more formal conversations, where the speakers don't know each other, the speakers may use structures such as indirect questions (e.g. 'Could you let me know if ...?') and more formal expressions (e.g. 'I apologise for ... ') in order to be more polite. This is also reflected through intonation and tone.

4. Recognise different speakers' viewpoints.

This is similar to locating specific information except that you will need to pay close attention to *who* is giving the information or, in this case, the person expressing the viewpoint. Speakers in the Listening test may often have similar viewpoints, which can be expressed through paraphrasing or synonymous language, or they may have contrasting viewpoints and very different opinions.

You could prepare for this by listening to topical podcasts or news stories. Begin by noting the topic and then make notes on the different speakers' viewpoints – you could draw a smiley face for speakers who agree with the viewpoints being expressed and an unhappy face for people who don't agree, or you could note down key phrases that express their views.

3 Plan/map/diagram labelling

What do you have to do?

Complete the gaps in a visual presentation of information by selecting answers from a given list or by using a specified number of words.

> **Tip:** If there is a list of options, there will be more options than there are answers. Therefore you will <u>not</u> use all the options given.

What language skills will you need?

1. Recognise the type of the presented information.

For this task, you will need to comprehend the information presented in a plan, map or diagram. You can prepare for this by researching these three types and learning what distinguishes them.

A *plan* is a schematic drawing of how something like a building is made.

A *map* shows a specific area and the most important places within that area.

A *diagram* usually shows a process or how something works.

2. Understand a visual representation of information.

You will need to be able to understand the information within a plan, map or diagram in this task. Prepare for this by researching simple plans, maps or diagrams – you can go online and search for some examples of these in English. Choose one and write a title or a very short summary of what the plan, map or diagram is about, e.g. 'College interviews' or 'The map shows students where to go for the interview at college.' Then look at the labels (or the key information and details) on the visual representation and check you understand them. Use your dictionary to check any new language and/or write a new label in your first language.

These two activities will help you achieve a quick general understanding of the listening text as well as a more detailed understanding of the important details. You could even look at a plan, map or diagram in your first language and then translate a summary and all the key information into English.

3. Understand a gapped description in relation to the visual representation.

> Once you can understand a visual representation (see point 2 above), you will be better able to relate this to a text description. You can approach the description as a simple reading task – first, skim read the description to check that your assessment of the visual representation matches the description, and then look carefully at the gaps. Reading is the secondary skill being tested in the Listening section of IELTS. Decide which type of information is missing in the gaps. For example, is it a number or a word? Is it a place, a building or a street? Then go back to the visual representation and the key information you have identified, and start to match the gaps and the information. When you have completed the gaps, remember to quickly read through your answers again and check they make logical sense.

4. Understand language that expresses directions and the relationship between different locations.

> There are many ways in which the speakers will talk about the plan, map or diagram, but they will always use language relating to directions and locations.

> Use your dictionary to check the meaning of any new words in the list below. These relate to a map or plan. You could also add words and phrases to this list.

Common language

adjoining	next to
after you get there	north/south/east/west
anti-clockwise/clockwise	outside the …
beside	running alongside
if you go through the entrance	the second room on your right
just past there	when you see

---

4 Form/table/flow-chart completion

What do you have to do?

Complete the gaps in a piece of information by using a specified number of words or by selecting answers from a given list. The information is presented as a form, table or flow-chart (i.e. not a continuous block of text).

> **Tip:** Check your answers don't exceed the number of words stated in the instructions or you will lose marks.

What language skills will you need?

1. Recognise the type of the presented information.

> As in *Listening 3 Plan/map/diagram labelling*, you will need to comprehend the information in a form, table or flow-chart. You can prepare by researching these three types and learning what distinguishes them.

> A *form* shows information required for a specific purpose, such as an order form or a membership form for a gym.

> A *table* shows information in a simple grid of rows and columns with headings.

> A *flow-chart* shows a process or sequence of how something works. The chart will include different sections and directional arrows.

2. Understand a visual representation of information.

> You will need to be able to understand a form, table or flow-chart in this task.
> See *Listening 3 Plan/map/diagram labelling*, point 2.

3. Predict possible types of answers.

> Before the recording starts, use the time to read the information in detail. Look at the gaps and decide what type of information is missing. Use any headings or section names to help you. For example, is the missing word a name/noun, a measurement or an adjective? Make a note of the type of information you will need to listen for; if you think you will need to listen for a noun or name, write the letter 'n' next to the question or write the abbreviation 'no.' for answers that are numbers or measurements. When the recording starts, use these notes to focus your attention on the relevant details.

Tip: Contractions, e.g. *isn't, you're,* are not tested. Hyphenated words count as one word.

4. Locate specific individual words or phrases.

Use your predictions and notes from point 3 above to help you focus on the specific details, and words or phrases that fit the gaps.

Tip: The answers should be exactly the same words as on the recording. You don't need to change the words in any way to use them as answers.

5 Sentence completion

What do you have to do?

Complete the gaps (using a specified number of words) in a set of sentences.

Tip: The instructions will state the number of words and numbers allowed in your answers. You can write a number with numerals (e.g. 1,000) or words (one thousand).

What language skills will you need?

1. Skim read a short piece of text.

Before the recording begins, read the heading and skim the sentences. Think of the sentences as an incomplete summary of the conversation, so reading the sentences before listening to the recording means you will already have some very useful knowledge about the conversation before you listen to it.

The heading will tell you what the topic is and the sentences will give you more information about the specific points that the speakers will discuss. There could be up to ten sentences, so skim read them as quickly and efficiently as possible.

2. Identify key words in the sentences.

Read the sentences again and underline the key words. There will usually be two to three key words in each sentence. For example, *Trips depart on _____* . Identifying the verb *depart* as a key word means you can focus on listening for information surrounding the departure of a trip. The preposition *on* tells us that the answer will probably be a day, such as *Monday* or *every Tuesday*.

Tip: The task is not testing your general knowledge of the world so don't complete a gap using your own knowledge or speculation about a subject. The answers must be words or phrases from the recording.

3. Understand language that expresses causal relationships.

Many conversations include information about causal relationships, i.e. the relationship between an event, situation or action (a cause) and its consequence(s) (effect(s)).

Being aware of the language used to express cause and effect will help you to identify and understand the relationship between two things.

Use your dictionary to check the meaning of any new words in the list below. You could also add words and phrases to this list.

Common language			
affect	bring about	hence	the consequence of
another result of	consequently	lead to	therefore
as a result of	due to	owing to	thus

Tip: Poor spelling and grammar are penalised in the test – you will lose marks and receive a lower band score. Make sure your answers are spelt correctly and are grammatically correct.

6 Short-answer questions

What do you have to do?

Write short answers (the instructions will specify the number of words) for the questions.

What language skills will you need?

> **Tip:** Short-answer questions are usually used with monologues and are therefore common in Part 2 and Part 4.

1. Understand a variety of question types.

> The question words are the first words for you to focus on in this task. Underline the question words in each question and think carefully about the type of information that is required in the answer. For example:

> | | |
> |---|---|
> | *How long ... ?* | a period of time, e.g. three hours |
> | *Where ... ?* | a location |
> | *Which type ... ?* | an example from a group of things |
> | *How ... ?* | a manner or an approach / a description or an explanation |
> | *Who ... ?* | a person or group of people |
> | *When ... ?* | a specific point of time, e.g. next summer |
> | *What ... ?* | a specific thing, group or object |

2. Identify key words in the questions.

> This is similar to *Listening 5 Sentence completion, point 2.* However, with this task, the key words are in a set of questions rather than a set of sentences.

> After underlining the question words (see point 1 above), read the other words in the question and identify the key words. These will typically be nouns, verbs, or modals. Grammatical words like articles, prepositions or auxiliary verbs are unlikely to carry important information. For example:

> *How long is the bus journey from the city centre to the airport?*

> By identifying the above key words, you can focus your attention on the length of time (not the cost, for example) for a journey by bus (not train, for example) from one specific place to another specific place.

3. Brainstorm language before listening.

> Before the recording begins, and after you have identified key words, you may have a few seconds to quickly think about the language you might hear. For example, for the bus journey example in point 2 above, you could brainstorm a few words and phrases related to this – timetable, it takes about, every 15 minutes, get on/off, route. You may hear the language you have brainstormed, but you may not! Nevertheless, brainstorming is still a useful strategy; it deepens your focus on the information you need and also encourages you to be open and receptive to any relevant language you hear on the recording.

4. Listen for concrete facts, such as places, prices or times.

> In this task, the answers are usually concrete facts, such as addresses and street names, prices and costs, or dates, days and times. You can prepare for this task by listening to adverts online or on the radio. As you listen, make a note of the following:

> * name and/or location
> * price(s)
> * date/day/time.

> If possible, you could also make a note of other information such as telephone numbers, websites or special offers.

> Then look again at the list of concrete facts you identified and write questions for each of them. Try to think of two or more ways to ask for the information in the answer. This will help build your awareness of the different type of questions you may hear in the test.

> **Tip:** The recording will include information that is relevant to the questions as well as information that is irrelevant (and is therefore the incorrect answer). This is done to test your ability to listen correctly for specific information.

Academic Reading

This table shows the format of the Academic Reading section of the IELTS Test.

Timing	Number of passages	Number of questions	Write answers	Topics and styles
60 minutes	3	40	on the answer sheet	The topics are general interest and non-specialist. The passages are sourced from books, journals, magazines and newspapers, and are written in a variety of styles, e.g. narrative, descriptive or discursive/argumentative. At least one passage will contain a logical argument. There will be a simple glossary for any technical terms used in a passage. The passages may also contain visual elements, such as diagrams, graphs or illustrations.

Each question is worth one mark. Incorrect spelling and grammar will be penalised. Scores are then translated into the IELTS 9-band scale and can be whole bands (e.g. 6) or half bands (e.g. 6.5).

Unlike the Listening Test, no extra time is allowed for transferring answers to the answer sheet. This is to be done within the 60 minutes allowed for the Academic Reading Test.

Questions and required skills

The questions are presented through one of eleven task types. The eleven task types are:

1 Multiple choice

What do you have to do?

Choose answers (or complete sentences) from a number of alternatives, and write the correct letter of the answer on the answer sheet.

The number of required answers will be stated in the instructions. There are three possible formats:

- choose the best answer (i.e. only <u>one</u>) from four alternatives (A, B, C or D)
- choose the <u>two</u> best answers from five alternatives (A, B, C, D or E)
- choose the <u>three</u> best answers from seven alternatives (A, B, C, D, E, F or G).

The questions follow the order of the passage.

This task is used with any type of passage.

What language skills will you need?

1. Skim read a passage for general understanding.

   This is an essential skill for all English language students, whether taking the IELTS test or not. When skimming a passage, you are reading it quite quickly – you aren't trying to understand every individual word – and your aim is to get a general understanding of the passage. After skimming, you should be able to give a short summary of what it is about.

   To practise this, choose a passage you haven't read before; it could be a passage from a course book or an article online. Give yourself a time limit (two to three minutes) and set a timer. This will encourage you to read the passage faster than you might normally read it. Then write a few notes summarising the passage. If possible, work with a partner. You each skim read a different passage. Then take turns explaining your passage to each other.

2. Scan read for specific points of the passage.

> Unlike point 1 above, this skill requires you to locate specific points in the passage. You will be searching for a specific word, phrase or piece of information, such as an opinion or a result. The general topic of the passage is not important for this skill, usually because you have already ascertained that by skim reading previously. When you have found the specific point, underline or circle it. Then you can review that point against the question and decide if you have located the correct information and therefore have the correct answer.

2 Identifying information

What do you have to do?

Decide if a set of statements agree with the information in the passage, and write 'true', 'false' or 'not given' on the answer sheet.

The questions follow the order of the passage.

This task is used for passages that are more factual.

What language skills will you need?

1. Understand the different meaning of 'true', 'false' and 'not given' answers.

> It is important to understand what these three options mean; if you don't, you may unintentionally select the incorrect option:

> *true* = the information in the statement is included in the passage, and the statement agrees with the passage. In other words, the information is the same in both the statement and the passage.

> *false* = there is information about the topic of the statement in the passage, but the passage contradicts the statement.

> *not given* = the information in the statement is <u>not</u> included in the passage, and therefore the statement cannot be true or false.

2. Locate and recognise specific points of information in the passage.

> See *Reading 1 Multiple choice*, point 2.

> **Tip:** Remember to use only the information in the passage for your answers. This is a test of your reading skills, not your general knowledge of the world and other subjects.

3. Deal with unknown words in the passage.

> Whilst the Academic Reading test does not directly test vocabulary, it does indirectly test how broad your lexical knowledge is and how you cope with unknown words.

> Therefore, regular practice in expanding your vocabulary is an important habit for the IELTS test taker. Make sure you keep good vocabulary records and regularly revise new vocabulary to consolidate your knowledge. Try testing yourself. For example:

> - think of ten words related to the environment
> - write definitions or translations for language related to employment
> - use five new words in a conversation, an email or a message each day.

> When you meet an unknown word in a passage, try to first identify the type of word. Is it a noun or an adverb, for example? Then read the sentence with the unknown word again and think carefully about the overall meaning of the sentence. Can you guess what the word might mean? Use the sentences before and after to help you with more context. You can practise this with any passage from your course book or a passage online.

> **Tip:** It is highly unlikely that you will know the meaning of every single word in a passage, so use a strategy described above to help you work out the meaning.

3 Identifying writer's views/claims

What do you have to do?

Decide if a set of statements agree with the writer's views/claims in the passage, and write 'yes', 'no' or 'not given' on the answer sheet.

The questions follow the order of the passage. This task is used for discursive or argumentative passages.

What language skills will you need?

1. Understand the different meaning of 'yes', 'no' and 'not given' answers.

> As with *Reading 2 Identifying information* above, it is important to understand what these three options mean in order to select the correct one:
>
> *yes* = the views/claims of the writer agree with the statement and are therefore the same as the statement.
>
> *no* = the views/claims of the writer disagree with the statement and are therefore the opposite of the statement.
>
> *not given* = the views/claims of the writer on this point are not included in the passage and are therefore not verified or refuted.

2. Understand the narrative and flow of a discursive/argumentative passage.

> Similar to *Reading 1 Multiple choice, point 2*, select an appropriate passage and skim read it. Make notes on how the argument develops and/or tell a partner about the passage.

3. Locate and recognise opinions and ideas expressed by a writer.

> See *Reading 1 Multiple choice*, point 2.

> **Tip:** A writer's opinions and ideas are not facts!

4. Deal with unknown words in the passage.

> See *Reading 2 Identifying information*, point 3.

4 Matching information

What do you have to do?

Match a set of information with the lettered paragraphs/sections of a passage, and write the letters of the correct paragraphs/sections on the answer sheet.

(If a paragraph/section can be chosen more than once, this will be stated in the instructions.)

The questions don't follow the order of the passage.

This task is used with any type of passage.

What language skills will you need?

1. Identify the key words in the set of information.

> See *Listening 5 Sentence completion*, point 2.

2. Scan read for specific information in each paragraph/section of a passage.

> See *Reading 1 Multiple choice*, point 2.

> For this task you need to locate specific information in the paragraphs/sections of a text. You will not necessarily need to find information in every paragraph/section, but there may be more than one piece of information in a given paragraph/section. This task is used with a variety of texts as it tests a range of reading skills, from locating detail to recognising a summary or definition.

> The types of information you may have to find include an example, a reason, a definition, a description, a comparison, a summary or an explanation.

5 Matching headings

What do you have to do?

Match a set of numbered headings (with lower-case Roman numerals) to the correct paragraphs/sections (labelled alphabetically) of a passage, and write the numeral of the correct heading on the answer sheet.

(If a paragraph/section can be chosen more than once, this will be stated in the instructions.)

This task is used with passages that have paragraphs/sections with distinct themes or topics.

What language skills will you need?

1. Skim read a whole passage and recognise the main idea of each paragraph/section.

   You can practise for this task with any passage that contains a number of different paragraphs/sections. Look for suitable passages in your course book or find one online or in a newspaper. (Try to start with a passage of four or five sections and build up to one with around eight sections.) When you have found a suitable passage, skim read for overall gist. What is the writer's purpose in writing? For example, does the writer describe something or offer an explanation? Then skim read each paragraph/section and either identify the topic sentence or make a note of the main idea of that paragraph/section.

   In the IELTS test, you can identify the key words in the headings (see *Listening 5 Sentence completion, point 2*) and then try to match your notes to the list of headings.

   Tip: Remember that there are always more headings than paragraphs/sections.

2. Recognise the difference between the main idea of a paragraph/section and supporting ideas.

   Be aware that this task asks you to match the main idea of a paragraph/section to a heading, and not supporting ideas (unlike *Listening 4 Matching information*, which requires you to match specific information). A paragraph/section about a college programme may also include details about one or two classes, but these details are supporting information only; the main idea is the whole college programme.

   Tip: The topic sentence is usually the first sentence of a paragraph/section and it clearly states the main idea or message of that paragraph/section.

   Tip: You might not use every paragraph/section in your answers, and you might use one paragraph/section more than once.

6 Matching features

What do you have to do?

Match a set of statements or information to a list of features (labelled alphabetically) from the passage, and write the letter of the correct feature on the answer sheet.

(If some features can be chosen more than once, this will be stated in the instructions.)

This task is used with factual and opinion-based discursive passages.

What language skills will you need?

1. Identify the key words in a set of statements/information and a list of features.

   See *Listening 5 Sentence completion, point 2*.

   Tip: In the test, spend a few minutes thinking about synonyms of the key words and other ways that the ideas or concepts could be described.

2. Recognise the relationship between statements/information and features.

   Use the key words you identified to scan read the passage for synonyms and similar words or phrases. This will help you focus on the relevant information and not get distracted by irrelevant or distracting information. When you find language that appears to relate to the feature, underline or circle it and write the letter of the feature. (This helps you to easily pinpoint possible answers and avoids confusion with other features/

17

answers). Read through the statements/information and features again, and check your initial ideas. Does the statement/information clearly match a feature? If it does, choose this for your answer. If it doesn't, scan read again to find a better match.

7 Matching sentence endings

What do you have to do?

Match a set of sentence beginnings about the passage to a set of sentence endings, and write the letter of the correct sentence ending on the answer sheet.

The questions follow the order of the passage.

This task is used with any type of passage.

What language skills will you need?

Identify the key words in a sentence beginning.

> See *Listening 5 Sentence completion*, point 2.

> Identifying key words in the sentence beginning will help you to focus on, and possibly predict, what language and information the sentence ending might include. When practising this task type in this book, you could try covering the sentence endings and writing your own sentence endings. Then look at the set of sentence endings provided and check if any are similar to your own ideas.

Tip: Remember that there are more sentence endings than are needed. When you have completed this task, check for a second time that the extra sentence endings (i.e. the ones you did <u>not</u> match) don't match any of the sentence beginnings.

8 Sentence completion

What do you have to do?

Complete gapped sentences with a specific number of words taken from the passage, and write the words on the answer sheet.

The questions follow the order of the passage.

This task is used with any type of passage.

What language skills will you need?

1. Skim read a passage for general understanding.

> See *Reading 1 Multiple choice*, point 1.

2. Scan read a passage to locate specific words.

> See *Reading 1 Multiple choice*, point 2.

3. Choose the correct number of words for each gapped sentence.

> This may appear to be a simple skill or an obvious one, but it is imperative to read the instructions carefully and write only the specified number of words (from the passage) as your answer. If you write more or fewer words than are stated in the instructions, you will be penalised and lose the mark.

> Make a note of your answer and, before transferring your answer to the answer sheet, check that:

> 1. you have written the number of words specified in the instructions as your answer
> 2. the words in your answer are all included in the passage.

4. Deal with unknown words in the passage.

> See *Reading 2 Identifying information*, point 3.

9 Summary, note, table, flow-chart completion

What do you have to do?

Complete a gapped summary of a passage, either with a specific number of words taken from the passage or with the correct option from a list of answers, and write the words or answers on the answer sheet.

The questions do <u>not</u> follow the order of the passage.

This task is used with descriptive passages.

What language skills will you need?

1. Recognise the different types of summary.

> For this task, you will be asked to complete a summary that will appear in one of four formats. The same language skills are required for all four formats:
>
> *summary*: a short set of connected sentences with gaps.
>
> *note*: a short set or list of phrases with gaps.
>
> *table*: a table of information with gaps.
>
> *flow-chart*: a sequence of steps or stages connected with arrows with gaps.

2. Identify the type of word missing.

> After reading the gapped summary, think about what type of word is missing in each of the gaps. For example, is it a noun, an adjective or a number? Make a note of your ideas using a letter (*n* = noun) or an abbreviation (*adj* = adjective). Then, when you scan read for details, refer back to these notes to help you select the correct word (in the correct form) from the passage.

3. Locate and recognise details in the passage.

> See *Reading 1 Multiple choice*, point 2.

> **Tip:** The answers are usually found in one section of the passage.

10 Diagram label completion

What do you have to do?

Complete gapped labels (using a specified number of words) on a diagram described in the passage, and write the words on the answer sheet.

The questions do <u>not</u> follow the order of the passage.

This task is used with descriptive passages.

What language skills will you need?

> **Tip:** A *diagram* is a pictorial representation of the key points of a process or a description, e.g. a machine, a building.

1. Scan read for a detailed description in a passage.

> See *Reading 1 Multiple choice*, point 2.

> **Tip:** The description relating to the diagram is usually in one section of the passage.

2. Relate written information to a diagram.

> Similar to *Reading 1 Multiple choice, point 2*, select an appropriate passage and focus on the descriptive part. Read the description carefully and if there isn't a diagram, try to create one to express the information in the description. If there is a diagram, cover the description and write a short summary of the diagram.

These activities will help you to better understand the relationship between written information and the visual representation of the same information.

11 Short-answer questions

What do you have to do?

Write short answers (using a specified number of words taken from the passage) to questions about factual information in the passage, and write the answers on the answer sheet.

The questions follow the order of the passage.

This task is used with passages that contain a great amount of factual information.

What language skills will you need?

1. Identify the key words in the questions.

> See <u>Listening 5 Sentence completion</u>, point 2.

> After identifying the key words, think about the type of answers you will need to locate in the passage. For example, for the question *What <u>percentage</u> of <u>female employees</u> were <u>recruited</u> in the <u>last decade</u>?*, the answer will be a number. Note that the other key words tell you to focus on the type of employee (female, not male) and a specific timeframe (within the last ten years).

2. Skim read a whole passage and recognise the main idea of each paragraph or section.

> See <u>Reading 5 Matching headings</u>, point 1.

> After noting the main idea of each section, return to the questions and the key words. The questions follow the order of the passage, so work through each question in turn by matching information with your notes on the passage. For example, a paragraph or section about new female employees will relate to the question *What <u>percentage</u> of <u>female employees</u> were <u>recruited</u> in the <u>last decade</u>?*

3. Locate and recognise specific details.

> Following on from points 1 and 2 above, use your ideas about the type of answers to scan read the paragraph or section again and locate the specific words (or numbers) that answer the question. Underline or circle these words (or numbers), and refer back to the instructions to check how many words are allowed in your answer. Then choose the words (or numbers) for your answer.

Academic Writing

This table shows the format of the Writing section of the IELTS Test.

	Task 1	Task 2
Number of questions	1	1
The task	Write a description, summary or explanation of a visual representation of information provided as a graph, table, chart or diagram. For example, describe the stages in a process, summarise how something works or describe an event.	Write an essay to respond to the presented viewpoint, argument or problem.
Number of words to write	150 minimum	250 minimum
Timing (per task)	20 minutes (out of a total of 60 minutes)	40 minutes (out of a total of 60 minutes)
Write answers	on the answer sheet	

There are two tasks and both must be attempted. You do not have the option to choose a task.

A formal writing style should be used for both tasks.

Write a full and complete answer, and don't include notes or bullet points. Answers under the required minimum word limit will be penalised.

You are permitted to make notes on the question paper, but this will not be submitted with your answer sheet or included in the assessment of your answer.

You aren't permitted to copy language directly from the question paper.

Task 1 is worth half the marks of Task 2, as it is a shorter and comparatively simpler task.

Task 1 and Task 2 are assessed on four criteria:

1. Task achievement and response – You will be assessed on how appropriately, accurately and relevantly your answer addresses the task. In Task 1, you express the visual information provided in written form. The information relates to factual content only and there is no need to include your own opinions. However, in Task 2, you can include your own viewpoint and support it with examples from your own experience.

2. Coherence and cohesion – You will be assessed on *coherence* in your answer, i.e. whether it is well organised and links information and ideas in a clear and logical way. Your answer should also show *cohesion*, i.e. it uses appropriate connectors, pronouns and conjunctions to create a fluent piece of writing.

3. Lexical resource – You will be assessed on the range of vocabulary in your answer, and its accuracy and appropriacy for the task.

4. Grammatical range and accuracy – You will be assessed on the range and accuracy of grammar in your answer.

Scores are translated into the IELTS 9-band scale and can be whole bands (e.g. 6) or half bands (e.g. 6.5).

Questions and required skills

Task 1

What do you have to do?

Read and understand the information presented in the visual input (one or more graphs, tables, charts or diagrams) on the question paper. Write an account (in the style specified in the instructions) of the information using a minimum of 150 words.

The specified style for your answers is usually a description, a summary or an explanation.

Tip: Remember that Task 1 is worth half the marks of Task 2, so divide your time accordingly. Work on Task 1 for 20 minutes and work on Task 2 for 40 minutes.

What language skills will you need?

1. Identify the key words in the task and the most important information in the visual input.

Similar to many other parts of the IELTS test, the first skill you should utilise for this task is to read the question calmly and carefully. Under test conditions, it is easy to misread instructions or not read the complete task. Therefore, read the task a few times and underline or circle the key words. For example:

Summarise the information by selecting and reporting the main features, and make comparisons where relevant.

The above underlined key words show that what is required is a *summary* that focuses on the *main features* (not minor features) and may include *comparisons* if these features are *relevant* (there may be no need for comparisons).

Then look at the visual input and read the information there. The instructions state what the input is about, so you will already be aware of the context. Use the key words to locate the relevant information. This will help you prioritise relevant information over less important or irrelevant information.

Tip: Only include the most important points from the input so that your answer will be completely relevant. Minor points or surplus details should be omitted.

Tip: You can practise for this task by looking at graphs, tables, charts or diagrams online or in newspapers or magazines, and describing the information in them using a few sentences.

2. Plan and organise your answer.

Once you are confident that you know what you have to do, you can organise your response. Think about:

- What information needs to be included? (What does not need to be included?)
- What is the most logical order in which to present this information?
- How many paragraphs are necessary? One or more?

Tip: Plan your answer for Task 1 carefully.

1. [2 minutes] Read the instructions for the task and the visual information.
2. [4 minutes] Use your question paper to make a paragraph plan and rough notes on what information will be in each one.
3. [10 minutes] Write your full answer on the answer sheet. Use your paragraph plan and notes to help you.
4. [4 minutes] Review your answer and check for any grammatical, spelling or punctuation errors. Also, check your word count is over 150 words. Make corrections if necessary.

3. Use accurate and appropriate language to write about the information.

As your answer will be assessed on your *lexical resource*, you need to learn, expand and practise your vocabulary before the test. Start to create lists of useful language for Task 1 and continue to add to the lists when you come across new relevant words. For example:

Useful language

To compare information:
although
approximately
By contrast, ...
far less/greater than
However, ...
In contrast, ...
like
nearly as high as
On the other hand, ...
slightly less/more
the same as
twice as much as
whereas
while

To talk about percentages:
10% – one in ten, a tenth
19% – less than a fifth
20% – a fifth
25% – one quarter
35% – just over a third
48% – just under half

50% – (a) half
60% – six in ten
75% – three quarters
98% – nearly all

To talk about changes in numbers:
double / halve
expand / shrink
go up / go down
increase / decrease
rise / fall

To talk about data or numbers:
amount
figure
level
number
part
proportion
quantity
rate
share
size

Tip: Choose a word or phrase you don't know or don't use very often, and write it in a sentence. Repeat this with five other words or phrases. Use your dictionary to help you.

4. Check and correct your answer.

Like point 1, this is another essential skill that will prevent you from losing marks. When you have completed your answer, read through it again and go through a simple checklist such as:
- Have you responded to the task in full? Have you missed anything?
- Have you included all the relevant information? Is there anything irrelevant that you can remove?
- Is your answer well staged and logical?
- Have you used correct punctuation?
- Are there any grammatical errors?
- Are there any spelling errors?

Tip: Remember that your style should not be informal. This is a formal, academic context and your choice of language and style should reflect that.

Make any necessary corrections and review the answer again.

You can practise reviewing by making the review a regular part of any written work you produce. You wouldn't write an email to your teacher without quickly reviewing the content before sending it, and this is the same – but even more important! When you complete any piece of written work, read it again for errors or swap your work with a friend.

Peer checking is a very useful and productive way of developing your reviewing skills. When you read your friend's work, you are assuming the role of the reader (and the teacher). If your friend's work is well written, then it will be fluent and easy to read, and you will have no problems understanding the overall content. If the handwriting is untidy or there are grammatical errors and spelling mistakes, this will slow down your reading and it will make the work difficult to understand. Underline or circle the words or phrases that gave you problems and discuss these with your friend. Then you can both make any necessary corrections to your work and swap answers again for a final peer check. It is a great way to improve and develop your writing in a non-threatening environment, and will make you feel better prepared for the actual IELTS Writing test.

Tip: Keep a list of language errors that you often make. For example, the spelling of certain words, omitting an article, not using separate paragraphs for different ideas, and so on. Use this as your own personal checklist for written work when practising for the IELTS Writing test.

Task 2

What do you have to do?

Read and understand the task and the topic on the question paper. Write a discursive answer that includes issues that are relevant to the topic using a minimum of 250 words.

> **Tip:** Remember that Task 2 is worth double the marks for Task 1, so divide your time accordingly. Work on Task 1 for 20 minutes and work on Task 2 for 40 minutes.

What language skills will you need?

1. Identify the key words in the task and the given topic.

Similar to *Writing Task 1, point 1,* you should calmly and carefully read the task and topic. This will consist of a few sentences that present and describe, for example, a specific viewpoint on a topic. Underline or circle the key words. For example:

Some people _choose not to eat meat or any food_ derived from _animals_.

They believe it is a _good choice for their own health_ and that it will also have a _positive impact on the world_.

The topic here is veganism (i.e. the practice of abstaining from animal products in your diet) and animal rights, and the viewpoint is that of a vegan.

> **Tip:** You don't need to agree with the presented viewpoint – or disagree with it! You will be assessed on the presentation of your viewpoint, _not_ the viewpoint itself.

The task will ask you to discuss this viewpoint and present your opinions. Unlike Task 1, your personal opinions and experience are required here. You viewpoint may or may not be the same as the one given, or you may partially agree with it – there is no right or wrong answer. The important point is that you present your personal viewpoint well, explain your opinions clearly and logically, and give examples from your own knowledge or experience.

2. Plan and organise your answer.

> **Tip:** The topic is highly likely to be one that you have encountered before, whether through your English language class or in your daily life. It won't be an unfamiliar topic requiring specialised knowledge or vocabulary.

Similar to *Writing Task 1, point 2,* planning is the next important stage in preparing your answer. For Task 2, it is a good idea to think quietly for a couple of minutes and brainstorm your thoughts about the viewpoint. You can make notes on the question paper or draw a simple mind map to start accessing and organising your ideas. Then review your notes or mind map and remove any points that are not relevant to the topic or task. Finally, you can start to organise the remaining relevant ideas into a paragraph plan.

> **Tip:** Plan your answer for Task 2 carefully.

1. [2 minutes] Read the instructions for the task.
2. [2 minutes] Brainstorm your ideas on what you can include in your answer.
3. [8 minutes] Use your question paper to make a paragraph plan and rough notes on what information will be in each one.
4. [20 minutes] Write your full answer on the answer sheet. Use your paragraph plan and notes to help you.
5. [8 minutes] Review your answer and check for any grammatical, spelling or punctuation errors. Also, check your word count is over 250 words. Make corrections if necessary.

> **Tip:** Start to get familiar with roughly how many lines and/or pages you use. This will make it easier for you to plan the scope of your answer as well as help with timing in the IELTS Writing test.

3. Present relevant evidence or examples to support your ideas.

As part of your planning, you will have brainstormed and/or made notes on examples to support your ideas. Wherever possible, do try to give an example to support or illustrate your ideas and opinions, but make sure that the examples are relevant to the task and the topic. These can be personal experiences that you have had. For example, perhaps you or someone you know has tried a vegan diet or lifestyle and so you could include your/their experience of this. Alternatively, you may have seen a video or listened to a podcast about diets, the food chain, animal rights or another closely related topic, and you could therefore include some relevant and interesting information from these sources.

Tip: Keep your answer relevant to the topic. Including irrelevant details will lose you marks for *Task achievement and response*.

To practise for Task 2, you could write a paragraph giving your viewpoint on different topics, remembering to support your viewpoint with examples and evidence from your own experience. You could choose your own idea for a topic or try one of the examples below:

Education – the best age to learn a new subject
Environment – an individual can have a global impact
Family – it is challenging to work in a family business
Sports – anyone can be a good sportsperson with practice
Technology – it improves our lives at work and at home
Travel – experiencing other cultures is the best way to learn about yourself

Writing these paragraphs will help you get into the habit of naturally supporting your viewpoint with evidence, as well as developing the skill of thinking in a more critical way about topics. This skill will prove useful in all academic and professional contexts.

4. Use accurate and appropriate language to write about the topic.

Tip: Read the task carefully. If it is about a specific area of technology, do <u>not</u> write a general answer on technology.

As with *Writing Task 1, point 3*, your answer will be assessed on your *lexical resource*, so your choice of language is an important part of the task. It will also help you to present your viewpoint and structure your answer well.

Try to develop lists of useful language for Task 2 and add to these when you come across new relevant words or phrases. For example:

Useful language

To present your viewpoint:
By contrast, ...
In my opinion, ...
In my personal experience, ...
In spite of the fact that ...
It does not necessarily follow that ...
It follows that ...
It is also true that ...
It is my belief that
There are many examples of ...
There is no/little doubt that ...
Therefore, it appears that ...

To talk about pros and cons:
A key benefit/drawback ...
Another positive/negative result of ...
One noticeable trend is ...

One of the advantages/disadvantages is ...
The best thing about ...
The main advantage/disadvantage of ... over ... is ...
The positive/negative aspect of ...
The positive/negative impact of ...

To talk about groups of people:
clients
contestants
customers
humans
individuals
members
participants
passengers
visitors

Tip: Choose three phrases to present your viewpoint and three phrases to talk about pros and cons, and write a short piece on one of the example topics in *Writing Task 2, point 3*.

5. Check and correct your answer.

See <u>Writing Task 1, point 4</u>.

Speaking

This table shows the format of the Speaking section of the IELTS Test.

Part	The task	Timing (per part)	Timing (total)
1 Introduction and interview	Answer general questions about yourself and some everyday topics.	4–5 minutes	11–14 minutes
2 Long turn	Read a topic card. Prepare and give a talk about it. When you have finished your talk, answer the examiner's questions.	3–4 minutes (including preparation time)	
3 Discussion	Answer further questions related to the topic of Part 2.	4–5 minutes	

This is an interactive test, where your spoken interaction with the examiner is assessed. It is very similar to a real-life interaction with another English speaker.

The examiner is a certified IELTS examiner and qualified teacher. All examiners are approved and trained to deliver and assess the test.

Your test will be recorded for the purpose of assessment only.

The IELTS Speaking test will take place by video call or in a separate room with the examiner, and usually another examiner known as the *interlocutor* will be present. The interlocutor will not take part in the test and will not ask you any questions. Their role is to observe and assess.

The examiner's questions are taken from an official list, so all the questions are appropriate for the IELTS Speaking test and are of a consistent level of difficulty.

The IELTS Speaking test is assessed on four criteria:

1. Fluency and coherence – You will be assessed on *fluency*, i.e. your ability to speak continually (i.e. without many hesitations, pauses or repetitions) and at a standard pace (not very fast or very slow). Your answer should also show *coherence,* i.e. you are able to connect your ideas and language in a logical and clear manner whilst speaking, for example, using cohesive devices (such as connectors and conjunctions) within and between the sentences of an answer.

2. Lexical resource – You will be assessed on the range of vocabulary you use and the accuracy of your usage. For example, you should use a broad range of vocabulary that is appropriate to the topic and/or task. You should also demonstrate your ability to interact in a conversation and to paraphrase when necessary.

3. Grammatical range and accuracy – As for *Lexical resource*, you will be assessed on the range of grammatical structures you use and the accuracy of your usage, for example, the length and complexity of your sentences, and the number of grammatical errors you make.

4. Pronunciation – You will be assessed on your ability to produce comprehensible speech that the examiner will be able to understand easily. For example, an answer that contains incorrect pronunciation of words, incorrect sentence stress, or language from the speaker's first language will receive a lower score.

Scores are translated into the IELTS 9-band scale and can be whole bands (e.g. 6) or half bands (e.g. 6.5).

Questions and required skills

Part 1

What do you have to do?

Listen to the examiner introduce himself/herself and then confirm your own identity (i.e. say your name). Answer the examiner's questions about everyday topics, e.g. home, family, work, studies or interests.

What language skills will you need?

1. Understand and answer questions about everyday topics.

Part 1 is designed to settle you into the task and allow you and the examiner to introduce yourselves. The questions will all be about everyday topics and will be similar to questions you might ask, or be asked, when meeting someone new.

You can practise for this by working with a friend and taking turns to ask each other simple questions (e.g. about your home, family, work, studies or interests) and giving your answers. Alternatively, you could write a question for yourself and set it as an alarm or reminder on your mobile for another day. Then, when the alarm/reminder goes off, you can answer the question as spontaneously as you can.

Tip: Don't worry if you are nervous at the start of the IELTS Speaking test. The questions in Part 1 are intended to help you relax and do your best.

2. Express opinions or give information on everyday topics.

Although the questions in Part 1 are relatively straightforward, make sure you give full answers using complete sentences. For example, the answer *I have a big family* is too short and does not give you the opportunity to demonstrate your lexical resource or grammatical range. A better answer might be:

I come from a very large family and I have five siblings. I'm the eldest and I help to take care of my younger sister, who's at junior school. Most of my extended family live nearby and we meet up all the time.

Tip: A relevant longer answer allows you to demonstrate the four criteria on which the IELTS Speaking test is assessed (i.e. Fluency and coherence, Lexical resource, Grammatical range and accuracy, Pronunciation).

Remember that your answer will be assessed according to the language you choose to use as well as the way you structure your reply and interact with the examiner. Therefore, it is advisable to learn useful phrases to include in your response. For example:

Useful language

To ask the examiner to repeat a question:
Could you repeat the question, please?
Sorry, would you mind repeating the question?

To ask the examiner to clarify a question:
I'm sorry, but I'm afraid I didn't understand the question.
Sorry, could I clarify what you mean? Do you want me to ... ?

To talk about yourself:
At the moment, I'm taking classes at ...
I grew up in ...
I'm currently working as a ...
I'm hoping to ...
In my case, ...
I've been living in ... for/since ...

To give yourself 'thinking time':
I'd have to say that ...
That's an interesting question ...
Well, let me see.

Tip: Don't forget that you are allowed to ask the examiner to repeat a question or to request clarification of a question or word.

Part 2

What do you have to do?

Read the instructions on a topic card and prepare to give a talk on the specified topic. Talk for one to two minutes about the specified topic. Listen to the examiner ask one or two additional questions on the same topic, and respond to these questions.

What language skills will you need?

1. Identify key words on the topic card and plan a response.

As for *Writing Task 2, point 1,* you should calmly and carefully read the topic card and, if necessary, ask the examiner for clarification, for example, if you don't understand a word on the topic card or you aren't sure of the oral instructions you have been given.

Then you can start to prepare your response. You have one minute for this and you will be given a pencil and paper to make notes for your talk. Firstly, underline or circle the key words on the topic card, including the bullet points. For example:

Describe your <u>favourite TV show</u>.

You should say:

* the <u>name</u> of the programme and <u>where it is set</u>
* what <u>kind</u> of programme it is
* what it is <u>about</u>

and explain <u>why you enjoy it</u>.

Then make a short list or a simple mind map of the information you want to include in your talk. If you have time, you could also note specific examples or language relevant to the topic. Add numbers to your notes or mind map so that you know the order of the points you will make in your talk.

Tip: Your notes will <u>not</u> be included as part of your assessment, so they don't need to be neat or clear for anyone else to read.

The examiner will tell you when one minute has passed and you must stop making notes. The examiner will then ask you to begin your talk.

2. Use appropriate language for the topic.

You can prepare for this by making vocabulary learning a key part of your general language learning as well as your revision for the IELTS exam. One way of doing this is to revise vocabulary you have learned and continue to add more words and phrases to sets of words. For example, you could add the following phrases to the topic of employment:

achieve work-life balance
aim for a promotion
get a pay rise
have the opportunity to travel
join a new company
receive a good benefits package

You should also try to read English language materials extensively. You could read online articles, short novels, newspapers or even social media accounts. The more reading you do, the greater your exposure to vocabulary and grammar in a natural context. This will, in turn, help you to increase your vocabulary as you will need to look up new words or check meanings. You could even read something and then create a vocabulary list or mind map of language connected to the topic.

Tip: As for Writing Task 2, you can draw on your own experience and include examples or evidence from your own life in this part.

3. Organise your ideas coherently and logically.

Remember that you are being assessed not only on the language you use, but also the way you present and order your ideas to the examiner. This is important in real life; the ability to present a point coherently and clearly, and in a way that is easy for the listener to understand, is essential in many academic and professional settings.

You can manage and structure the flow of your talk using the language below:

Useful language

To begin and introduce your talk:
I'd like to talk about …
I've chosen to present the topic of …
May I begin now?

To move on to another point:
As for …
I'd like to also consider …
Let me now talk about …
Moving on to …

To give examples or offer further explanation:
A good example of this is …
Another thing is …
As an example, …
In other words, …
To better explain this point, …
To illustrate this point, I'd like to tell you about …

To conclude your talk:
So, all in all, …
To conclude then, …
To sum up, …
Thank you for listening to my talk.

Tip: Make sure you use the notes you made for your talk and make sure you include all the points on the task card.

4. Speak at length on a given topic.

Including the **Useful language** in *Speaking Part 2, point 3* will help you plan the timing of each stage of your talk. This will ensure you give an answer of the required length, rather than one that is too short and doesn't allow the examiner to observe your spoken skills and language competence.

As a guide, the maximum times allowed for the stages in your talk are:

i)   15 seconds   introduce and begin your talk

ii) 90 seconds   talk about each of the three bullet points

or

ii) 30 seconds   first bullet point and details

iii) 30 seconds   second bullet point and details

iv) 30 seconds   third bullet point and details

v)   15 seconds   conclude your talk and thank the examiner

Tip: The examiner will tell you when your two minutes have passed and you will then need to end your talk.

You can practise for this talk by carrying out a similar speaking task by yourself or with a friend. Pick a topic from the list below and give yourself 30–60 seconds to prepare and make notes or create a mind map. (You can use the timer on your mobile phone or ask a friend to time you and tell you when the time has passed.)

- a book/film you recently enjoyed
- a person who has inspired you
- a place you like to visit
- a sport or activity you like doing
- a subject you enjoy learning

Remember to include some of the **Useful language** from *Speaking Part 2, point 3,* so refer to this list and choose some suitable phrases to include in your talk. Then give your talk for at least one minute (again, use the timer on your mobile phone or your friend can tell you when the time has passed) and give extra information and details when possible. You may find it difficult to talk for that long or you may find it easy; either way, practising the timing will help you become better aware of the amount of speaking required for the IELTS Speaking test.

Take turns to practise giving a talk with a partner. When it is your time to listen, tick the phrases in the **Useful language** list that your friend uses. You can even note down good examples of vocabulary and grammar (e.g. 'the book was recently adapted into an award-winning film') and any errors that you observe or any points that weren't clear. If you are practising by yourself, record your talk on your mobile phone. Then you can listen back to your talk and assess it yourself on the length, the **Useful language** phrases used and any language errors.

Part 3

What do you have to do?

Listen to the examiner ask further questions that are related to the topic in Part 2 but allow for greater depth of discussion, and then respond to these questions.

What language skills will you need?

1. Understand and answer abstract or detailed questions on a topic.

As for *Speaking Part 1, point 1,* you will need to respond to the examiner's questions. In this part, the questions will be more complex (compared to the ones in Part 1) and will require you to give a longer and more considered response.

You can practise for this by choosing a topic from *Speaking Part 2, point 4* (or selecting another common topic) and having a discussion with a friend. Try to ask each other questions that require the other person to express their viewpoint.

Tip: If you don't understand a question or a word in the question, remember you can ask the examiner to explain and clarify.

2. Express your opinions on a topic and speculate about more abstract ideas.

This skill is one that we use frequently and easily in real life as it is natural to express our opinion on topics or make speculations about something. This helps us to develop our thoughts and our own understanding of a topic. As in real life, you may have a number of different thoughts about a topic or you may completely disagree with another person's viewpoint. In Part 3, you need to express or explain your thoughts or make speculations; there are no right or wrong answers.

In the IELTS Speaking test, you can present and organise your thoughts using the phrases below:

Useful language

To agree with an opinion:
I couldn't agree more.
That's my view exactly.
Yes, I think that's true.

To partially agree with an opinion:
I agree with that to an extent. However, ...
I don't entirely agree because I feel that ...
I think that depends on ...

To disagree with an opinion:
I'm afraid that isn't an opinion I share.
I'm not so sure about that. I'd say that ...
I wouldn't say that is necessarily true.
To be (perfectly) honest, ...

To talk about the future and probability:
I'd say it's definitely true that ...
I'm fairly certain that ...
It seems unlikely that ...
It's doubtful whether ...
It's likely that ...

To make general statements:
In general, ...
In my country, most people ...
It depends on the circumstances but ...
It's widely accepted that ...
Many people believe that ...

Tip: You can practise for this by selecting phrases from the categories in **Useful language** above and completing them with your own opinions about different topics.

Test 1

LISTENING

PART 1   *Questions 1–10*

Questions 1–3

Choose the correct letter, A, B or C.

1   Which special event takes place in September?

   A   their mother's birthday

   B   their parents' wedding anniversary

   C   their father's birthday

2   On Saturday evening the people attending the workshop

   A   talk about their artwork.

   B   listen to a talk.

   C   spend some time painting.

3   The people attending the workshop

   A   have to provide their own food.

   B   do not have to pay extra for meals.

   C   get a discount if they supply their own food.

Questions 4–10

Complete the form below.

*Write **NO MORE THAN TWO WORDS AND/OR A NUMBER** for each answer.*

Swansfield Painting Weekend **Booking Form**

Name: John Meacher

Address: **(4)** _____, Blandfield

Postcode: **(5)** _____

Preferred technique:

☐ watercolour

☐ **(6)** _____

☐ oil

☐ pen and ink

Dates:

☐ 17–19 July

☐ **(7)** _____ August

☐ 11–13 September

How would you describe your level? **(8)** _____

Do you have any special dietary requirements?

☐ vegetarian

☐ vegan

☐ allergies

☐ other: I don't eat **(9)** _____

Discount code: **(10)** _____

PART 2　　　　　*Questions 11–20*

02

Questions 11–15

Complete the notes below.

*Write **NO MORE THAN TWO WORDS AND/OR A NUMBER** for each answer.*

Notice of Traffic Re-routing

The re-routing plans are an attempt to reduce traffic during

(11) _____.

Stage 1 will commence on (12) _____.

Please send us your views of the project by (13) _____.

In order to keep traffic moving, access to the High Street will be

(14) _____.

(15) _____ will not be allowed on the High Street.

Questions 16–17

Choose TWO letters, A–E.

Which **TWO** roads will not be affected by the changes?

    A Malvern Road

    B Lincoln Road

    C Hazelhurst Road

    D Elmdon Avenue

    E Botteville Road

Questions 18–20

Choose THREE letters, A–G.

Which **THREE** groups are unhappy about the project?

    A emergency services

    B local residents

    C shopkeepers

    D pedestrians

    E delivery drivers

    F cyclists

    G parents

PART 3   *Questions 21–30*

03

Questions 21–22

Choose the correct letter, A, B or C.

21 What is Stephen's problem?

   A He cannot finish assignments on time.

   B He is not very organised.

   C His friends are getting better results than him.

22 The counsellor believes that some students at university

   A are not used to taking responsibility for their studies.

   B often need more help from their teachers.

   C find it difficult to ask for help.

Questions 23–25

Choose THREE letters, A–G.

Which **THREE** things does Stephen have a problem with?

   A staying out late with friends

   B getting anxious about his assignments

   C not having enough time

   D not having access to the study materials he needs

   E spending too much money

   F feeling lonely

   G deciding what is important

Questions 26–30

Complete the sentences below.

*Write **NO MORE THAN TWO WORDS** for each answer.*

Suggestion	Purpose
Calendar	It will provide an **(26)** _____ of the year. It will help you remember important dates.
Diary. Get one with **(27)** _____ per day.	Use this to **(28)** _____ the week. The best time to write in it is **(29)** _____ .
Write a to-do list.	Completing the tasks will make you feel **(30)** _____ .

PART 4   *Questions 31–40*

04

Questions 31–34

Choose the correct letter, A, B or C.

31 In the past, scientists believed that our brain

   A developed new cells after adulthood.

   B was left unprotected after an injury.

   C stopped developing at a certain time in our lives.

32 The latest research shows that our brains

   A have become more effective at learning new skills.

   B continue to change throughout our lives.

   C work in a similar way to a computer.

33 What did Paul Bach-y-Rita claim his research showed?

   A The brain can develop new neural connections to enable sight.

   B Brain scans can help blind people see.

   C There were a number of causes of sight loss.

34 Scientists working with taxi drivers

   A set them certain memory tests.

   B compared their brains to those of other drivers.

   C spent years doing their research.

Questions 35–37

Complete the sentences below.

Write NO MORE THAN ONE WORD for each answer.

35 Experiences gained when we _____ can lead to new connections being formed in the brain.

36 The elderly can help themselves by doing _____ training exercises.

37 Changing the _____ we use for everyday activities can have an impact on our brain.

Questions 38–40

Choose THREE letters, A–G.

Which **THREE** things should make us cautious about the possibilities of neuroplasticity?

    A Successful experiments have not been repeated.

    B Patients with brain damage have to work extremely hard to achieve results.

    C Neuroplasticity is a recently discovered phenomenon.

    D There are thousands of connections in the brain we do not understand.

    E We cannot always be sure that treatments will work.

    F We cannot all expect to play a musical instrument.

    G To some extent, success is dependent on how old we are.

READING

READING PASSAGE 1

*You should spend about 20 minutes on **Questions 1–14**, which are based on Reading Passage 1 below.*

Grey water

In Abu Dhabi, where fresh water sources are very limited, sustainable water management is a high priority. The region receives on average just 120 millimetres of rainfall every year but the country is seeing demand for water increase by almost 40% annually. In this situation, it is clear that Abu Dhabi needs to boost the efficiency of water use by increasing water recycling and using treated water safely. An example of how this can be done can be seen at one of Abu Dhabi's airport hotels, which is saving a quarter of its water by recycling grey water. The hotel's new grey water recycling system is reported to save 735,000 litres of water per month, or 60 litres for every one of its guests.

Every building where people live or work, such as homes, hotels, schools and offices uses two types of water, potable and non-potable. Put simply, potable water is drinking water and non-potable water is used for washing and cleaning. Non-potable water is further divided into grey and black water. Black water is waste water that has been contaminated because it has been used to carry away human waste from toilets, for example, and cannot be reused without extensive biological or chemical treatment. Grey water, however, requires less treatment prior to reuse, and although it cannot be used for drinking, as in the case of the hotel, it can help make significant savings to water usage by being used again for different purposes.

Grey water usually comes from showers, washing machines, sinks, dishwashers, and so on, and because of this it contains fats and oils from products such as soap and washing powder as well as flakes of skin and food waste. It typically makes up approximately 6% of a household's waste water but contains fewer harmful bacteria and less nitrogen than black or waste water. However, if it is recycled properly, around 70 litres of drinking water per person per day can be saved by domestic households. To separate grey water from black water, a separate water system is needed in the building because different pipes are required to keep grey water away from the contaminated water and flow it into the recycling process.

When the grey water undergoes biological cleaning, the water is collected from various sources around the house and fed into a course filter and surge tank. This serves two purposes: first of all, a valve regulates air and water flow into the surge tank so that an even flow and pressure is maintained. This is important for the filtering process to work properly and ensure an even flow of grey water through the filter. The water is then pumped into a second filtration tank, which contains natural materials. In this second tank, the water passes through different layers. The first filtration layer is made up of sand, which traps larger waste particles between the grains. Below this layer there are other layers made up of soil, finer sand and then coarse sand. Each layer traps more and more waste, thus purifying the water as it passes through. A lot of the purifying takes place in the soil layer, where microorganisms feed on the organic waste in the grey water and reproduce. Finally, the water flows through gravel or small stones to allow it to drain out of the system.

It is then pumped into a UV tank for a final mechanical treatment. In the UV tanks, ultraviolet light sterilises the water by killing any remaining microorganisms. Further filtration may also be applied after this. At this point, the water can be reused, not for drinking but for flushing toilets, or outdoor uses like washing the car or watering plants.

In contrast, the mechanical process for treating grey water is much simpler. It usually involves collecting the water from sinks, showers, etc. and passing it through a series of filters, each with a membrane that is finer than that of the previous filter. Chemicals, usually chlorine, can then be used to disinfect the water and it can also be treated with UV light.

In hot dry countries such as Abu Dhabi and in other environmentally sensitive areas, the benefits of recycling grey water are obvious. The main one is that it reduces the pressures on public water supplies. Moreover, the amount of polluted water entering rivers is reduced and the problem of poisonous blue-green algae in water reservoirs is also significantly reduced. Furthermore, grey water recycling can save on water bills in the long term.

However, grey water recycling can be expensive if it involves putting new or extra pipes into a building to move the grey water into the purification system. Furthermore, even after filtration and cleaning, the water still contains chemicals and microorganisms which limit its uses. There are few risks to human health when recycled grey water is used properly; one possible risk comes from eating fruit and vegetables that have been grown with it but the danger seems to be minimal. It is clear that commercial and domestic water use needs to be taken more seriously, and single-use water systems are hard to justify in a world of ever greater water scarcity.

Questions 1–5

Look at the descriptions (Questions 1–5) and the list of quantities below.

Match each description with the correct quantity.

Write the correct letter, A–E, in boxes 1–5 on your answer sheet.

1 how much rainwater falls annually in Abu Dhabi
2 how much water an airport hotel is saving by reusing waste water
3 how much domestic waste water is grey water
4 how much water is recycled per person staying at an airport hotel
5 how much potable water can be saved daily per person by recycling grey water

---

Quantities

A 60 litres

B 25%

C approximately 70 litres

D 120 millimetres

E 6%

Questions 6–10

Look at the diagram below and complete the sentences.

*Choose **NO MORE THAN TWO WORDS** from the passage for each answer.*

Write your answers in boxes 6–10 on your answer sheet.

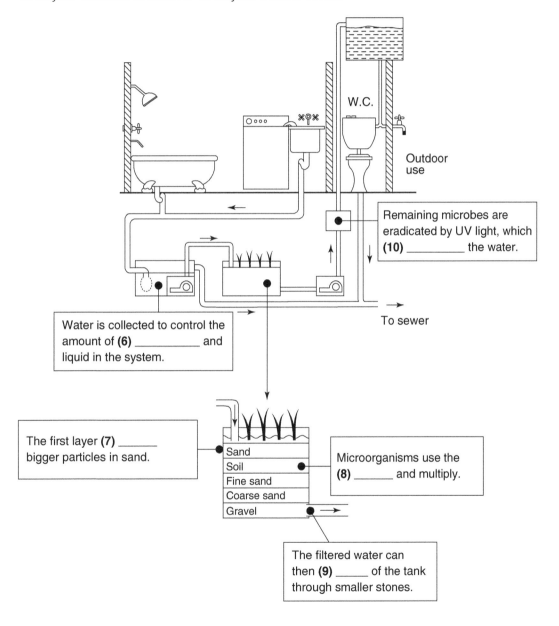

W.C.

Outdoor use

Remaining microbes are eradicated by UV light, which **(10)** _____ the water.

Water is collected to control the amount of **(6)** _____ and liquid in the system.

To sewer

The first layer **(7)** _____ bigger particles in sand.

Sand
Soil
Fine sand
Coarse sand
Gravel

Microorganisms use the **(8)** _____ and multiply.

The filtered water can then **(9)** _____ of the tank through smaller stones.

Questions 11–14

Do the following statements agree with the information given in Reading Passage 1?

In boxes 11–14 on your answer sheet, write

TRUE	*if the statement agrees with the information*
FALSE	*if the statement contradicts the information*
NOT GIVEN	*if there is no information on this*

11 Grey water recycling reduces the amount of pollution entering water reserves.

12 Grey water recycling can be expensive if it involves plumbing work.

13 Filtering grey water leaves the water completely free from chemicals and microorganisms.

14 Vegetables and fruit grown with grey water may be more likely to get crop diseases.

READING PASSAGE 2

*You should spend about 20 minutes on **Questions 15–28**, which are based on Reading Passage 2 below.*

Born to run

People run for many different reasons: for fun, for exercise, to raise money for charities, and so on. Over the past decades, running has become an essential part of many health routines because of the publicity about its beneficial effects. It is claimed that it is good for our heart, it reduces stress and it helps to prevent diseases like diabetes. But what if running is more than just a way of keeping fit? Perhaps we need to run because it is part of what makes us human.

Evolutionary biologists point to the physical characteristics that have made our species one of the greatest runners on Earth. Scientists like Professor Daniel Lieberman of Harvard University maintain that our ancestors' need to run long distances in hot conditions led to evolutionary adaptations, such as the ability to lose heat through our sweat; skin with relatively little hair so we cool down as we run; large powerful muscles like the gluteus maximus, which controls hip and thigh movements; the Achilles tendon, which stores and releases energy for each step or jump we make; and a short vertical neck that keeps our head stable as we run, in contrast to animals whose heads bob up and down for balance.

Professor Lieberman explains that the features of the human neck that evolved to keep the head stable when we run were vital because they gave us an evolutionary advantage. This ability enabled us to scan what is in front of us while we are running and it helped us avoid falling and tripping. It meant that apart from being foragers, who look for plants, roots and berries for food, we could also become hunters. We could now get food from animals, which is richer in protein, and Lieberman contends that this enabled the evolution of the large human brain.

All of these adaptations give humans the ability to run much further than many animals. This means they can persistence hunt. Persistence or endurance hunting gives the hunter, who may be slower than their prey over short distances, the ability to track and follow an animal over very long distances until it is exhausted, then killed. It is a strategy still used by humans today. The hunter-gatherer tribes of the Kalahari Desert will track an antelope for hours over distances of more than 30 kilometres until it is too exhausted to go further.

Our ability to run long distances also means we can run half-marathons, marathons and even ultramarathons, where people run huge distances every day for days. However, many researchers suggest that running, particularly extensive running, can have adverse effects. The list of possible injuries is long and they have been well documented, especially injuries around joints in the hips and knees. Studies of runners dating back to 1973 as well as more recent studies have found a correlation between running and osteoporosis (or weakening of the bones). Research by Melonie Burrows at the University of East London found that long distance female runners have lower bone density, a sign of osteoporosis, than women who did little exercise. Studies by James O'Keefe and others at the Mayo

Foundation for Medical Education found abnormalities in the structure of the hearts of athletes who did extreme running such as ultramarathons.

Despite these findings, other studies have found that running long distances actually strengthens the parts of the knee that are impacted by running. Furthermore, where damage occurs in the knee, this is reversed six months later. It also seems that our hip joints are able to withstand or tolerate the impacts from running. It has therefore been suggested that because our bodies have evolved to run, they have also evolved to self-repair damage to joints caused by the activity, and that in fact, running makes these joints stronger in the long term.

Other studies show that running improves the condition of our hearts and lungs, and reduces blood pressure, weight and the risk of many other diseases such as diabetes and cancer. A study led by Duck-chul Lee at Iowa State University followed 55,000 adults for over 15 years and concluded that running for just 50 minutes a week increases average life expectancy by three years. The study also found that people who ran consistently had up to 50% lower risk of heart disease.

Questions 15–20

Look at the statements (Questions 15–20) and the list of researchers below.

Match each statement with the researcher who made the claim.

*Write the correct letter, **A–D**, in boxes 15–20 on your answer sheet.*
NB You may use any letter more than once.

15 The bones of women who run long distances are weaker than those of other women.

16 Ultramarathon runners can develop hearts that are not the same as those of other people.

17 Humans evolved to run great distances in high temperatures.

18 Muscles in our body have adapted to help us run.

19 Running just under an hour a week helps us live longer.

20 Having a neck that keeps the head still when we move gives humans an evolutionary advantage.

Researchers
A Duck-chul Lee
B Daniel Lieberman
C James O'Keefe
D Melonie Burrows

Questions 21–24

Complete the notes below.

Choose **ONE WORD ONLY** *from the passage for each answer.*

Write your answers in boxes 21–24 on your answer sheet.

Physical developments

Neck: to keep our head **(21)** _____ when we move

Skin: not much hair so we can keep **(22)** _____ as we run

    ability to sweat when it is **(23)** _____

Gluteus maximus: at the top of our legs to move hips and thighs

Achilles tendon: to **(24)** _____ the energy we need
    so that we can run

Questions 25–28

Complete the summary of the last three paragraphs using the list of words, A–G, below.

Write the correct letter, A–G, in boxes 25–28 on your answer sheet.

Research dating from 1973 has found a correlation between running and
(25) _____ bones. More recent research has discovered that some athletes who run extreme distances have **(26)** _____ abnormalities in their hearts. However, both hip and knee joints are **(27)** _____ of withstanding the physical strains from running and can self-repair. It seems that running even a little every week can enable us to live **(28)** _____ by three years.

A	stronger	**B**	weakened	**C**	structural
D	muscular	**E**	capable	**F**	longer
G	fit				

READING PASSAGE 3

*You should spend about 20 minutes on **Questions 29–40**, which are based on Reading Passage 3 below.*

Life at the limit

What are the physical limits to life in extreme environments? Although microbes are the Earth's simplest organisms, they live in places where it is impossible for more complex life forms to survive. Some microbes are able to thrive in the water surrounding deep sea hydrothermal vents, which emit water heated up to 400°C. At the other extreme, some microbes can survive in sub-zero temperatures. In fact, marine microbes living in all regions of the ocean make up over 98% of the total organisms living in the ocean. But what exactly are the limits to survival? Can organisms live in places that lack nutrients, and how long can they survive?

The middle of the Pacific Ocean, in an area known as the South Pacific Gyre, is the place furthest from any land, and it lacks nutrients or signs of life. According to Steven D'Hondt, an oceanographer at the University of Rhode Island, it is the deadest spot in the ocean. It seemed to be the obvious place to look for limits of life on Earth, and microbes have, in fact, been found far beneath this oceanic desert. Researchers think that they have been there for at least 100 million years. The previous record for longevity was held by microbes that had survived for 15 million years but this most recent discovery exceeds that tenfold and raises some intriguing questions.

The microbes from the South Pacific Gyre were discovered by geomicrobiologist Yuki Morono of the Japan Agency for Marine-Earth Science and Technology. Morono wanted to know whether organisms are able to survive where there is very little to sustain them. He drilled 5,700 metres below the seabed and extracted clay samples. The samples were found to contain oxygen, enough to allow the microbes to live, although the clay was extremely poor in nutrients. When Morono and his team then introduced nutrients into the samples, they were absorbed by the microbes that were living in the clay. Within a few days, the microbes started to multiply and 557 days later they were still forming thriving communities.

How the organisms survived for so long is a remarkable puzzle that scientists are trying to understand. The microbes are under intense pressure from miles of mud and water above them and do not have food or sunlight. Under inhospitable conditions, some microbes can form spores, or endospores. In this inactive state, they can stay dormant in order to survive extended periods of starvation. But the Pacific microbes had not formed these spores, suggesting two different possibilities.

A microbe can either reproduce by dividing or it can conserve its energy and maintain only its most basic functions. One possibility is that in the unfavourable conditions under the South Pacific floor, the microbes could have been dividing very slowly over centuries. In this case, the microbes in Morono's study may be the descendants of microbes from an even more distant past. However, at the depth where the microbes were found, there is so little nutrition that it seems unlikely that they would have the energy to divide and multiply. In fact, it seems that the most they could do is to self-repair. But if that is the case, and the microbes are not reproducing, they must have been living at the very edge of life for millions of years. This would mean that their metabolism can slow down so much that they can survive with only the tiniest amounts of nutrients. To the researchers, it seemed almost impossible that the microbes would be able to wake up and grow but they did just that.

The study is globally important and, as Yuki Morono stated, it shows that some of the simplest living creatures in the world 'do not actually have the concept of lifespan'. Unfortunately, the research is very difficult to replicate because different areas of the seabed have different compositions and therefore different environments, so is this a unique find? Scientists have collected samples of material from the sub-seabed that are 200 million years old; could they hold even older organisms? This points to another question: at which point under the seafloor does life end and what are the conditions that limit life? These are important questions, not only for life on Earth but also for potential life on other planets. According to Bo Barker Jørgensen from Aarhus University, 'low food and energy seem not to set the ultimate limit for life on Earth'. So, could life exist on places such as Mars or Jupiter's moons? If a planet seems to be uninhabitable, perhaps life may still exist in some form beneath the extra-terrestrial surface.

Questions 29–31

Choose the correct letter, A, B, C or D.

Write the correct letter in boxes 29–31 on your answer sheet.

29 In the first paragraph, the writer states that microbes

    A compete with each other for nutrients in extreme environments.

    B can flourish where other forms of life cannot live.

    C prefer to live in areas rich in nutrients.

    D can survive temperatures lower than −98°C.

30 Which statement is NOT true about the South Pacific Gyre, according to the second paragraph?

    A It is the part of the ocean furthest away from land.

    B There are no means of supporting life there.

    C It is a good place to investigate the limits of life on Earth.

    D It is impossible for living creatures to survive there.

31 The team led by Yuki Morono

    A discovered a complex mixture of chemicals under the ocean.

    B extracted oxygen from the clay in samples taken from the ocean.

    C provided the microbes with nutrients that increased their activity.

    D waited for 557 days for the microbes to start forming colonies.

Questions 32–37

Do the following statements agree with the information given in Reading Passage 3?

In boxes 32–37 on your answer sheet, write

> **TRUE**   *if the statement agrees with the information*
> **FALSE**   *if the statement contradicts the information*
> **NOT GIVEN**   *if there is no information on this*

32 Scientists believe the microbes they discovered in the South Pacific Gyre could have lived for 100 million years.

33 In situations of physical stress, microbes form endospores.

34 The microbes in the South Pacific Gyre can survive greater pressure from mud and water than microbes in other parts of the ocean.

35 Scientists discovered that microbes from the South Pacific Gyre reproduce very slowly.

36 If the microbes under the sea floor in the South Pacific Gyre were not dividing, they were surviving for millions of years.

37 The microbes from the South Pacific Gyre had survived without oxygen or nutrients.

Questions 38–40

Complete the summary below.

*Choose **ONE WORD ONLY** from the passage for each answer.*

Write your answers in boxes 38–40 on your answer sheet.

It seems microorganisms do not have limits to their **(38)** _____. However, this is hard to confirm because different conditions exist in the seabed and therefore it is hard to **(39)** _____ the study. According to some scientists, having very little **(40)** _____ or food is not a barrier to life.

WRITING TASK 1

You should spend about 20 minutes on this task.

The table below shows the projected growth of global freight by 2050 and how this will affect carbon dioxide (CO_2) emissions.

Summarise the information by selecting and reporting the main features, and make comparisons where relevant.

Growth of global freight by 2050 and projected carbon emissions

	Freight volume (in billion tons/km)		Growth (in %)	CO_2 emission (in million tons)		Growth (in %)
	2010	2050		2010	2050	
Air	191	1 111	482	150	767	411
Road	6 388	30 945	384	1 118	4 519	304
Rail	4 262	19 126	349	62	217	250
Sea	60 053	256 433	327	779	2 630	238
	70 894	307 615	334	2 108	8 132	286

Write at least 150 words.

WRITING TASK 2

You should spend about 40 minutes on this task.

Write about the following topic:

> *Some people think that e-books will eventually replace traditional paper-based books. Others, however, believe that both versions will continue to exist side by side.*
>
> *Discuss both these views and give your own opinion.*

Give reasons for your answer and include any relevant examples from your own knowledge or experience.

Write at least 250 words.

PART 1: Introduction and interview

Listen to Track 05, pressing pause after each question to answer.

05

PART 2: Individual long turn

Before you read the task card, listen to Track 06.

06

Describe a shop you enjoy going to.

You should say

      what the shop is called

      what it sells

      what kind of people shop there

and say what it is about the shop that you like.

PART 3: Two-way discussion

Listen to Track 07, pressing pause after each question to answer.

07

Test 2

PART 1   Questions 1–10

Complete the form below.

*Write **NO MORE THAN TWO WORDS AND/OR A NUMBER** for each answer.*

Rightway Furnishings Complaint Form		
Order reference number: **(1)** _____		
Customer name: Thomas **(2)** _____		
Date order placed: **(3)** _____		
ITEM	PROBLEM	ACTION TO BE TAKEN
Hamilton three-seater sofa	Part of the sofa was **(4)** _____ Leg scratched	**(5)** _____
Regent rug	Wrong **(6)** _____ Different size to advertised	Customer to telephone back **(7)** _____
Morrison coffee table	Wrong instructions sent The four **(8)** _____ were missing	Report issue to **(9)** _____ team
Additional notes: Send **(10)** _____ to customer		

53

Questions 11–13

Choose the correct letter, A, B or C.

11 Julie explains that
  A last year's festival was called off.
  B there have been four festivals so far.
  C there is a chance the festival will be cancelled.

12 One of the new members of the organising committee
  A works in the industry.
  B has planned festivals in the past.
  C judges competitions.

13 This year's festival
  A has more things for visitors to do.
  B starts earlier than usual.
  C will be recorded.

Questions 14–17

Complete the notes below.

*Write **NO MORE THAN TWO WORDS AND/OR A NUMBER** for each answer.*

Hagley Food Festival

Friday to Sunday: 12.00 p.m.– **(14)** _____

Special offer: Buy a **(15)** _____ for only £15.
£10 for children under 16.

Please use the car park and avoid parking in **(16)** _____.

Free transport to and from the station every **(17)** _____.

Questions 18–20

Choose THREE letters, A–G.

Which **THREE** things can visitors do at the festival?

    A get the autograph of a celebrity chef
    B take their child to a cookery lesson
    C help a local charity
    D try food from Vietnam
    E donate a cookery book
    F demonstrate their cookery skills
    G learn how to grow organic vegetables

Questions 21–24

Choose the correct letter, A, B or C.

21 Lee explains that
    A students in their final year have to stay on campus.
    B he can be certain of getting a place on campus if necessary.
    C there is only one hall available on campus.

22 Students living in Broomfield Hall
    A pay quite a lot of rent.
    B hold frequent parties.
    C share showers and toilets.

23 Rooms in Crifield
    A offer pleasant views of the countryside.
    B are near a building site.
    C are more affordable.

24 The house on the High Street
    A only has two rooms to rent.
    B is suitable for two students.
    C is on a busy road.

Questions 25–26

Choose TWO letters, A–E.

Which **TWO** things are true about the second house?

    A It is not available to tenants yet.
    B There is a room that people share.
    C It needs some furniture.
    D It has a garden.
    E It is in a quiet location.

Questions 27–30

Choose the correct letter, A, B or C.

27 Susan

    A has already been invited to share accommodation.

    B has decided what she is going to do.

    C wanted to live with friends on her course.

28 Before viewing the property, Susan has to

    A attend some final lectures.

    B speak to her tutor.

    C complete some work.

29 Why do Lee and Susan need to find a third person quickly?

    A Forms need to be completed.

    B The house might be taken by someone else.

    C They want to avoid paying a larger deposit.

30 Susan thinks

    A she might have a problem finding a third person.

    B it is better to view the property before asking anyone to join them.

    C all her friends have arranged accommodation.

11

Question 31

Choose the correct letter, A, B or C.

31 Many inexperienced entrepreneurs

   A convince themselves there are a lot of potential customers.

   B ask someone to build them a website dedicated to their product.

   C come up with some of their best ideas at night.

Questions 32–34

Choose THREE letters, A–G.

Which **THREE** things stop some people doing market research?

   A They have had success in the past without doing it.

   B They think they know their customers' needs.

   C They have had feedback that market research is not reliable.

   D They do not want to be given bad news.

   E They think it is a mistake to spend money on it.

   F They think they cannot afford to do it.

   G They do not understand research techniques.

Questions 35–36

Choose the correct letter, A, B or C.

35 Selling to a wide range of people

    A can be very expensive.

    B is easier online.

    C does not appeal to everyone.

36 If you are entering a competitive market,

    A focus on keeping your prices as low as possible.

    B do not tell anyone what you plan to offer.

    C consider offering a unique product or service.

Questions 37–40

Complete the sentences below.

*Write **NO MORE THAN TWO WORDS** for each answer.*

37 Feedback can be more easily obtained when you have an _____ presence.

38 You can find out what your visitors' _____ are from your most visited social media posts.

39 Send visitors to a _____ for more detailed information.

40 Consider providing a _____ of your product in order to get feedback.

READING PASSAGE 1

*You should spend about 20 minutes on **Questions 1–14**, which are based on Reading Passage 1 below.*

Moon base

On 16 July 1969, two American astronauts, Neil Armstrong and Buzz Aldrin, made the first landing on the Moon when the Eagle lunar module touched down in the Sea of Tranquility and Armstrong stepped onto the lunar surface. At that time, it seemed almost impossible that humans would not colonise the Moon in the near future but the cost of sending people to live there was just too great. Instead, individual national space agencies have been sending robots called orbiters and rovers in place of humans. These are able to bring back and transmit a huge amount of data to help us understand the Moon better and then colonise it.

Although it is difficult to take people back to the Moon, it is not impossible. We can transport people but the logistical challenge of keeping them there is a very different thing. However, we have two of the components necessary to make this work: power from the Sun and minerals on the Moon itself. Scientists and researchers are already busy in laboratories and simulation facilities on Earth, testing their ideas for a lunar base.

The most fundamental requirement for keeping people on the Moon is oxygen, a component of the air we breathe. Fortunately, the surface of the Moon is covered with rocks and lunar soil known as regolith, which is 42–45% oxygen. Harvesting the oxygen from the regolith will be very energy intensive, but the American space agency NASA has developed and tested robots capable of doing this. Oxygen is, of course, one of the components needed to produce water, the next vital requirement for sustaining life. The other component of water is hydrogen, but because hydrogen is not present on the Moon as a free chemical, there are two options. Either we take it to the Moon in liquid form or we extract it from water. In 2018 NASA confirmed that water is indeed present on the Moon in the form of ice at the lunar poles. It is estimated that there could be 10 billion tons of water there. Some of the water would be used to sustain life, but most of it would be converted into fuel by electrolysing it into its constituent parts: oxygen and hydrogen. Electrolysis, however, requires a great deal of energy and this will need to be sourced from the Sun.

A town in Norway, Rjukan, has given scientists a lead on how to do this. Rjukan used to lack sunlight for long periods of time until giant solar mirrors were positioned on high points above the town in order to reflect sunlight down into it. On the Moon, water could be obtained by reflecting sunlight onto ice within the craters from giant reflectors positioned at high points or mountains near the craters. The melted water could then be moved to a processing plant, where it would be split into hydrogen and oxygen using solar electricity. The hydrogen could then be used to fuel vehicles or fed to fuel cells to supply energy to the lunar base, and the oxygen could be used in the air supply. As well as being used to obtain water, the Sun's energy could also be used to provide power to the base. Lunar soil contains almost all the minerals necessary to build solar panels and in theory, the potential to harvest solar electricity is unlimited. However, because the lunar night lasts for 354 hours, it is important to place solar panels in regions of the Moon that receive the most sunlight. Fortunately, the Moon's poles get sunlight 75–80% of the time and this is also where ice is located, making the poles ideal places to establish the base station.

What will the Moon base be constructed from? The Moon's surface is constantly bombarded by cosmic radiation and small asteroids because it has no protecting atmosphere or magnetic field. This makes it a dangerous place to live so shelter is vital. There are three options. One would be to build a Moon base on Earth and transport it to the Moon via a spaceship in lunar orbit, but the costs of doing this would be prohibitive. A better solution would be to make bricks from the lunar soil. Architects in Vienna have already shown that such bricks can be used to form walls and domes, and it is thought that they would be strong enough to stand up to moonquakes. A third option would be to use caves and geographical features such as crater walls as shelters. Researchers in the Canary Islands are currently practising how to explore lunar caves by driving rovers into caves and tubes formed by volcanic lava.

Humans have not been on the Moon for decades, but preparations to establish a base there are now well under way, and lessons learned from a future Moon base will help us to explore even further: Mars, Europa and beyond.

Questions 1–5

Do the following statements agree with the information given in Reading Passage 1?

In boxes 1–5 on your answer sheet, write

TRUE	*if the statement agrees with the information*
FALSE	*if the statement contradicts the information*
NOT GIVEN	*if there is no information on this*

1   In the late 1960s it seemed likely that humans would build a city on the Moon.

2   Machines are able to send large amounts of information about the Moon back to Earth.

3   It is difficult to take people to the Moon and bring them back safely.

4   Solar power and lunar minerals make it possible to establish a base on the Moon.

5   Tests to see if a lunar base is possible are taking place on the Moon.

Questions 6–9

Complete each sentence with the correct ending, A–G, below.

Write the correct letter, A–G, in boxes 6–9 on your answer sheet.

6 It will not be necessary to transport supplies from Earth to build and sustain a Moon base because

7 We know that we can extract oxygen from lunar rocks because

8 Hydrogen will have to be extracted from ice on the Moon because

9 We know that some of the techniques needed to establish a Moon base will work because

---

A they would be cheaper to manufacture on the Moon.

B this has already been done successfully with robots.

C it is quite easy to duplicate on the Moon.

D resources found on the Moon could be used instead.

E they have already been tested on Earth.

F it is composed of oxygen and hydrogen.

G it will be needed to fuel vehicles and power a Moon base.

Questions 10–13

Complete the summary below.

*Choose **NO MORE THAN TWO WORDS** from paragraph 4 for each answer.*

Write your answers in boxes 10–13 on your answer sheet.

New techniques, for example, the use of mirrors to light the town of Rjukan in Norway, can be applied on the Moon. Sunlight could be **(10)** _____ onto the Moon's ice to melt it. The water could then be split into hydrogen and oxygen, and the hydrogen could be used as **(11)** _____. Lunar soil contains the minerals needed to make **(12)** _____ to generate electricity. In order to collect sunlight during the lunar night, these would be located at the **(13)** _____.

Question 14

*Choose the correct letter, **A**, **B**, **C** or **D**.*

Write the correct letter in box 14 on your answer sheet.

14 Which option for shelter is NOT mentioned in paragraph 5?

    A taking radiation proof shelters to the Moon

    B staying on a spaceship in orbit around the Moon

    C using materials found on the Moon's surface to make bricks

    D finding shelter in natural features such as crater walls and lunar caves

READING PASSAGE 2

You should spend about 20 minutes on **Questions 15–26**, *which are based on Reading Passage 2 below.*

Peer to peer banking

In 1994 Microsoft's founder, Bill Gates, said that although banking is necessary, banks are not. At a time when many traditional institutions and ways of doing things are changing, banking is changing too. There are now new ways of accessing loans and lending money. Thanks to the rise of alternative finance, people can raise and invest money outside the traditional banking system and the regulations and rules that banks have to follow. This has taken many forms, such as crowdfunding, revenue-based finance and peer to peer finance. Crowdfunding is when specific projects raise money by asking a large number of people to invest a small amount of money in return for shares. In revenue-based finance, investors provide money to a company in return for a fixed percentage of the earnings. Peer to peer (P2P) banking also bypasses traditional banks by helping individuals give direct loans to other individuals. Prior to these financial vehicles, it was difficult to invest in new companies without having a considerable amount of money.

In traditional banking, an institution usually works as a financial middleman, regulating the transactions between lenders and borrowers. The banks check the financial status and credit rating of the lender and offer security to the borrower. A credit rating is a score given to an individual that measures how risky it is to lend to that person, based on a prediction of their ability to pay back their loan. P2P banking, on the other hand, works without the traditional checks offered by the banking system. The process is relatively simple. If someone is interested in borrowing money, they complete an online application form on a P2P lending company platform. The online P2P organisation assesses the application and the credit rating of the person making the application. At this point, an interest rate at which the applicant can borrow money is assigned to them. When the application is approved, the applicant is given various options for borrowing and paying back the money and can choose among them. The interesting development here is that, depending on the platform, the investor and the lender are able to select their preferred client depending on the conditions that are on offer. The borrower then makes monthly repayments that include the added interest on the loan. The company that owns the online platform charges a fee to both borrowers and lenders for the services it provides and this is how it generates its profit – almost like a dating agency matching the suitability of the people involved.

Because P2P banks are online, they do not have to pay for a physical high street presence, which can be expensive. Nor do they need to have large teams of staff because lenders and borrowers are matched using a computer algorithm that assesses the credit status of each party. Consequently, the savings made can then be passed to their customers through better interest rates or reduced fees for their services.

Two indicators of the success of P2P banks are their wide customer base and the accuracy of their credit rating processes. P2P companies assess credit worthiness through their own artificial intelligence software, which takes hundreds or thousands of factors into account when someone applies for a loan. This process is done though analysing big data – the process of examining huge amounts of information to make decisions. The good news for P2P lenders is that so far, the number of bad debts has been relatively low. This is a key point in a process that relies on trust or the knowledge that if you lend money, you will get it back, plus more, after a period of time. This is significant because P2P banks do not have the same financial guarantees that governments require traditional banks to offer. They also do not have the same capital reserves that allow savers or investors to get their money back if the P2P bank fails.

The loan/investment model developed by P2P banks enables them to reach people who would not normally qualify for a loan from a traditional bank or who would not normally consider themselves to be an investor. For example, if a small business does not meet the narrow rules for borrowing from a traditional bank, they may be able to get a loan through P2P; and potential investors are finding the higher rates of interest attractive. Because of this, consumers now have more choice about where they invest and borrow, and traditional banks face a threat to their business.

So, what is the future for banking and P2P financial platforms? Possibly a lot will depend on the question of trust mentioned before. Big banks still have the advantages of large cash reserves, legal backing and government guarantees – all the safeguards not available to people putting their money into P2P banks. But for people with limited access to money and small businesses struggling to find financing, P2P lending is already changing the way people bank. Traditional banks will have to think about their response to competition from P2P banking, but for P2P companies the future looks full of opportunities in financial sectors such as insurance, house purchasing, loans for students, and so on.

Questions 15–17

*Complete each sentence with the correct ending, **A–F**, below.*

*Write the correct letter, **A–F**, in boxes 15–17 on your answer sheet.*

15 The availability of alternative finance means that people can now raise money even if they do not meet _____.

16 Alternative finance allows individuals with limited finances to invest in _____.

17 One of the roles of traditional banks is to manage and check _____.

A new companies.

B the process of making loans and investments.

C a lot of money to buy shares in safe companies.

D the traditional structures of banks.

E the requirements traditional banks ask for.

F a fixed percentage.

G companies that are too risky to invest in.

Questions 18–22

Complete the flow-chart below.

*Choose **NO MORE THAN TWO WORDS** from the passage for each answer.*

Write your answers in boxes 18–22 on your answer sheet.

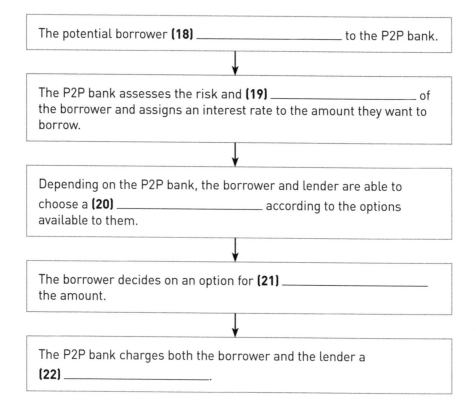

The potential borrower **(18)** _____ to the P2P bank.

↓

The P2P bank assesses the risk and **(19)** _____ of the borrower and assigns an interest rate to the amount they want to borrow.

↓

Depending on the P2P bank, the borrower and lender are able to choose a **(20)** _____ according to the options available to them.

↓

The borrower decides on an option for **(21)** _____ the amount.

↓

The P2P bank charges both the borrower and the lender a **(22)** _____.

Questions 23–24

Choose TWO letters, A–D.

Write the correct letters in boxes 23 and 24 on your answer sheet.

Which **TWO** advantages of P2P banks are mentioned by the writer of the text?

    A P2P banks save money by not having buildings on the high street.

    B The number of bad debts for P2P banks has been lower than traditional banks.

    C P2P banks are not in competition with traditional banks.

    D P2P banks do not need a lot of staff because they use other means to assess credit risk.

Questions 25–26

Choose TWO letters, A–D.

Write the correct letters in boxes 25 and 26 on your answer sheet.

Which **TWO** advantages of traditional banks are mentioned by the writer of the text?

    A Traditional banks have a wider customer base.

    B Governments make traditional banks guarantee savings, so customers can be sure most of their money is safe.

    C Traditional banks have large reserves of cash.

    D Traditional banks have attractive rates of interest for borrowers and lenders.

READING PASSAGE 3

*You should spend about 20 minutes on **Questions 27–40**, which are based on Reading Passage 3 below.*

Questions 27–31

*Reading Passage 3 has six sections, **A–F**.*

Choose the correct heading for each section from the list of headings below.

*Write the correct number, **i–ix**, in boxes 27–31 on your answer sheet.*

List of Headings

i   Bird migration and their routes

ii   Memorising the sky for migration purposes

iii   Using the Earth's magnetic field to navigate

iv   Humans sense Earth's magnetism like birds

v   Studies show that birds get lost over the ocean

vi   Evidence shows birds use scents to guide them

vii   Ways used to navigate migration routes

viii   Familiar places guide birds across the land

ix   The navigation strategy most used by birds

Example	*Answer*
Section **A**	i

27   Section **B**

28   Section **C**

29   Section **D**

30   Section **E**

31   Section **F**

The long-distance navigators

A Every year between late July and October, the Arctic tern leaves its breeding grounds in the Arctic and flies over 19,000 kilometres to the Antarctic. The bird therefore sees two summers a year, once in the northern hemisphere and then again in the southern hemisphere. The Arctic tern is by no means the only bird to undertake long journeys. It is estimated that one in five bird species migrates, a feat that requires great endurance, stamina and strength. The migration patterns of birds are not random. They are very precise and follow flight routes called flyways, which connect a bird's breeding grounds with its wintering grounds, and they include stopovers for food and rest. The Americas Flyway, for example, is the route that birds take from their North American breeding grounds to wintering places in the Caribbean and South America, and the African-Eurasian Flyway connects breeding grounds in Europe and northern Asia with wintering grounds in Africa. Migration is largely driven by the weather and the availability of food. Birds in the southern hemisphere fly north, and birds in the northern hemisphere go south, seeking food and places to mate and rear their young.

B Birds have a variety of methods by which they are able to find their way across these flyways year in, year out. It seems that birds employ different geopositioning strategies according to the conditions encountered during migration. They seem able to use the position of the sun and stars, the Earth's magnetic field, smells and even landmarks to find their way, depending on which is available to them during the journey.

C When the chicks of migrating birds are born, they imprint, or intuitively learn, the map of the sky and stars as they grow in order to orientate themselves. In one famous experiment, Stephen Emlen placed Indigo buntings in a planetarium, where patterns of stars and planets are projected onto the ceiling. When the stars were projected in different positions, the birds changed position according to the new sky map, thus showing their awareness of the position of the stars.

D Obviously, birds cannot use a sky map when the weather is overcast so they must have other means to guide them on their journey. One possibility is that they use the Earth's magnetic field. How they do this is a mystery because the field is so weak. However, experiments have pointed to evidence that birds use the magnetic field in two ways. Researchers have discovered receptors, or chemicals, in their retinas and it is thought that these enable birds to sense the direction of the magnetic north. When these chemicals are exposed to light, they generate electrons that are sensitive to magnetism. If this is the case, north and south could look different to migratory birds, in effect allowing them to 'see' the magnetic field. Other researchers suggest that that birds can also sense magnetism using a molecule called magnetite. Magnetite contains iron and orientates to the north like the needle on a compass. Scientists have found magnetite on the beak of some birds and nerves that carry information about the magnetic field to their brain so that the birds can in effect 'feel' the magnetism. It seems that birds are able to sense the strength of the magnetic field, which is stronger at the poles and weaker at the equator. Traces of magnetite have also been found in humans but our ability to sense magnetic currents is far less developed than in other animals.

E   There is also some evidence that birds use their sense of smell to find their way across long distances. Researchers in the UK, Spain and Italy experimented on seabirds by temporarily blocking their sense of smell using chemicals and then tracking their paths home. The birds could find their way normally when they approached land where aromas and odours are present but were less efficient at finding their direction over the sea, suggesting that smell is very important for them in piloting their routes.

F   Visual clues have long been thought to be a navigational tool for birds. 'Previewing' experiments, where birds were allowed or denied visual access to a familiar site before releasing them, indicated that they use a 'familiar area map'. It seems that birds may build up a visual memory of landmarks that allows them to successfully navigate around places they have already visited. Birds that migrate in daylight often follow natural features like mountains, rivers and lakes. It has even been suggested that they follow man-made features such as roads.

Questions 32–40

Complete the notes below.

*Choose **NO MORE THAN TWO WORDS** from the passage for each answer.*

Write your answers in boxes 32–40 on your answer sheet.

Research and experiments

Imprinting: Experiment took place in a **(32)** _____. Birds aligned themselves to the **(33)** _____ when it was changed.

Magnetic field: Chemicals in birds' **(34)** _____ become sensitive to magnetism when exposed to **(35)** _____. As a result, north and south appear **(36)** _____ to birds.

Magnetite found on the **(37)** _____ of birds. Magnetite allows birds to sense strength of magnetic field.

Smell: Sense of smell taken away using **(38)** _____. Birds flew normally near land but were not as **(39)** _____ navigating over the sea.

Previewing: Preventing **(40)** _____ to familiar places showed birds use natural features to navigate.

WRITING

WRITING TASK 1

You should spend about 20 minutes on this task.

The two charts below show the percentage of mothers and fathers in part-time and full-time employment between 1997 and 2017.

Summarise the information by selecting and reporting the main features, and make comparisons where relevant.

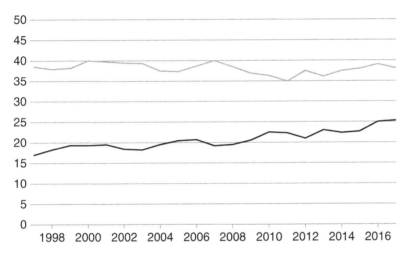

Percentage of mothers with a youngest child aged three or four years old, who are in full-time and part-time employment, England, 1997 to 2017

% —— full-time —— part-time

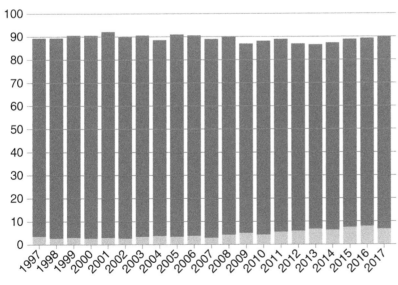

Percentage of fathers with a youngest child aged three or four years old, who work full-time and part-time, England, 1997 to 2017

% ■ Part-time ▨ Full-time

Write at least 150 words.

WRITING TASK 2

You should spend about 40 minutes on this task.

Write about the following topic:

> *In some countries, loneliness and isolation amongst older people is increasing and leading to mental health issues.*
>
> *What do you think are the causes of loneliness and what measures could be taken to solve it?*

Give reasons for your answer and include any relevant examples from your own knowledge or experience.

Write at least 250 words.

SPEAKING

PART 1: Introduction and interview

Listen to Track 12, pressing pause after each question to answer.

12

PART 2: Individual long turn

Before you read the task card, listen to Track 13.

13

Describe a meal you like to eat.

You should say

      what the meal is

      how often you eat it

      if you eat it at home or in a restaurant

and say why you like it so much.

PART 3: Two-way discussion

Listen to Track 14, pressing pause after each question to answer.

14

Test 3

PART 1   *Questions 1–10*

15

Complete the form below.

*Write **NO MORE THAN THREE WORDS AND/OR A NUMBER** for each answer.*

Jamieson's Ltd
Job Application

Applicant's name: Tessa Murphy

Placement of job advertisement: on the **(1)** _____

Post: (2) _____

Current occupation/Studies

Degree in **(3)** _____

Work experience

Period: January–May: Stacey's Boutique

Role: **(4)** _____

Responsibilities: served customers and assisted the manager to arrange the **(5)** _____

Skills: dealing with money and customers

Period: **(6)** _____: Summer school

Role: social organiser

Responsibilities: **(7)** _____ and evening events

Skills: working as part of a team

Hobbies and interests

Reading

Going to **(8)** _____

Availability

Possible starting date: **(9)** _____

Unavailable on **(10)** _____

PART 2

Questions 11–17

Label the plan below.

*Write **NO MORE THAN TWO WORDS** for each answer.*

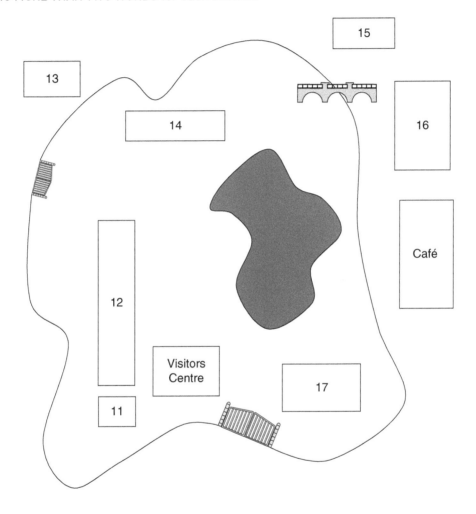

Questions 18–20

Choose the correct letter, A, B or C.

18 The duck pond

    A is quite shallow.

    B often has people falling in.

    C is closed to visitors due to heavy rain.

19 Visitors to the farm

    A should not handle the animals before eating.

    B often forget to wash their hands.

    C should try to keep the hand wash stations clean.

20 Visitors needing first aid should

    A phone for help.

    B speak to someone at the main desk.

    C go to the first aiders near the farm.

PART 3

Questions 21–30

Questions 21–24

Choose the correct letter, A, B or C.

21 Work experience

    A is usually organised by the student.

    B is a necessary part of the degree.

    C sometimes takes place at the university.

22 Students will be paid if

    A they take time off in the summer.

    B they are on placement for a year.

    C they show they are responsible.

23 Companies that offer work experience placements

    A sometimes hold competitions.

    B expect you to know how to use databases and spreadsheets.

    C often have more than one student applying.

24 Students attending an interview

    A should expect it to be formal.

    B should prepare for it.

    C should chat with the Careers Service first.

Questions 25–26

Choose TWO letters, A–E.

Which **TWO** things does the Careers Service help with?

    A identifying your strengths

    B dealing with problems at the company

    C supporting students with work-based assessments

    D keeping a record of your experiences

    E helping with academic work

Questions 27–30

Complete the summary below.

Write ONE WORD ONLY for each answer.

Look forward to your work experience

Your year in industry will be a memorable experience and of enormous benefit in the future. If it goes well, it will confirm that your choice of **(27)** _____ has been a wise one. At the very least, the year spent at the company will give you the chance to **(28)** _____ the kind of work you are interested in. If you make a positive **(29)** _____, you may be offered a job when you finish your degree. There is also a good chance that you will make some **(30)** _____ who may prove useful in the future.

PART 4   *Questions 31–40*

Questions 31–32

Choose the correct letter, A, B or C.

31 The substance that makes up spider silk

    A changes its form when it leaves the spider's body.

    B consists of five different proteins.

    C is commonly found in garden plants.

32 Spider silk

    A is similar in strength to steel.

    B can stretch 30 times its length.

    C is not affected by freezing temperatures.

Questions 33–36

Complete the sentences below.

*Write **NO MORE THAN TWO WORDS** for each answer.*

33 The _____ used spider silk to treat people who were bleeding.

34 Spider silk was used by Indigenous Australians as _____.

35 Scientists have used spider silk to grow human skin to treat _____.

36 There is interest in using spider silk in airbags in cars to reduce the _____ on the body.

Questions 37–40

Which method of producing silk matches the information in the sentences?

*Choose your answers from the box and write the correct letter, **A–D**, next to questions 37–40.*

A cows' cells
B goats' milk
C silkworms
D synthetic silk

37 It could be used to help wounds heal.

38 It is stronger than a particular man-made material.

39 It requires no further work after the silk is spun.

40 It could produce large quantities of silk protein.

READING

READING PASSAGE 1

*You should spend about 20 minutes on **Questions 1–14**, which are based on Reading Passage 1 below.*

The Change Curve

Change is inevitable in any sphere of life. Although the results of change can bring great benefits, the process of change can be intensely traumatic, involve loss of choice, power and status, and when change happens in the workplace, it can even lead to loss of jobs. Many businesses and organisations use a model called the Change Curve to understand and manage how people react to change and the stages they go through before they accept it.

The concept of the Change Curve is based on work by psychiatrist Elisabeth Kübler-Ross. Her book *On Death & Dying,* published in 1969, dealt with the trauma and shock that people who are facing the end of life experience and how their families are also affected. Kübler-Ross proposed several stages of grief as a way of helping patients face death and their relatives deal with its effects. Kübler-Ross's ideas were groundbreaking but have since become one of the bases of grief support and counselling. Moreover, because the ideas give a framework for dealing with personal trauma and change and for helping people adjust emotionally to significant life events, the model has been adopted by organisational theory and business management.

It is worth noting that Kübler-Ross's original work described 10–13 stages of grief rather than the simpler four-stage version used by organisations, and that she did not intend them to be regarded as individual stages to be passed through in a fixed order but rather as phases of dealing with grief, which people may experience more than once at different times.

When change is introduced, in stage 1, people's first reactions may be shock or denial as their normality is threatened. Their refusal to accept the facts is a natural defensive reaction and it is important to understand this in order to help them move beyond this stage. Even when people know about a change in advance and understand the need for it, they still need to be informed of what is happening to them and their workplace. At this stage, it is important to communicate with people and to give them the sense that they are being included in the process.

If stage 1 is handled well, stage 2, a critical stage, will be smoother than if stage 1 is badly handled. In stage 2, people start to react to the change and this may generate feelings of anger, resentment or fear. They may feel angry with themselves, their workmates and even their friends. For an organisation, this is the point at which a team can fall apart and the working environment can become chaotic. Good management is crucial now and it must consider the impact the change is having on people and their emotions and address any objections they may have. Furthermore, change may affect people differently. For example, some may find that their skills are no longer useful and that their position is being threatened or undermined. Reactions to change are highly personal so it is important to listen to people and monitor the situation and, if necessary, show that you are listening by taking action in response.

Stage 3 is when the organisation begins to assimilate the changes and come out of the crisis. At this point, the changes have become real to people and they have begun to accept them. They will begin to learn in practical terms what the changes mean for them and will do this more easily if they are helped and supported to do so. Therefore, training will be important, and time for this will need to be scheduled. The organisation's productivity may slip as people begin to work with the changes instead of against them. People will stop focusing on the past and start to learn what is good about the changes and what they need to do to adapt. When they have the right skills and training to cope, the organisation can move forward again.

The final stage, stage 4, is when people embrace the new reality and begin to see the benefits. They then start seeing opportunities and build new plans and hopes. Some may actually acknowledge that the change has been for the best, while others may accept the new status quo because they have no other option. During this stage, the organisation will become more productive. At this point, it is a good idea to acknowledge the difficulties and turmoil people have been through and celebrate the success of the change.

Questions 1–8

Look at the following descriptions (Questions 1–8) and the stages below.

Match each description with the stage in which it occurs.

Write the correct letter, A–D, in boxes 1–8 on your answer sheet.

NB   You may use any letter more than once.

1   Common feelings are hate, bitterness and alarm about the changes.
2   Programmes to help and train people are important.
3   People reject the reality of what is happening.
4   People start to acknowledge and work with the new situation.
5   Relationships between colleagues become problematic and the working environment no longer functions properly.
6   It is important to explain forthcoming changes so that people feel involved.
7   It is important to acknowledge the positive aspects of the change and show appreciation for the way people have dealt with difficulties.
8   People start planning for their future in the new circumstances.

A stage 1
B stage 2
C stage 3
D stage 4

Questions 9–12

Do the following statements agree with the information given in Reading Passage 1?

In boxes 9–12 on your answer sheet, write

TRUE	*if the statement agrees with the information*
FALSE	*if the statement contradicts the information*
NOT GIVEN	*if there is no information on this*

9 The Change Curve is a model of human behaviour that helps us understand why organisations change.

10 The ideas for the Change Curve were based on ideas used in counselling people who were dying.

11 Kübler-Ross's ideas give us a way of understanding how people adapt to significant national events.

12 A more complex version of Kübler-Ross's stages is used by organisations to understand change.

Questions 13–14

Choose TWO letters, A–E.

Write the correct letters in boxes 13 and 14 on your answer sheet.

Which **TWO** pieces of information are mentioned by the writer of the text in paragraphs 5–7?

A During stage 3, the productivity of a company increases as people get used to changes.

B It is not worth spending money on training staff because they are not focused on their jobs.

C Some people only accept changes because there is no other choice.

D Changes are harder to process when people receive no support.

E Managers can prevent people from feeling any stress by communicating with staff.

READING PASSAGE 2

You should spend about 20 minutes on Questions 15–29, which are based on Reading Passage 2 below.

Space Junk

Since the Soviet Union successfully launched the first man-made satellite, Sputnik 1, in 1957, about 5,000 more satellites have been put into orbit around the Earth. About 2,000 of these are active and although the rest are now dead, they remain in orbit, together with parts from all the rockets that carried them there. These remnants are often referred to as space junk, space trash or orbital debris. The debris ranges in size from 1–10 centimetres and there are estimated to be around half a million pieces with an additional 23,000 fragments bigger than 10 centimetres. These larger pieces can be observed and tracked from the ground. The waste is found in all zones of the Earth's orbit: low Earth orbit, which is within 2,000 kilometres of the Earth's surface; medium orbit, which is between 2,000 and 36,000 kilometres from the Earth's surface; and high orbit, which is beyond that. Most satellites are in low Earth orbit, as is the International Space Station (ISS). The problem is that most of the space debris is found there too and this is becoming a huge problem.

Some of the debris in low Earth orbit is eventually captured by the Earth's gravity and burns up when it enters the Earth's atmosphere or reaches its surface. However, most of the space junk stays in low Earth orbit and this can have several unwanted consequences. In 2009, almost 500 miles above Siberia, there was a collision between the obsolete Russian satellite Cosmos 2251 and the working US communication satellite Iridium 33. The satellites collided with each other at a speed of 11.7 kilometres per second and produced more than 2,000 pieces of debris. This was the first time two satellites were actually observed hitting each other in space, and the fragments from that collision could be seen spreading out over a very wide area over the following months.

Even though the area within low Earth orbit is vast, the speed at which pieces of junk travel means that they are deadly at the infrequent times they encounter another object. In 2006 a small piece of space junk hit the ISS and damaged one of its windows. Later, in 2014, the ISS had to make an emergency manoeuvre to avoid a piece of junk from the Russian Cosmos 2251 satellite smashing into it. The potential disaster was only averted because a supply vehicle that was docked with the space station fired its thrusters and raised the ISS by one kilometre out of the path of the space junk. This example illustrates the first problem with the debris: satellites need to carry out important work but are in constant danger of being damaged or destroyed. The ISS was designed to withstand impacts from debris up to one centimetre in size but in order to prevent it being hit by larger objects, scientists have to watch for space junk and try to move the station out of harm's way if necessary; the lives of the people on board could be at risk so it is extremely important to monitor the paths of the pieces of debris. However, it is very difficult to accurately plot the course of a debris fragment and so the ISS is only moved when there is *probability* of a strike. The junk from Cosmos 2251 was spotted only six hours before it passed within three kilometres of the ISS's position. As debris is broken into smaller and smaller pieces, tracking it becomes increasingly difficult.

The second problem is what happens when we launch satellites and rockets in the future. Some scientists describe space junk as an umbrella or ring around the Earth, which any future launch will need to punch through to go into space. No one really knows how bad the problem has to get before it prevents us putting objects into space or makes it very expensive to do so. The astrophysicist Donald Kessler, who used to work for NASA, calculated that if there is enough junk in orbit, collisions between pieces would create high-velocity smaller pieces of debris that would then hit even more objects, resulting in a chain reaction, producing more and more destructive pieces of debris. The problem is made worse when satellites remain in space after their working lives or when they are destroyed deliberately. An anti-satellite test in 2007 destroyed an obsolete weather satellite, creating 3,000 pieces of space debris, and a missile strike in 2019 scattered thousands more pieces into orbit. The gradual accumulation of space junk caused by debris colliding and creating more junk is called the Kessler syndrome and it will build up over the next 100 years. Eventually, the time between collisions will become shorter and shorter, and it is predicted that a cloud of deadly space junk will circle the planet.

Kessler believes that we need legislation that requires countries to build satellites that re-enter the atmosphere after their mission has ended and impose penalties on countries that do not do this. The problem is that the damage is already done and even if everyone keeps to the rules, collisions are still happening and the amount of debris is growing. This points to a second aspect of the potential solution: clean up the biggest pieces. The larger debris could be tracked and removed; Kessler believes that if we could take just five objects per year out of orbit, the problem would stabilise. Although this sounds simple, satellites travel at great speeds and some are very large. Ideas for dealing with inactive satellites include removing them using harpoons or nets based on the ISS. A satellite service station that would repair satellites and extend their working lives has also been proposed. Whichever solution is brought forward, however, it will need international cooperation and this could be more difficult to achieve than catching the wayward satellites.

Questions 15–19

*Complete each sentence with the correct ending, **A–H**, below.*

*Write the correct letter, **A–H**, in boxes 15–19 on your answer sheet.*

15 A large number of the satellites that orbit the Earth
16 Pieces of space junk that are larger than 10 centimetres
17 Pieces of debris that have resulted from collisions
18 Some objects that are in low Earth orbit
19 Collisions that happen at high speed

A can be found mostly in the same orbit area as the International Space Station.

B produce even more debris that travels large distances.

C are above Siberia.

D are no longer active.

E can be seen and followed from Earth.

F are among the 5,000 satellites that are circling the Earth.

G burn up and are destroyed as they fall back to ground.

H circle the planet in the medium Earth orbit.

Questions 20–23

Choose the correct letter, A, B, C or D.

Write the correct letter in boxes 20–23 on your answer sheet.

20 The International Space Station managed to avoid a piece of space junk because

    A one of its windows was damaged.

    B a supply vehicle moved it out of its path.

    C scientists did not want to smash a Russian satellite.

    D space junk travels at incredible speeds.

21 Because both satellites and space debris are in low Earth orbit,

    A satellites are built to withstand impact.

    B there is a high probability of collisions happening.

    C scientists try to accurately predict the orbit of the debris.

    D the International Space Station is frequently moved to avoid them.

22 The amount of junk in space will NOT lead to

    A more expensive space flights.

    B a huge ball of space junk around the Earth.

    C easier tracking of orbiting fragments.

    D a chain reaction of pieces of debris hitting each other and creating more junk.

23 The problem of space junk is being made worse due to

    A the intentional destruction of old satellites.

    B the high concentration of pieces of debris.

    C inactive satellites not returning to Earth.

    D a lack of understanding of the extent of the problem.

Questions 24–29

Complete the summary below.

Choose NO MORE THAN THREE WORDS from the passage for each answer.

Write your answers in boxes 24–29 on your answer sheet.

Solutions to the Kessler syndrome include introducing laws that force countries to launch satellites that can (24) _____
the Earth's atmosphere at the end of their life and make them pay
(25) _____ if they do not do this. At the
same time, we need to (26) _____ the situation
by removing larger objects from low Earth orbit. This is difficult because of the
(27) _____ of such objects, but ideas include
catching them with (28) _____, or building a
(29) _____ to extend their active lives.

READING PASSAGE 3

You should spend about 20 minutes on Questions 30–40, which are based on Reading Passage 3 below.

The Tree of Life

A   The baobab tree has a very distinctive appearance, with a large, round trunk and branches that look like roots reaching into the air. The latter gained it the name of the 'upside-down tree' but it is also known by other names. The origin of the word 'baobab' is not clear; it may come from the Arabic *bu hibab,* referring to a fruit with many seeds, or from the medieval Latin *bahobab,* apparently from a central African language. It grows in arid regions of the southern hemisphere and has evolved unique ways of surviving in water-scarce environments. The tree is common throughout sub-Saharan Africa, Madagascar and north-western Australia. It is impressive, not just because of its appearance and ability to survive in harsh climates, but also because of its size. In Zimbabwe, one baobab grew so big that 40 adults could fit inside it. A baobab can grow 25 metres high and as it gets older, the middle of the trunk becomes hollowed out. The hollow trunk is used as shelter by animals, and humans too have used it for a variety of purposes; one tree was even used as a prison cell. Indeed, the baobab is one of the biggest flowering plants in the world and produces fruits that are prized by people and animals alike for food.

B   Baobabs are long lived but unlike other trees, it is very difficult, if not impossible, to discover their age by counting annual growth rings in the trunk because their growth rings are very faint. Instead, researchers use radiocarbon dating to analyse samples from trees. The oldest specimen found so far was 2,500 years old. The trees have a staged growth pattern that was observed by the naturalist Von Breitenbach, who described four phases. The first is the young or sapling phase, which lasts until the tree is 15 years old. During this phase, it reaches a height of about six metres. The second phase is the cone phase, which lasts until the tree is 60–70 years old. This is the period when growth is the fastest and the tree reaches about 15 metres in height. In the third phase, the bottle phase, the trunk broadens out to produce the tree's iconic shape, and at 200–300 years old, it gains a height of about 20 metres. During the old age phase, the trunk expands further and becomes hollow. The tree eventually dies aged 500–800 years, although some individuals survive much longer.

C   A master of water management, the baobab can hold up to 120,000 litres of water in its trunk, which is incredibly useful for animals and humans in times of drought. Both are able to pierce the tree to access the water, and this is probably why many trees can be found along trade routes in Africa. The trunk is not a single structure but is composed of many stems fused together. This creates gaps in the trunk to capture precious water, which can be absorbed later by the tree – unless people or animals find it first.

D The tree first flowers after 20 years of age and the flowering period can be up to 6 weeks. The flowers appear in early summer (October to December in the southern hemisphere) and they are extraordinary. White in colour, heavy and large, they open during the evening simultaneously and survive for just 24 hours. When they open, they have a sweet smell but the scent becomes unpleasant later on as they turn brown and then fall. The flowers are pollinated mainly by fruit bats, which are attracted by the strong smell, and to a lesser extent by bushbabies as well as various insects. After flowering, the baobab produces large fruit pods about 20 centimetres long, which hang down from the tree. The pods take six months to ripen before falling to the ground, from where they can be harvested. Inside are small black seeds that are covered with a white powdery substance that tastes lemony and delicious and is a valuable food source. The fruit has many uses: it can be made into a drink that is high in vitamins C and B2, and it has been used to treat fevers; the seeds are pressed into oil or roasted as snacks; and the shell can be made into a musical percussion instrument.

E Like many giant trees, an old baobab creates its own ecosystem. It supports the life of thousands of creatures, from the largest mammals to insects and other small animals that shelter in its crevices. Birds nest in its branches; baboons eat its fruit; bushbabies and fruit bats drink the nectar. Little wonder the baobab is sometimes called the 'tree of life'. However, like all living things, the baobab does eventually die and when this happens, it collapses quickly and disintegrates into fibres. Perhaps this has given rise to another of its names, the 'magic tree'; its disintegration is so fast that the tree simply seems to disappear.

Questions 30–32

Complete the sentences below.

Choose ONE WORD ONLY from the passage for each answer.

Write your answers in boxes 30–32 on your answer sheet.

30 The baobab is called the 'upside-down tree' because its _____ stick into the air like tree roots.

31 It is also called the 'tree of life' because many creatures depend on it for water, food, _____ and as a place to live.

32 Because the baobab _____ so quickly at the end of its life, people also call it the 'magic tree'.

Questions 33–35

Complete the table below.

*Choose **NO MORE THAN TWO WORDS** from the passage for each answer.*

Write your answers in boxes 33–35 on your answer sheet.

Age (years)	Phase	Height	Feature
10–15	sapling	3–6 metres	–
60–70	(33) _____	5–15 metres	the tree's (34) _____ is the quickest
70–300	bottle	10–20 metres	the trunk (35) _____ and takes on the familiar baobab shape
300–800	old age	–	the tree trunk becomes hollow and expands

Questions 36–40

Reading Passage 3 has five paragraphs labelled A–E.

Which paragraph contains the following information?

Write the correct letter, A–E, in boxes 36–40 on your answer sheet.

36 how the baobab reproduces
37 the end of the baobab's life
38 how the baobab survives in dry conditions
39 the climate and regions in which the tree grows
40 how scientists date the trees

WRITING TASK 1

You should spend about 20 minutes on this task.

> The line graph below shows demographic trends in Scotland.
>
> Summarise the information by selecting and reporting the main features.

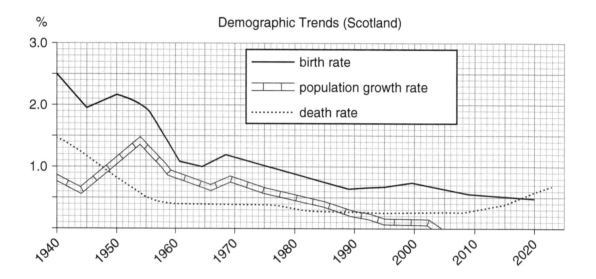

Write at least 150 words.

WRITING TASK 2

You should spend about 40 minutes on this task.

Write about the following topic:

> Given the increase in the consumption of fast food amongst young people, the school curriculum should place far more emphasis on teaching the principles of good nutrition and the skills necessary to maintain a healthy diet.
>
> To what extent do you agree or disagree with this opinion?

Give reasons for your answer and include any relevant examples from your own knowledge or experience.

Write at least 250 words.

SPEAKING

PART 1: Introduction and interview

Listen to Track 19, pressing pause after each question to answer.

19

PART 2: Individual long turn

Before you read the task card, listen to Track 20.

20

Describe a building you have seen that made a big impression on you.

You should say

what the building was

when you went there

why you went there

and say what it is about the building that you liked.

PART 3: Two-way discussion

Listen to Track 21, pressing pause after each question to answer.

21

Test 4

PART 1   *Questions 1–10*

Questions 1–3

Choose the correct letter, A, B or C.

1 The food will be placed
   A in the office.
   B in the training room.
   C outside the training room.

2 The company is only providing food at lunchtime because
   A attendees will already have had breakfast.
   B breakfast is more expensive than lunch.
   C there is only enough money to provide lunch.

3 Which of the following people will be at the lunch?
   A the manager
   B the secretary
   C the trainer

Questions 4–10

Complete the form below.

*Write **NO MORE THAN TWO WORDS AND/OR A NUMBER** for each answer.*

Corporate Catering Order Form

Date of event: **(4)** _____

Delivery time: **(5)** _____

Number of people: **(6)** _____

Standard Buffet	Premium Buffet
Sandwiches	Sandwiches
Crisps	Crisps
Hot and cold drinks	Salad bowl
	Fruit
	Cakes
	Hot and cold drinks
Cost: **(7)** _____	Cost: £5.50

Dietary requirements: 1 person requires **(8)** _____ food.

Contact person: Carol **(9)** _____

Telephone number: 455 2298, Extension **(10)** _____

23

Questions 11–20

Complete the leaflet below.

Write **NO MORE THAN THREE WORDS AND/OR A NUMBER** *for each answer.*

Stay Safe During a Heatwave

- In the daytime try to limit the amount of **(11)** _____ in rooms.

- At night, when the temperature is cooler, keep windows open.

- Are you using air conditioning? Pay attention to your
  (12) _____.

- Spray cold water on your face or take a **(13)** _____.

- Your wrists and the back of your neck are your body's
  (14) _____. Place a cold cloth on these areas.

- Eat a healthy diet to replace the nutrients you lose through
  (15) _____. Drink plenty of water!

- Try to stay at home between **(16)** _____ as this is the hottest part of the day.

- If you go out in the sun, wear a hat or use an **(17)** _____.

- Wear loose-fitting clothes made from **(18)** _____.

- Take it easy when doing any **(19)** _____.

- Remember your neighbours, especially if they are elderly or have
  (20) _____.

PART 3

Questions 21–30

Questions 21–25

*Choose the correct letter, **A**, **B** or **C**.*

21 The student did not speak with Professor Collins because
    A she did not have the time.
    B she could not get an appointment with him.
    C he is not around at the moment.

22 When doing assignments, many students
    A are surprised to find how difficult they are to write.
    B often fail to get the required grades.
    C do not provide a full answer.

23 The tutor says that words like 'analyse', 'discuss' and 'evaluate'
    A each require a completely different response.
    B will often have the same meaning.
    C can be difficult to understand.

24 The danger of using certain sources on the internet is that
    A the assignment may receive a lower grade.
    B they are full of promotions and adverts.
    C they are sometimes written by politicians.

25 The books on a reading list
    A express fewer opinions than the internet.
    B are more critical of other authors.
    C have been assessed by other experts.

Questions 26–30

Complete the sentences below.

*Write **NO MORE THAN TWO WORDS** for each answer.*

Proofreading checklist

- Make sure you express yourself clearly.

- Your paragraphs must be **(26)** _____ and in an order that makes sense to the reader.

- Check you have given a full answer to the question.

- The points you have made should be **(27)** _____. Don't write just anything to get to the required word count.

- Avoid the use of informal language.

- Pay attention to any **(28)** _____ and spelling.

- Check your **(29)** _____ are grammatically correct.

- Check your **(30)** _____ to make sure you have expressed yourself effectively.

PART 4 · Questions 31–40

25

Questions 31–32

Choose **TWO** *letters, A–E.*

Which **TWO** things can result from a lack of strength training?

    A A person will not get the benefit of natural activities.

    B A person will not do as well in their sport as they could.

    C An athlete can no longer practise their sport.

    D A person will not be able to visit the gym.

    E A person's injuries will get worse.

Questions 33–37

Choose the correct letter, A, B or C.

33 An injury caused by a fall
  A tends to be unexpected.
  B needs to be dealt with urgently.
  C is often caused by weak muscles.

34 Athletes who do more than one sport
  A place too much pressure on their bodies.
  B are in particular need of strength training.
  C avoid overworking one part of the body.

35 Injuries can be avoided
  A if an athlete makes fewer repetitive movements.
  B if muscles that are not used as much are exercised.
  C if an athlete can learn to keep their balance.

36 A strength training programme
  A should also help you move more freely.
  B will reduce daily aches and pains.
  C is only suitable for particular sports.

37 What problem do older athletes face?
  A They eat a poorer diet than younger athletes.
  B They are unable to continue doing their chosen sport.
  C They lose muscle mass.

Questions 38–40

Complete the sentences below.

*Write **NO MORE THAN TWO WORDS** for each answer.*

38 Athletes are often less able to practise their sport during the

_____.

39 Seeing improvements brought about by strength training can help athletes develop

a _____.

40 If athletes are prevented from doing their sport for a long time, strength training can help

them remain _____.

READING PASSAGE 1

*You should spend about 20 minutes on **Questions 1–14**, which are based on Reading Passage 1 below.*

Coastal defences

The world's coastlines are constantly being reshaped and reworked by the sea. Coastal erosion is one of the natural phenomena that contribute to the creation and destruction of our shores and one of the main processes that form beaches, dunes, mud flats, reefs and marshes along the coast. These different shoreline features have a wide range of functions: they provide habitats for wildlife, prevent flooding and protect fresh water resources inland, and, of course, they provide opportunities for leisure activities like sunbathing. As human activity along the coast continues to increase with the development of towns and industries, managing erosion is becoming a problem of growing importance. The risk of flooding due to rising sea levels, attributed to the effects of global warming, makes finding a solution to erosion a priority. As well as protecting natural habitats, coastal management involves saving homes and businesses from damage or destruction, and failing to do this can have severe consequences for society and the economy.

Coastlines are changed by the sea in two ways: erosion and longshore drift. Erosion happens through different processes, but essentially the action of the sea wears down features of the coastal landscape such as cliffs, beaches and sand dunes before washing them away. Longshore drift happens when waves approach a beach at an angle and move sediment along the coast until eventually the beach changes its shape. The beach may even disappear from its original location and re-form (as sediment is deposited) further down the coast.

There are three basic approaches to coastline management. The first one is to maintain the existing coastal defences but not to build new ones. The second is to build new defences further out at sea in order to reduce pressure on existing defences and even extend the coastline. The third is to retreat, in other words, to move people, homes and businesses away from disappearing coastlines. When the preferred option is to attempt to stop coastline erosion, either hard or soft engineering options can be used.

Hard engineering options are expensive and, in all probability, short term. They tend to have a significant effect on the landscape and environment because of their size and visual impact. Furthermore, they are expensive to build and maintain. Common coastal hard engineering methods are to build a sea wall or groynes; each type of barrier is designed to combat an aspect of coastal change, and in some places more than one type of sea defence can be seen. Sea walls are built at the edge of a coastline and are usually made from reinforced concrete to make them stronger. The walls prevent the sea from washing away the bottom of cliffs, causing the cliffs to fall into the sea. The walls can be vertical, curved or mound walls. Vertical walls were mainly used in the past and are the simplest type of wall. Unfortunately, they are also the most easily damaged by waves as their foundations can be undermined by the sea. Curved seawalls serve to push the waves back out to sea, and the curve prevents water from crashing over the top of the wall. However, deflecting the energy of the waves simply means that erosion takes place further down the coast. Mound sea walls use a mixture of loose material, such as rock and concrete, which has the advantage of absorbing the energy of the waves rather than deflecting it, and cost much less to build. However, they are less effective in storms and have shorter lives than solid sea walls.

Groynes are low walls built at a right angle to the coastline and are used to minimise the effect of longshore drift. They can be built from wood, stones and/or concrete, and are used in groups to break the beach into sections. As a wave hits the side of a groyne, its power is reduced and the material being carried by it is deposited at the side of the groyne. Groynes are less expensive than sea walls to put in place but like mound sea walls, they have a short lifespan.

The alternatives to hard engineering schemes are soft engineering techniques. They are low-cost solutions that have little immediate effectiveness against coastal erosion but are much more sustainable. There are two main kinds of soft engineering options. The first is beach nourishment, which replaces the sand and pebbles washed away by the sea. This avoids the need for expensive sea walls but sand needs to be moved constantly to maintain the beach. Unfortunately, because this option does not stop natural erosion by the sea, a larger quantity of material is deposited further down the coast. The second option, managed retreat, avoids coastal management and construction projects and allows areas of the coast to erode and flood naturally. Managed retreat usually takes place in areas of low economic value. The advantage of this method is that it encourages the development of beaches and salt marshes, two kinds of environments that are natural defences against the sea. The second advantage is, of course, that it is cheap.

Coastal management is difficult as local people, farmers and the agricultural industry, environmentalists, tourist authorities and other economic interests will have different opinions about what should be done. The importance of the issue is obvious from just one statistic: 45% of the world's population live within 100 kilometres of the coast. As sea levels rise and storm energy increases, the problems of coastal management are going to become ever more intense and pressing.

Questions 1–5

Complete the summary using the list of words, A–I, below.

Write the correct letter, A–I, in boxes 1–5 on your answer sheet.

Coastal erosion can create several different types of **(1)** _____, which have many different **(2)** _____ in the changing coastal environment. These include providing environments for wildlife to live, stopping floods and protecting water supplies. The increasing **(3)** _____ of homes and businesses on or near the coast means that managing our coastline is a(n) **(4)** _____ for many countries around the world. If this cannot be done effectively, there could be severe effects on **(5)** _____.

A crisis	**B** priority	**C** landscape
D management	**E** economy	**F** roles
G society	**H** resources	**I** development

Questions 6–8

Complete the sentences below.

Choose ONE WORD ONLY from the passage for each answer.

Write your answers in boxes 6–8 on your answer sheet.

6 Erosion occurs when features of the coast are worn down by the sea's
_____.

7 Shorelines are reshaped when materials are washed down the coast because waves hit beaches at an _____.

8 Beaches can move and _____ some distance away from their original position.

Questions 9–12

Complete the flow-chart below.

Choose **ONE WORD** *from the passage for each answer.*

Write your answers in boxes 9–12 on your answer sheet.

```
┌────────────────────────────────┐
│   Engineered Coastal Defences   │
└────────────────────────────────┘
```

Sea walls

vertical
✓ simple to build
X the foundations are often
(9) _____ by the sea

curved
✓ stop waves **(10)** _____
over the wall
X reflect wave energy back to the
sea

mound
✓ capable of **(11)** _____
wave energy
X need replacing often

Groynes

vertical
✓ less expensive than walls
X do not have a long
(12) _____

Groynes

Vertical sea wall

Curved sea wall

Questions 13–14

Choose the correct letter, A, B, C or D.

Write the correct letter in boxes 13–14 on your answer sheet.

13 Which statement is NOT TRUE about beach nourishment?

A Sea walls are not needed.

B Coastal materials have to be replaced often.

C More coastal material is carried further down the coast.

D It involves building roads to bring materials to the coast.

14 Which statement is TRUE about managed retreat?

A Salt marshes and cliffs are usually created as a result.

B It is used in areas of little commercial interest.

C Not a lot of land is lost to the sea.

D The costs of managed retreat are high.

READING PASSAGE 2

*You should spend about 20 minutes on **Questions 15–29**, which are based on Reading Passage 2 below.*

Team working

The ability to work in a team is one that is prized by employers and educationalists alike. It is often requested in job advertisements and displayed on CVs. When employers list their most important skills for promotion, 86% list team working skills. The willingness and ability to work with a group of people towards a single target has become increasingly important in an era when soft skills like communication, creativity, critical thinking and collaboration are essential in work and study. Today's teams are different from those of the past because a team is likely to change membership more often, will be more socially diverse and its members could be located over a wider area – even globally.

In 1965 psychologist Bruce Tuckman recognised that team building goes through different stages, from a collection of individuals to a fully functioning unit. Tuckman did not study groups himself; he reviewed articles about group development. He found that the articles described two features that all the groups had in common: individual interactions and the task activity. Tuckman recognised that groups evolve and he suggested that they do so via four stages that he called forming, storming, norming and performing. Briefly, in the first stage, 'forming', people are getting to know each other and finding their roles in the new hierarchy. In the second stage, 'storming', there are conflicts between members as differences emerge about issues such as what the team is being asked to do and how to do it. In the third phase, 'norming', team members start to work together. They establish processes about who will do what, when and how, and there is a growing sense of cooperation in the team. In the fourth stage, 'performing', the team now has a shared set of norms and has learned how to work well together. The individual members focus less on their position in the team and how to work together and more on their tasks. Tuckman later added a further, final stage, 'adjourning', to his model. In this final stage, the team stops working together, celebrates its success and reflects on its performance and achievements.

The value of Tuckman's model is that it enables us to see team working as a process dependent on interpersonal relationships and the team's interaction with the task. It gives managers and educators a simple, staged model to help them form teams and support the team members as they try to understand where they are in the process. According to the model, all teams are likely to go through these stages in this order, and although it is also possible to go backwards, for example from storming to forming, when a team does this, it must go through the other stages in the same order again. However, the model has been criticised and alternatives have been proposed. Firstly, Tuckman's model was not based on first-hand observations and evidence, and it seems that where the model has been tested, the reality was different from that predicted by the model. A study by the Monterey Naval Postgraduate School showed that only 2% of the teams observed went through all four stages. Furthermore, storming, or conflict, continues throughout the duration of the team's life and conflict happens frequently. Secondly, Tuckman's model excluded external factors such as the nature of the task the group has been given and how this affects progress. Thirdly, the model predicts stability and specialisation: the longer the team stays together, the better it becomes at its task or tasks.

The problem is that when teams become too specialised, this leads to silo working, where teams focus on one task and become territorial about sharing ideas, knowledge and expertise with others in the organisation. In fact, some researchers, like Klaus Schauser at the University of California, have suggested that there is a sixth stage to Tuckman's model: stagnation. Newer companies, especially in the technology sector, require agile – or flexible – teams, and have built their company culture around a process called reteaming, or breaking up teams to build new ones. This enables team members to move between groups so that teams learn from each other. Some online gaming and music streaming companies are noted for their reteaming techniques, believing that this gives them the flexibility to move with their markets and to change and adapt swiftly. One way to re-organise teams is to create situations where a team has to make an effort to recruit new members and there is an ongoing effort to bring in new people. Another way is to let a team grow until it is big enough to divide into two teams; the advantage is that both teams are used to working with each other and so are now two effective working groups. When there is a single temporary problem to solve, volunteers can come together to form a temporary task team. After the work on the problem is completed, the team breaks up and the members re-join their old group. Finally, team members can swap places between teams in order to share learning across the organisation.

Questions 15–19

Complete the table below.

Choose ONE WORD ONLY from the passage for each answer.

Write your answers in boxes 15–19 on your answer sheet.

Stage	Behaviours
Forming	People become acquainted with each other and learn where they fit into the group's **(15)** _____.
Storming	Differences **(16)** _____ in the team about the task members are being asked to do and the way to do it.
Norming	Team **(17)** _____ improves as people learn how to work with each other.
Performing	The team understands how to work together according to agreed **(18)** _____.
Adjourning	The team breaks up and can think about its **(19)** _____ and successes.

Questions 20–21

Choose TWO letters, A–E.

Write the correct letters in boxes 20 and 21 on your answer sheet.

The list below describes some of the features of Tuckman's model.

Which **TWO** points are mentioned by the writer of the text?

    A It regards team working as a process dependent on good managers.

    B It helps managers support their staff as they try to form working teams.

    C It helps managers monitor the performance of their teams.

    D It is based on research carried out by Tuckman in the workplace.

    E It proposes that teams can return to a previous stage before moving to the next one.

Questions 22–23

Choose TWO letters, A–E.

Write the correct letters in boxes 22 and 23 on your answer sheet.

The list below describes some of the shortcomings of Tuckman's model.

Which **TWO** points are mentioned by the writer of the text?

    A It only applies to schools of postgraduate studies.

    B It incorrectly forecasts that teams become unstable and unable to perform well.

    C It does not predict how long a team can stay together.

    D It does not consider outside influences that affect people's work.

    E It does not predict what actually happens at work.

Questions 24–29

Do the following statements agree with the information given in Reading Passage 2?

In boxes 24–29 on your answer sheet, write

> **TRUE** if the statement agrees with the information
> **FALSE** if the statement contradicts the information
> **NOT GIVEN** if there is no information on this

24 Modern tech companies do not like people working in a team for more than six months.

25 Technology companies routinely dissolve teams to form new ones.

26 Reteaming means that technology companies cannot respond quickly to changes in the market.

27 Technology companies routinely recruit new team members from outside the company.

28 Some teams are left to grow until they are big enough to make two smaller teams.

29 Sometimes, people from one team will join another to make a new temporary team focused on a single task.

READING PASSAGE 3

You should spend about 20 minutes on **Questions 30–40***, which are based on Reading Passage 3 below.*

Artificial curation

We all know that too much information can be a bad thing – this is as true in daily life as it is in business. Filtering useful from useless information has become a growing problem, bringing confusion with it, but this is where data curation can help. Curating data involves finding and displaying patterns in large volumes of disconnected and messy data to create meaningful information and suggestions for the end user. The process of data collection to inform business and consumer choice has developed from collecting information via questionnaires and interviews to digitalising information and using technology to gather and interpret data. The latter requires huge databases for computer algorithms (sets of computer instructions) to search and find patterns in order to predict what choices we might make. The use of algorithms is called AI curation, and from shopping to social media, it is part of our lives.

AI curation involves designing computer algorithms that work with large amounts of data. The data is gathered from people's past internet use, for example, searches, purchases, likes and bookmarks. The algorithm looks for patterns in this historical data and uses these patterns to predict the user's choices. The patterns and predictions help the algorithm search and sort through the huge volume of information on the internet and present items that the user has previously looked for or liked or bought. For example, if a person has searched for a particular product online, the algorithm may make suggestions for other products or websites the person might be interested in. If the consumer goes on to click through to the website or to buy something that has been recommended, then the algorithm has found a winning pattern for that individual.

Algorithms make it possible to collect data about a target audience and consequently, they determine which adverts we see as we browse the internet as well as which news stories are shown to us. The purpose of this is to increase our engagement with a particular company or website and thus generate revenue. AI curation has other benefits too. In the recent past, when we wanted information about the news, we went to a news site and if we were interested in sports news, for example, we searched for sports news within that news site. With AI curation, based on our searches and our likes, we have the sports news brought directly to us. Users see what they are mostly interested in and, conversely, see less of what they don't want to. They can therefore build a relationship with websites they frequently visit as content and products are personalised for them, building loyalty and trust. Finally, they are able to focus on certain information and build up specialist knowledge about the things they are interested in. They can even connect with other users who are interested in the same subject and form communities based on that particular topic.

Although algorithms are good to some extent at curating virtual information for us and putting forward suggestions, some companies are moving away from AI and back to human recommendations. Humans have always played a role in some areas of internet curation, particularly news or stories where people have to moderate or make a choice about what is suitable or not for an audience. There have been several cases where algorithms have spread stories that were partially or wholly untrue or presented content that was not suitable for younger people. Some social media companies are bringing back human editors because algorithms cannot distinguish between stories that have on-the-record sources and stories that are simply made up. The other thing a recommendation algorithm can't do is to tell you why it is desirable to use a product – what makes it great or different or better than a rival product. Neither can it give its recommendation the human touch, and people usually prefer recommendations from other people. The problem with human curation, however, is that there just isn't enough of it to deal with all the information, particularly when algorithms are cheaper and much more efficient.

It seems that the best way forward is a solution that uses both AI and human curation. One news company that works in this way starts by asking its users to pick articles for others to read. These stories form the basis for algorithms to work with. The algorithms then gather similar stories for the next stage. When the algorithm has compiled stories from various internet sources, a human editor fine-tunes the selection for the audience. For example, if the AI curator is asked for stories about famous people, it may deliver sensational or even misleading stories because these are the ones that have received the most clicks. At this point, the human curator intervenes and deletes inappropriate content in favour of better stories. It seems that putting a human curator alongside AI can give a better quality of curation and create trust in the recommendations as well as a personal connection that isn't offered by an algorithm alone.

Questions 30–32

Complete the sentences below.

Choose ONE WORD ONLY from the passage for each answer.

Write your answers in boxes 30–32 on your answer sheet.

30 The amount of data that is available to companies is too great to be useful and results in _____.

31 AI curation means that a computer program looks for and shows _____ in large amounts of data.

32 Technology is applied to digital information to collect and _____ the data.

Questions 33–34

Choose TWO letters, A–E.

Write the correct letters in boxes 33 and 34 on your answer sheet.

Which **TWO** things does an algorithm do?

    A It reviews past interactions by the user on the internet to gather data.

    B It helps to build relationships between the user and their preferred websites.

    C It uses people's responses to create advertisements.

    D It collects information from other algorithms.

    E It presents information that we do not want to see.

Questions 35–36

Choose TWO letters, A–E.

Write the correct letters in boxes 35 and 36 on your answer sheet.

Which **TWO** things can't an AI algorithm do?

    A provide certain kinds of information more directly

    B distinguish between stories that have valid sources and those that don't

    C recommend items that are appropriate for the user

    D find sources quickly and efficiently

    E find stories about famous people

Questions 37–40

Complete the flow-chart below.

*Choose **ONE WORD ONLY** from the passage for each answer.*

Write your answers in boxes 37–40 on your answer sheet.

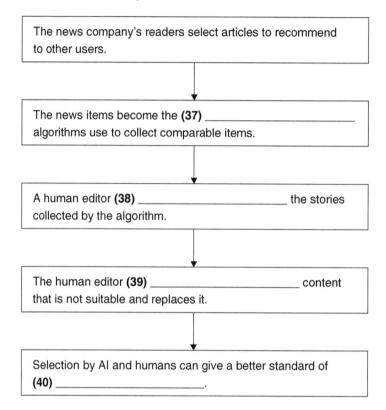

The news company's readers select articles to recommend to other users.

↓

The news items become the **(37)** _____ algorithms use to collect comparable items.

↓

A human editor **(38)** _____ the stories collected by the algorithm.

↓

The human editor **(39)** _____ content that is not suitable and replaces it.

↓

Selection by AI and humans can give a better standard of **(40)** _____.

WRITING

WRITING TASK 1

You should spend about 20 minutes on this task.

> *The diagram below shows a recommended recruitment process for new staff.*
>
> *Summarise the information by selecting and reporting the main features.*

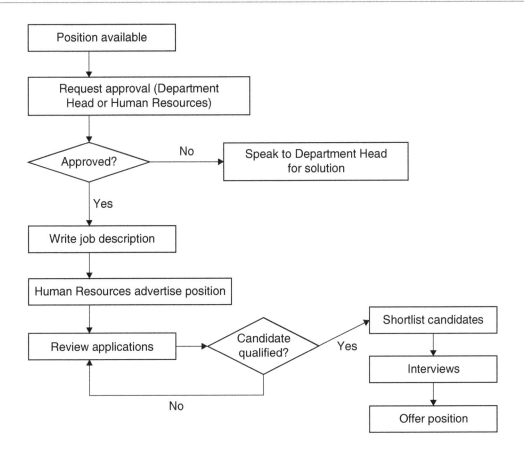

Write at least 150 words.

WRITING TASK 2

You should spend about 40 minutes on this task.

Write about the following topic:

> *Popular social media bloggers and vloggers have become a significant influence for those who follow them.*
>
> *How do social media influencers impact on an audience's purchasing decisions?*
> *Is this a positive or negative development?*

Give reasons for your answer and include any relevant examples from your own knowledge or experience.

Write at least 250 words.

SPEAKING

PART 1: Introduction and interview

Listen to Track 26, pressing pause after each question to answer.

PART 2: Individual long turn

Before you read the task card, listen to Track 27.

Describe a present you were given that you particularly liked.

You should say

what the present was

why you received it

who gave it to you

and say what it is about the present that you liked.

PART 3: Two-way discussion

Listen to Track 28, pressing pause after each question to answer.

General Training Test A

READING

SECTION 1   Questions 1–14

Read the text below and answer questions 1–14.

Questions 1–5

The text has six paragraphs, A–F.

Choose the correct heading for paragraphs A–D and F from the list of headings below.

Write the correct number, i–ix, in boxes 1–5 on your answer sheet.

List of Headings
i   Registering your belongings
ii   Items you should not include in your boxes
iii   Storing your stuff whatever your needs
iv   Taking what you need
v   Charges and fees
vi   Collection day
vii   Using technology to keep your things safe
viii   Tips for packing
ix   What we are responsible for

1   Paragraph **A**

2   Paragraph **B**

3   Paragraph **C**

4   Paragraph **D**

Example	*Answer*
Paragraph **E**	**ii**

5   Paragraph **F**

BoxIt – Moving Students

A If you're moving in or moving out of your student accommodation, you might need a helping hand. At BoxIt we're here to help you move and store your stuff wherever you are, box by box. Because you just pay by the box, you don't pay more than you have to. Whether you're making room for a new purchase, need somewhere to store your things over the holidays, taking a year out or just need more space at home, we'd love to help.

B We store suitcases, cycles, sacks and stacks of other stuff in our secure sites. If you need packing materials, tell us and we'll send them to you. You can upload photos of the things in each box to your own BoxIt account to remind yourself what is where, and then download our app to track your belongings as they move. We'll take your things to our secure warehouse until you're ready for us to bring them back to you. When you're ready to move, give BoxIt a call and we'll deliver your things to your desired location the next day.

C When you're ready, book the delivery of your boxes online. Just let us know what you need to be stored and we'll send one of our friendly staff to pick your things up for free, but remember that if the address we are delivering your boxes to is further than 25 miles from where we picked them up, there is an additional charge. Collections are free from Monday to Friday if we collect between 8 a.m. and 8 p.m. If you'd like a precise time or a weekend collection, these cost a bit more.

D Think about what you're going to put in your boxes and how you're going to put them in before you start. Go through your things and decide what you want to store, give away, throw away or donate to charity. Make sure you've got all you need to move your things – you can order everything from us. You'll need strong boxes – don't use old supermarket boxes – they could let you down. Line your box with bubble wrap all along the inside and then put the softer items like clothes at the bottom and top of the box and your most valuable things in the middle. Don't leave any empty space in your box – this makes your box weaker and it could get squashed and damage the things inside, and not filling the box also means you need more boxes so it costs you money. And don't put too much into your box – keep it under 25 kilos in weight; if you can't lift it, we probably won't be able to either.

E If you pack the following items in your boxes, we can't be responsible for any damage to your things when we're moving them:

- Knives and sharp objects not suitably covered up and wrapped
- Musical instruments in soft cases
- Food, including sauces (e.g. soy sauce and ketchup)
- Antiques (breakable and fragile)
- Pets or any other living creature
- Any item that emits fumes or odours
- Mirrors or large glass items

F Make sure the driver can easily get into your place and that you or someone you trust is at your address for the full duration of the collection time, with your boxes and other items on the ground floor ready to be picked up. And remember: there are also other things you need to do before you go. Leave your room tidy and clean for the inventory checkout; report any faults like the lights not working so that you don't get charged for them; remember to return your keys and leave a forwarding address for any letters.

Questions 6-14

*The text has six paragraphs, **A-F**.*

For which paragraph are the following statements true?

*Write the correct letter, **A-F**, in boxes 6-14 on your answer sheet.*
__NB__ You may use any letter more than once.

6 Before you start to pack, you should decide what you want to keep.

7 You need to pay more if you want BoxIt to come at a time you choose.

8 You can store just one box or more.

9 You should not put anything that has a strong smell in a box.

10 BoxIt do not charge to take your things to storage.

11 Put the items that are precious to you in the middle of your box.

12 The company has software that tells you where your things are.

13 If you do not report any faults or damage to your room, you could be asked to pay for them.

14 It can be more expensive if you do not pack your box fully.

SECTION 2　　　　　*Questions 15–28*

Read the text below and answer questions 15–21.

Taking care of your mental health

A Everyone at some point can feel worried or anxious, homesick or isolated because they don't fit in. This often happens when you change your location or when changes happen to you, and the truth is that this happens to lots of people; it's a normal part of life. It's been recognised that around one third of students will experience poor mental health during their studies. Studying with us is no different but we recognise that taking care of your mental health and physical well-being is necessary for a successful college experience.

B College counselling services can help you maintain a healthy psychological outlook when things get difficult. We offer individual support and face-to-face counselling sessions, individual drop-in sessions, as well as workshops and short courses. There's lots of support for you at the college and this brief guide gives you advice on looking after your mental health and where you can get support if you need it. So, what can you do to look after your mental health when you're facing difficulties?

C People need people and a network of friends and family is extremely important. Your studies will take up a lot of your time and it's easy to become too focused on your academic work to the exclusion of normal life and other people, particularly around exam and assessment periods. Put aside time to talk to family and friends and identify ways to make new friends, but don't forget to take an interest in your old friends and ask them how they are and what they're doing.

D Physical fitness is closely connected to well-being. Exercise releases chemicals in your brain that can positively change your mood. Having goals or challenges linked to physical activity can also improve your mental well-being by enhancing feelings of control, self-esteem and efficiency. Do some physical activity that suits you and that you enjoy but if you don't go to the gym or do a sport, at least you could use the stairs when you go upstairs, go for a walk at lunchtime or get off the bus one stop before your usual one and walk the rest of the way.

E Greater awareness of what's happening at the moment can improve your mental well-being. This involves taking notice of your thoughts and feelings, your body and other things around you. Taking up a free-time activity like music, yoga, walking or hiking can relax and calm you and focus you on what's happening now.

F Doing something kind for someone is also a great way to increase your feelings of well-being. Research shows that doing something for another person once a week for six weeks is associated with an increase in happiness. Try doing something for a friend or relative, volunteer to help with something and tell people around you that you appreciate them. They might say the same thing back to you!

121

G Research shows that learning new skills improves your self-esteem, gives you a sense of direction and helps you to connect with others. Like doing physical activity, learning new things gives you a challenge and a focus away from the things you're doing day to day. Make sure your new skill is broken down stage by stage and that these stages are easily achieved so that you feel a sense of accomplishment. How about learning to play a new sport, taking up a hobby like cooking, or helping someone with their interest?

Questions 15–21

The text has seven paragraphs, A–G.

Which paragraph mentions the following?

Write the correct letter, A–G, in boxes 15–21 on your answer sheet.

15 You can have an individual consultation about your mental health whenever you wish.

16 Good physical and mental health is important if you want to do well academically.

17 Students can focus excessively on their studies at certain times.

18 If you spend a little time every week being caring and considerate, you will probably feel happier.

19 Being active can help you feel more in control of yourself.

20 You can reduce stress by being aware of your surroundings and what you are thinking and feeling.

21 When you learn something different, you feel that you have accomplished something.

Questions 22–28

Read the text below and answer questions 22–28.

How stress can affect us

It is quite normal to feel under pressure, and pressure can sometimes be a positive force: it can make us feel energised, take action and get results. But if the pressure becomes too much and we tip over into feeling stressed, then it can have a negative impact on us and our health. We refer to this state as stress. However, because stress is a very subjective phenomenon, it lacks a precise medical definition and can mean different things in different contexts. We might talk about stressful situations when we have lots to do or worry about and don't have any control over what is happening. Alternatively, we might talk about how we feel when we are anxious or under pressure.

Although stress isn't a mental condition, it can lead to mental health problems or make existing problems deteriorate. If, for example, it is difficult for us to manage our stress, we could become anxious or depressed. The former is when we are worried, tense or afraid about things that could happen in the future and is a natural response when we believe that we are under threat. Depression is a mental state in which we feel isolated, are unable to relate to other people and, among other things, lack self-confidence. Then we find coping with daily life hard and may avoid communication with other people, which makes the problems of stress worse.

Tiredness, headaches or an upset stomach could be the first physical clues that we are stressed. We often find it hard to sleep or eat well, and a poor diet and lack of sleep can affect our physical health. When we are in poor health, this, in turn, can make us feel more stressed emotionally.

Stress is a natural response to a threat, often referred to as the fight, flight or freeze response. Humans, like other animals, have instinctive ways of reacting to physical dangers such as being chased by a wild animal, and when we are threatened, our bodies release the hormones cortisol, norepinephrine and adrenaline. These hormones make us more alert so that we can react faster either to fight for our lives or to run away from the danger, and they make our hearts beat more quickly so that blood is sent to where it is needed most. After the threat has passed, our bodies release other hormones to help our muscles relax. Cortisol, norepinephrine and adrenaline can also be produced when we feel emotionally threatened in stressful situations, but they may take a long time to return to normal levels. The long-term activation of the stress-response system and the overexposure to stress hormones that follows can disrupt almost all the body's processes and leave us at increased risk of many health problems. This can make us feel physically unwell and could affect our health in the longer term.

Questions 22–28

Do the following statements agree with the information given in the text?

In boxes 22–28 on your answer sheet, write

TRUE	*if the statement agrees with the information*
FALSE	*if the statement contradicts the information*
NOT GIVEN	*if there is no information on this*

22 Stress can result from the pressure to do well in exams.

23 Stress can be defined precisely.

24 Stress can make existing psychological problems worse.

25 Anxiety is when we feel lonely and unable to connect with other people.

26 People suffering from depression often feel that life is boring.

27 Stress can have physical effects that make the condition worse.

28 Hormones released during stressful periods can affect our long-term health.

SECTION 3   Questions 29–40

Read the text below and answer questions 29–40.

The European Eel

One of the most mysterious and endangered fish in Europe is the European eel. Eels live long and complex lives and during their lifetime will travel thousands of miles, transforming themselves as they go. They can grow up to one metre long and have long, snake-like bodies with one pair of small fins at the sides. They are secretive creatures; most of their early life at sea is a mystery and when they come inland during their adult lives, they are nocturnal, living under stones and burrowing into mud during the day. They can live between seven and 85 years, with an average lifespan of 55 years, and much of this time is spent out of sight.

The European eel is a 'catadromous' fish: it is born at sea and spawns or reproduces there; then it migrates to inland waters to eat and grow. European eels can be found from Russia and Finland to as far south as the coasts of Morocco, Egypt and the countries around the Black Sea. They spend most of their adult lives in freshwater rivers, streams and estuaries before returning to the open ocean to lay eggs. We know quite a lot about the eels' adult lives but big questions remain about their migration. It was only very recently that scientists following eels with electronic tracking devices along part of their route discovered that the adults do not migrate directly to their breeding grounds. Instead, they follow ocean currents far south of their destination and then catch another current to go north later. They are a solitary species for most of their life and do not join other eels in schools or groups.

In the course of their life, eels pass through a number of very different stages, marked by changes in size, shape and colour. The European eels' life begins near Bermuda in the deep waters of the Sargasso Sea, in the middle of the North Atlantic, where the eggs hatch into transparent larvae called leptocephalus. The Sargasso is noted for its calm blue waters and the Sargassum seaweed that grows there, which the European eels use as cover, drifting with the Gulf Stream as it moves north-eastwards across the Atlantic. This 4,000-mile journey lasts over a year before the eels reach European and North African shores. They gather in the estuaries of rivers in the form of transparent miniature eels called glass eels to continue their migration inland. As glass eels leave the open ocean to enter the estuaries and ascend rivers, they gain colour and are known as elvers. Their migration occurs in late winter, early spring and through the summer months. For the next six to 20 years, the eels grow, putting on weight, becoming longer and developing yellow undersides. This is their yellow eel stage, when they travel continuously upstream toward lower temperatures and less salty waters, possibly also in reaction to crowded waters downstream. During their upriver journey, eels have been observed climbing obstacles such as dams to reach their breeding grounds and also leaving the water altogether and entering fields to eat slugs and worms. After migrating upstream, the male eels grow and feed for six to twelve years, the females for nine to 20 years, before returning to the sea to reproduce. Moving back to the sea, their stomachs dissolve, their skin turns silver and they are called silver eels. They seem to be stimulated to move downstream at night when there is a new moon or when the river is flooding.

Eels were once plentiful in Europe and were a source of food for many inhabitants. In the city of London, which is located on the river Thames, eel pie and jellied eels were a speciality in the poorer East End of the city. But now European eels are on the list of critically endangered species and their numbers have declined by around 90% since the 1970s. Researchers believe that this decrease happens at the glass eel stage, which is when the species is most at risk. In the past 40 years, the number of glass eels arriving in Europe has fallen by around 95%. Several reasons seem to be responsible for the decline. Artificial blocks to their natural migration routes, like weirs and dams, hydropower and water-pumping stations could be preventing the eels reaching their freshwater breeding grounds. Overfishing, pesticides and parasites are also believed to be part of the problem. Researchers in Portugal have found that rising temperatures and acidic waters are posing yet another threat. Dr Reinhold Hanel at the Thunen Institute in Germany also believes that climate change is harming eels by changing the ocean currents along their migration routes to and from the Sargasso Sea so that fewer glass eels are able to drift across to European shores. He stated that for fish that cross oceans and move between fresh and saltwater as eels do, climate change is yet another pressure. These vulnerable fish face so many dangers on their long journeys that the impact of man-made risks is proving too much for their survival.

Questions 29–30

Choose the correct letter, A, B, C or D.

Write your answers in boxes 29 and 30 on your answer sheet.

29 Which of the following is mentioned by the writer?

    A The lifecycle of the European eel is well understood by researchers.

    B The European eel is long-lived and it changes very little during its lifetime.

    C The European eel grows a pair of fins along its back.

    D The European eel is active mainly during the night.

30 The migration route of the European eel back to the Sargasso Sea

    A follows the coasts of Morocco and Egypt.

    B starts in the rivers and estuaries of European countries.

    C has been fully traced by researchers.

    D is indirect and goes past its final destination.

Questions 31–35

Complete the flow-chart below.

Choose **ONE WORD ONLY** *from the text for each answer.*

Write your answers in boxes 31–35 on your answer sheet.

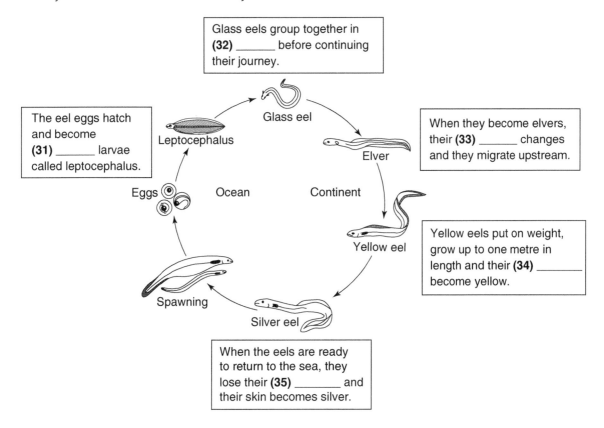

Glass eels group together in **(32)** _____ before continuing their journey.

Glass eel

The eel eggs hatch and become **(31)** _____ larvae called leptocephalus.

Leptocephalus

When they become elvers, their **(33)** _____ changes and they migrate upstream.

Elver

Eggs

Ocean

Continent

Yellow eel

Yellow eels put on weight, grow up to one metre in length and their **(34)** _____ become yellow.

Spawning

Silver eel

When the eels are ready to return to the sea, they lose their **(35)** _____ and their skin becomes silver.

Questions 36–40

Answer the questions below.

Choose NO MORE THAN TWO WORDS from the text for each answer.

Write your answers in boxes 36–40 on your answer sheet.

36 In which city were eels popular as food?

37 At which stage of the eel's life is it most in danger?

38 Which other threat, besides rising temperatures, did researchers in Portugal find harms the eel?

39 What is global warming changing?

40 What kind of risks are putting the eel's survival into question?

WRITING TASK 1

You should spend about 20 minutes on this task.

Your English-speaking friend is coming to visit you for the weekend.

Write a letter to your friend. In your letter
- explain how to get to your house from the station
- describe what you can do at the weekend
- offer advice on the weather and what he/she should bring to wear.

Write at least 150 words. You do NOT need to write any addresses.

Begin your letter as follows:

Dear ...,

WRITING TASK 2

You should spend about 40 minutes on this task.

Write about the following topic:

Some people think the best way to study a second language is in a country where it is spoken. Others believe it is possible to become proficient by staying in your own country and studying there.

Discuss both these views and give your own opinion.

Give reasons for your answer and include any relevant examples from your own knowledge or experience.

Write at least 250 words.

General Training Test B

SECTION 1   *Questions 1–13*

Read the text below and answer Questions 1–7.

Induction week programme

Welcome to your Accounting and Finance course induction. The induction is designed to give you information about your course, college support services and fun events provided by the Students' Union. Your induction week timetable is below.

A Day 1

10:00–12:00 Programme Leader session 1: Welcome and course overview
Other activities today include:
- Q&A at the library
- Careers Service: Placement and work experience drop-in
- Cooking demonstration – good food on a budget!
- The Big Friday Quiz

B Day 2

10:00–12:00 International Students: Meet the tutors at the English Language Centre to learn about its activities
Other activities today include:
- International Student Advice: Ask us about UK culture
- Careers Service: Placement and work experience drop-in
- Friends Hang Out

C Day 3

10:00–11:00 Programme Leader session 2: Economics and International Finance module
Other activities today include:
- Q&A at the Writing Shop
- Careers Service: Finding part-time work

D Day 4

10:00–11:00 Programme Leader session 3: Banking and Finance module
Other activities today include:
- Disability Service: Introduction to student support
- Careers Service: Drop-in
- International Student Advice: Visa advice

Questions 1–7

Look at the induction week events for days A–D above.

On which day will the following people get the information they need?

Write the correct letter, A–D, in boxes 1–7 on your answer sheet.
NB You may use any letter more than once.

1 a student from abroad who wants to find out about speaking classes in English

2 a student who wants to learn about their course in International Finance

3 a disabled student who wants to find out what help is available to them

4 a student who wants to make their own meals without spending a lot of money

5 a student who would like to work in the evening after studying

6 a student who wants to ask about how to stay in the country legally

7 a student who would like to improve their reports and essays

Questions 8–13

Read the text below and answer Questions 8–13.

This is email is to inform you about forthcoming construction work to the Central Building between the beginning of October and mid-November. The rules below are for your safety during the construction work and must be followed.

As you know, the Central Building is in urgent need of upgrading. Site management have therefore taken the decision to partially close sections of the building to make this possible. The work involves essential maintenance mainly to the corridors and ventilation system to make sure that they comply with current fire and safety regulations.

While work is in progress in these parts of the building, please try to find an alternative route that avoids them completely. If you need to access offices or rooms affected by the work, you must:

- let the site manager know that you would like to enter a particular room by completing a permission form and giving the date and time of entry
- wear the hard hat, mask and goggles provided so that you are protected from dust and falling objects
- make sure all electrical equipment is switched off – both the piece of equipment and the plug – when you leave in order to avoid fire hazards
- let the site manager know when you have left the area.

Please comply with these rules and remember that they are intended for your safety and to minimise the risk of accidents. If you have any further questions, please contact us and we will reply within 24 hours.

Questions 8–13

Do the following statements agree with the information given in the text?

In boxes 8–13 on your answer sheet, write

> **TRUE**   *if the statement agrees with the information*
> **FALSE**   *if the statement contradicts the information*
> **NOT GIVEN**   *if there is no information on this*

8   The staff kitchen will be upgraded.

9   The building falls below the standards of modern fire regulations.

10 The building work will take two months to complete.

11 Building work will be carried out mainly to hallways and air circulation systems.

12 If you want to go into a room affected by building work, you need to call the site manager.

13 The work will probably end earlier than scheduled.

Read the text below and answer questions 14–22.

Education Now – Online courses

At Education Now, all our online courses are free so anyone can be a student anywhere, any time. Here are some of our trending courses.

A *Songs: How to listen to a song*

Music and songs have always been part of human society. Discover what songs can tell us about human emotions and learn techniques for interpreting them. On this course, you will learn how to understand what you are listening to and learn to appreciate songs of all kinds. This course is designed for music lovers and anyone who wants to develop and expand their understanding of songs and songwriting.

What will you learn?

By the end of the course, you will be able to ...

- talk about how songs create their effects and describe how music becomes effective, accessible and compelling.
- develop an understanding of the role of songs in contemporary society.

What topics will you cover?

- Traditions: the history of popular music, where it comes from, how it has changed, and how it has been important to societies at different times and in different places.
- How songs work: songwriting techniques and the craft of writing a good song.

B *Business bookkeeping and personal finance*

Develop skills to manage finances in the 21st century. This course is for anyone interested in bookkeeping and financial accounting and will also be of interest to small business owners or those wanting to manage their own finances better.

What will you learn?

By the end of the course, you will have learned ...

- how money works and the skills to manage your personal finances.
- how profit or loss leads to income or debt.
- how to record and organise financial data and how to interpret the information.
- how to prepare a balance sheet and a profit and loss account.

What topics will you cover?

- The main aspects of financial accounting, such as assets, liabilities, revenue and expenses.
- Financial statements and their purposes.

C *Superfood: Truth and fiction*

Blueberries, kale and green tea have all been called superfoods. But what exactly is a superfood? Find out about the link between superfoods, society and health in this course.

What will you learn?

By the end of the course, you will …

- be able to define what a superfood is.
- evaluate the impact of the superfood phenomenon on society and the economy.

What topics will you cover?

- What is a superfood? Are superfoods different from other foods?
- How can we assess superfoods and their impact and role in our diet?
- Are there dangers connected to eating superfoods?

D How to get a graduate job

This course has been designed for students and graduates looking for guidance on how to land a graduate job more easily. It is also useful for anyone who would like to bring their job-hunting skills up to date.

What will you learn?

By the end of the course, you will …

- be able to write a professional CV.
- have developed the interview skills necessary to secure the job you want.

What topics will you cover?

- Everything you need to know about the graduate job market.
- How to stand out in a highly competitive graduate job application process.
- How to prepare for work and how to make a good impression in your new job.

Questions 14–22

Do the following statements agree with the information given in the text?

In boxes 14–22 on your answer sheet, write

TRUE	*if the statement agrees with the information*
FALSE	*if the statement contradicts the information*
NOT GIVEN	*if there is no information on this*

14 People have always expressed their feelings through music.

15 Course A will teach you how to write your own songs.

16 A knowledge of harmony is necessary if you want to do course A.

17 Course B teaches you about banking regulations and rules.

18 At the end of course B you will have a deep understanding of economics.

19 In course C you will learn about the economic effect of superfoods.

20 In course C you can learn which superfoods to include in a healthy diet.

21 Course D is useful for people with out-of-date job-hunting skills.

22 In course D you will learn how to apply for a job and how the job market works.

Read the text below and answer questions 23–28.

IT outages

When IT systems are offline for maintenance and upgrading, employees can feel upset and inconvenienced. However, it's a fact of working life that IT systems have to be taken offline periodically so having effective communications systems and practices are essential to take some of the pain out of the process and can avoid questions, confusion and lost productivity.

Communicate in advance

Whenever possible, provide plenty of notice about any planned downtime. This will help people organise their work in advance and plan accordingly. For example, if they know IT systems will be down for several hours one day in the week, they may decide to work at home or do tasks that don't require IT connectivity during that period.

Communicate more than once

People have lots to do at work and an IT outage a few weeks in the future won't be high on their priority list. Sending an email weeks or days in advance of a suspension of IT services isn't an effective way of informing people. It is much better to communicate several times leading up to the event and again shortly before it. Repeating your key message about the IT service helps to maintain awareness of the event.

Use multiple channels

In the same way that you need to inform people more than once about an IT outage, don't just communicate this via email; if you have several communication channels, use these as well. For example, old-fashioned posters in the staff canteen will remind everyone that scheduled maintenance is about to happen.

On-screen pop-ups

We're all used to notifications from our favourite apps on our mobile phones, and when a pop-up notification is flashed onto our screens at work, it has an immediate impact. Specialist software sends messages directly to the user. These messages cannot be dismissed and require a response so that you know they have been seen and hopefully read. For example, if the IT outage is due the next day, a reminder notification can be sent to all users so that they can prepare for it.

Using these simple suggestions can help everyone get smoothly through an IT outage by communicating facts, getting people's attention and preparing everyone in advance.

Questions 23–28

Complete the summary below.

Choose ONE WORD ONLY from the text for each answer.

Write your answers in boxes 23–28 on your answer sheet.

When IT systems are not available to people, it can cause **(23)** _____,
lost work and lots of questions. It is better to let people know in advance about any
(24) _____ that has been planned so they can adjust their work pattern. For
example, they may plan tasks away from the computer or work at **(25)** _____.
It is essential to tell people several times in different ways. By **(26)** _____
the main message and by using **(27)** _____ methods, for example, posters
in the staff café, you can get people's attention. Another good way to alert people is to send
(28) _____ messages to their computers as they work.

SECTION 3   *Questions 29–40*

Read the text below and answer questions 29–40.

Questions 29–34

The text below has six paragraphs, A–F.

Choose the correct heading for paragraphs B–F from the list of headings below.

Write the correct number, i–ix, in boxes 29–34 on your answer sheet.

List of Headings

i	Sticking with bad decisions
ii	Small and big decisions
iii	Avoiding losing
iv	Unhelpful emotions
v	Information overload
vi	First impressions
vii	The temptations of risk
viii	Understanding processes that influence choices
ix	Peer pressure
x	Making well-informed decisions

Example	*Answer*
Paragraph **A**	**viii**

29 Paragraph **B**

30 Paragraph **C**

31 Paragraph **D**

32 Paragraph **E**

33 Paragraph **F**

34 Paragraph **G**

Decisions, decisions

A We make decisions every minute of our lives, from large, life-changing ones about our careers or relationships to mundane, day-to-day ones, like which socks to wear or how to travel to work. But we often make decisions without considering what we are doing and sometimes our emotions get in the way of rational thought. Making good choices is a balance between reason and desire, knowing what has happened in the past and what you want in the future. Most people do this instinctively, without understanding the mental processes that influence our decisions, but what would happen if we understood these processes better? Researchers today are uncovering the hidden influences that direct us one way or the other when we make choices.

B 'Everyone loves a winner' is a common saying but surprisingly, people dislike losing more than they like winning and it actually takes a lot to tempt us to take a risk. Psychologist and economist Daniel Kahneman from Princeton University found that people do not like to bet money in a 50:50 situation unless they can win twice the amount they could lose. So, for example, although the chance of winning or losing is the same, most people will only bet $100 if they can win more than $200. This suggests that people are more likely to decide to stick with a current situation unless there is a powerful reason to change.

C When a decision needs to be made, emotions seem to get in the way. Daniel Fessler from the University of California asked a group of people to play a game in which they could either get a $15 reward or gamble with the money and risk getting nothing. In one version of the game, he made the people feel angry beforehand and found that men, but not women, gambled more when they were feeling annoyed.

D So, while emotions can sometimes influence us to make bad decisions, logically, the more information we have, the better decisions we should make. Unfortunately, researchers have found that this is not necessarily the case. Having too much data can be just as problematic as having too little. Ap Dijksterhuis and his colleagues at the University of Amsterdam gave two groups of subjects a problem: which car to choose. One group got a list describing just four features, such as how many miles a car had been driven, while the other group had a list of twelve features. Dijksterhuis found that the subjects who had fewer choices picked the best car for them, whereas the other group became confused by the number of features. Surprisingly, the latter group made the best decision when they did not analyse their options based on the features given and relied on gut instinct.

E Another factor that influences our decision-making is sunk cost. The supersonic jet Concorde is a good illustration of the sunk cost fallacy, where the British and French governments justified further spending on a project that would never make a profit because of the amount already spent on it. The sunk cost fallacy, in other words, is the belief that if you have already invested time or money in something, this justifies spending more time or money on it. The fallacy also influences decision-making on a much smaller scale. The more time or money we have invested in something, the more attached to it we are. Hal Arkes and Catherine Blumer at Ohio State University asked a group of students to imagine they had paid $100 for a trip. They were then told they could buy another holiday to a better resort but for a cheaper price. After they had bought both holidays, the students were told that the trips were on the same weekend and they had to choose one of them. Surprisingly, they chose the more expensive but worse deal – a decision based on the fallacy, not logic.

F   The way we behave around our friends has often been studied and it seems that their behaviour also strongly influences the decisions we take. At Arizona State University, researchers led by Robert Cialdini placed cards in hotel rooms asking guests to use their towels more than once, either a) to help the environment, or b) for the sake of future generations, or c) because most of the other guests in the hotel were doing so. The last reason turned out to be 30% more effective than the other two reasons. Social validation can be a major factor in decision-making so it is a good idea to ask yourself when you are making a decision whether it really is your own.

G   On the other hand, we make fast and competent judgements all the time about who we want to talk to and to trust. Alexander Todorov and Janine Willis from Princeton University found that people make judgements about qualities like aggressiveness, likability and attractiveness within the first 100 milliseconds of seeing a person for the first time. Even when the research subjects were given one second more time, they usually just became more confident about their initial choice. It seems that snap decisions and quick judgements can be valid ways of making decisions.

Questions 35–40

Look at the following statements (Questions 35–40) and the list of researchers below.

*Match each statement with the correct researcher, **A–F**.*

*Write the correct letter, **A–F**, in boxes 35–40 on your answer sheet.*
***NB** You may use any letter more than once.*

> **A** Alexander Todorov and Janine Willis
> **B** Daniel Kahneman
> **C** Robert Cialdini
> **D** Ap Dijksterhuis
> **E** Hal Arkes and Catherine Blumer
> **F** Daniel Fessler

35   It takes under a second for people to make judgements about others.

36   Social pressure affects our decision-making.

37   When people have spent time or money on something, they are reluctant to abandon it.

38   Having a lot of information does not always help when making decisions.

39   People dislike situations in which what they risk losing is equal to the amount they might gain.

40   Men are more likely to make bad choices than women when they are emotional.

WRITING

WRITING TASK 1

You should spend about 20 minutes on this task.

> You recently ate at a restaurant and were very dissatisfied with the experience.
> You complained to the waiter at the time but nothing was done.
>
> Write a letter to the restaurant manager. In your letter:
> * describe the problem you had
> * explain what happened when you complained to the waiter
> * say what you would like the manager to do.

Write at least 150 words. You do NOT need to write any addresses.

Begin your letter as follows:

Dear Sir or Madam,

WRITING TASK 2

You should spend about 40 minutes on this task.

Write about the following topic:

> *More people today are choosing to work for themselves rather than for a company or organisation.*
>
> *Why is this the case?*

Give reasons for your answer and include any relevant examples from your own knowledge or experience.

Write at least 250 words.

Mini-dictionary

 Some of the more difficult words from each of the Listening and Reading texts are defined here in this mini-dictionary. The definitions focus on the meanings of the words in the context in which they appear in the text. Definitions and examples are from *Collins COBUILD Key Words for IELTS (Advanced)*, *Collins COBUILD IELTS Dictionary* and *Collins COBUILD Advanced Dictionary*.

TEST 1: LISTENING

Part 1

bug /bʌg/ NOUN You can say that someone has been bitten by a particular **bug** when they suddenly become very enthusiastic about something. [INFORMAL] • *Roundhay Park in Leeds was the place I first got the fishing bug.*

posh /pɒʃ/ (posher, poshest) ADJECTIVE If you describe something as **posh**, you mean that it is smart, fashionable, and expensive. [INFORMAL] • *Celebrating a promotion, I took her to a posh hotel for a cocktail.*

Part 2

consultation /ˌkɒnsəl'teɪʃən/ (consultations) NOUN **Consultation** is discussion about something. • *The plans were drawn up in consultation with the World Health Organisation.*

iron out /ˌaɪən'aʊt/ (irons out, ironing out, ironed out) PHRASAL VERB If you **iron out** difficulties, you resolve them and bring them to an end. • *It was in the beginning, when we were still ironing out problems.*

pilot /'paɪlət/ (pilots) NOUN A **pilot** project is one which is used to test an idea before deciding whether to introduce it on a larger scale. • *It was a ten-year pilot project backed by the trade and industry department.*

premises /'premɪsɪz/ PLURAL NOUN The **premises** of a business or an institution are all the buildings and land that it occupies in one place. • *There is a kitchen on the premises.*

roll out /ˌrəʊl'aʊt/ (rolls out, rolling out, rolled out) PHRASAL VERB If a company **rolls out** a new product or service, or if the product or service **rolls out**, it is made available to the public. • *On Thursday Microsoft rolls out its new operating system.*

shelve /ʃelv/ (shelves, shelving, shelved) VERB If someone **shelves** a plan or project, they decide not to continue with it, either for a while or permanently. • *Sadly, the project has now been shelved.*

stir /stɜː/ PHRASE If an event **causes a stir**, it causes great excitement, shock, or anger among people. • *His film has caused a stir in America.*

Part 3

prioritise /praɪ'ɒrɪtaɪz, US -ɔːr-/ (prioritises, prioritising, prioritised) VERB If you **prioritise** the tasks that you have to do, you decide which are the most important and do them first. • *Make lists of what to do and prioritise your tasks.*

Part 4

ailment /'eɪlmənt/ (ailments) NOUN An **ailment** is an illness, especially one that is not very serious. • *The pharmacist can assist you with the treatment of common ailments.*

enhanced /ɪn'hɑːnst, -hænst/ ADJECTIVE Something that is **enhanced** has an improved value, quality, or attractiveness. • *We aim to provide an enhanced educational experience.*

hard-wired /ˌhɑːd'waɪəd/ ADJECTIVE A **hard-wired** part of a computer forms part of its hardware. • *The computer in the office was hard-wired into the network.*

neural /'njʊərəl, US nʊr-/ ADJECTIVE **Neural** means relating to a nerve or to the nervous system. [MEDICAL] • *They study the neural pathways in the brain.*

neuron /njʊərɒn, US nʊr-/ (neurons) NOUN A **neuron** is a cell which is part of the nervous system. Neurons send messages to and from the brain. [TECHNICAL] • *Information is transferred along each neuron by means of an electrical impulse.*

neuroplasticity /ˌnjʊərəʊplæ'stɪsɪti, US nʊr-/ NOUN **Neuroplasticity** is the ability of the brain to adapt itself following illness or injury. • *What are the wider implications of neuroplasticity?*

trait /treɪt/ (traits) NOUN A **trait** is a particular characteristic, quality, or tendency that someone or something has. • *Creativity is a human trait.*

trigger /'trɪgə/ (triggers, triggering, triggered) VERB If something **triggers** an event or situation, it causes it to begin to happen or exist. • *This was said to be the incident which triggered the outbreak of the First World War.*

TEST 1: READING

Passage 1

algae /'ældʒi, 'ælgaɪ/ NOUN **Algae** is a type of plant with no stems or leaves that grows in water or on damp surfaces. • *Research is being conducted in using algae to reduce greenhouse gas emissions.*

boost /buːst/ (boosts, boosting, boosted) VERB If one thing **boosts** another, it causes it to increase, improve, or be more successful. • *It wants the government to take action to boost the economy.*

coarse /kɔːs/ **(coarser, coarsest)** ADJECTIVE **Coarse** things have a rough texture because they consist of thick threads or large pieces. • *Ahead lay a beach of coarse sand.*

contaminated /kən'tæmɪneɪtɪd/ ADJECTIVE If something is **contaminated**, it has been made dirty or harmful by waste, dirt, chemicals, or radiation. • *Have any fish been contaminated in the Arctic Ocean?*

disinfect /ˌdɪsɪn'fekt/ **(disinfects, disinfecting, disinfected)** VERB If you **disinfect** something, you clean it using a substance that kills germs. • *Chlorine is used to disinfect water.*

domestic /də'mestɪk/ ADJECTIVE **Domestic** duties and activities are concerned with the running of a home and family. • *We made a plan for sharing domestic chores.*

drain /dreɪn/ **(drains, draining, drained)** VERB If you **drain** a liquid from a place or object, you remove the liquid by causing it to flow somewhere else. If a liquid **drains** somewhere, it flows there. • *Miners built the tunnel to drain water out of the mines.*

efficiency /ɪ'fɪʃənsi/ NOUN **Efficiency** is the quality of being able to do a task successfully, without wasting time or energy. • *There are many ways to increase agricultural efficiency in the poorer areas of the world.*

extensive /ɪk'stensɪv/ ADJECTIVE If something is **extensive**, it is very great. • *The blast caused extensive damage, shattering the ground-floor windows.*

filter /'fɪltə/ **(filters)** NOUN A **filter** is a device through which a substance is passed when it is being filtered. • *He discarded the paper coffee filter.*

flake /fleɪk/ **(flakes)** NOUN A **flake** is a small thin piece of something, especially one that has broken off a larger piece. • *The floor was covered with flakes of paint.*

flow /fləʊ/ **(flows, flowing, flowed)** VERB If a liquid, gas, or electrical current **flows** somewhere, it moves there steadily and continuously. • *The current flows into electric motors that drive the wheels.*

flush /flʌʃ/ **(flushes, flushing, flushed)** VERB When someone **flushes** a toilet after using it, they fill the toilet bowl with water in order to clean it, usually by pressing a handle or pulling a chain. You can also say that a toilet **flushes**. • *She flushed the toilet and went back in the bedroom.*

grain /greɪn/ **(grains)** NOUN A **grain** of something such as sand or salt is a tiny hard piece of it. • *Some of these pieces were hardly so large as a grain of sand.*

gravel /'grævəl/ NOUN **Gravel** consists of very small stones. It is often used to make paths. • *The entrance is a narrow gravel driveway with a broken-down gate.*

mechanical /mɪ'kænɪkəl/ ADJECTIVE **Mechanical** means relating to machines and engines and the way they work. • *The train had stopped due to a mechanical problem.*

membrane /'membreɪn/ **(membranes)** NOUN A **membrane** is a thin flexible piece of material. • *Mario was able to develop a microporous membrane that allowed water vapour to escape without allowing water into the shoe.*

potable /'pəʊtəbəl/ ADJECTIVE **Potable** water is clean and safe for drinking. [MAINLY US] • *Potable water was scarce in colonial times.*

prior /'praɪə/ PHRASE If something happens **prior to** a particular time or event, it happens before that time or event. [FORMAL] • *Prior to his Japan trip, he went to New York.*

scarcity /'skeəsɪti/ **(scarcities)** NOUN If there is a **scarcity** of something, there is not enough of it for the people who need it or want it. [FORMAL] • *We were worried about an ever-increasing scarcity of water.*

sterilise /'sterɪlaɪz/ **(sterlises, sterlising, sterilised)** VERB If you **sterilise** a thing or a place, you make it completely clean and free from germs. • *Sulphur is also used to sterilise equipment.*

surge tank /'sɜːdʒtæŋk/ **(surge tanks)** NOUN A **surge tank** is a tank that can absorb sudden large increases in water flow. [TECHNICAL] • *Using a simple surge tank can reduce unfavourable effects.*

sustainable /sə'steɪnəbəl/ ADJECTIVE You use **sustainable** to describe the use of natural resources when this use is kept at a steady level that is not likely to damage the environment. • *Try to buy wood that you know has come from a sustainable source.*

Passage 2

abnormality /ˌæbnɔː'mælɪti/ **(abnormalities)** NOUN An **abnormality** in something, especially in a person's body or behaviour, is an unusual part or feature of it that may be worrying or dangerous. [FORMAL] • *Further scans are required to confirm the diagnosis of an abnormality.*

Achilles tendon /əˌkɪliːz'tendən/ **(Achilles tendons)** NOUN Your **Achilles tendon** is the tendon inside the back of your leg just above your heel. • *He tore his Achilles tendon playing hockey.*

adaptation /ˌædæp'teɪʃən/ **(adaptation)** NOUN **Adaptation** is the act of changing something or changing your behaviour to make it suitable for a new purpose or situation. • *Most living creatures are capable of adaptation when compelled to do so.*

adverse /'ædvɜːs, US æd'vɜːrs/ ADJECTIVE **Adverse** decisions, conditions, or effects are unfavourable to you. • *Despite the adverse conditions, the road was finished in just eight months.*

blood pressure /'blʌdˌpreʃə/ NOUN Your **blood pressure** is the amount of force with which your blood flows around your body. • *This group was more likely to have high blood pressure.*

bob /bɒb/ **(bobs, bobbing, bobbed)** VERB If something **bobs** up and down, it moves up and down, like something does when it is floating on water. • *The raft bobbed up and down quietly.*

bone density /'bəʊn,densɪti/ NOUN **Bone density** is used to refer to the amount of minerals in a particular volume of bone. [MEDICAL] • *Weight-bearing exercise can increase bone density.*

consistently /kən'sɪstəntli/ ADVERB If someone does something **consistently**, they do it regularly, in the same way, or achieve the same level of success in it. • *It's something I have consistently denied.*

contend /kən'tend/ **(contends, contending, contended)** VERB If you **contend** that something is true, you state or argue that it is true. [FORMAL] • *'You were just looking,' contends Samantha. 'I was the one doing all the work.'*

correlation /,kɒrə'leɪʃən, US kɔːr-/ **(correlations)** NOUN A **correlation** between things is a connection or link between them. • *They wanted to prove the correlation between smoking and disease.*

diabetes /,daɪə'biːtiːz, US -tɪs/ NOUN **Diabetes** is a medical condition in which someone has too much sugar in their blood. • *They were carefully screened for diabetes.*

feature /'fiːtʃə/ **(features)** NOUN A **feature** of something is an interesting or important part or characteristic of it. • *The spacious gardens are a special feature of this property.*

forager /'fɒrɪdʒə, US fɔːr-/ **(foragers)** NOUN If you describe a person as a **forager**, you mean that they look for their own food, often in nature. • *There are also rural foragers for whom mushrooms are a key food source.*

impact /ɪm'pækt/ **(impacts, impacting, impacted)** VERB If one object **impacts** another, it hits it with great force. [FORMAL] • *According to the air force, the missile merely impacted the ground prematurely.*

joint /dʒɔɪnt/ **(joints)** NOUN A **joint** is a part of your body such as your elbow or knee where two bones meet and are able to move together. • *Her joints ache if she exercises.*

life expectancy /,laɪfɪk'spektənsi/ NOUN The **life expectancy** of a person, animal, or plant is the length of time that they are normally likely to live. • *They had longer life expectancies than their parents.*

osteoporosis /,ɒstiəʊpə'rəʊsɪs/ NOUN **Osteoporosis** is a condition in which your bones lose calcium and become more likely to break. [MEDICAL] • *She suffers from osteoporosis.*

persistence /pə'sɪstəns/ NOUN If you have **persistence**, you continue to do something even though it is difficult or other people are against it. • *Skill comes only with practice, patience and persistence.*

prey /preɪ/ NOUN A creature's **prey** are the creatures that it hunts and eats in order to live. • *Electric rays stun their prey with huge electrical discharges.*

protein /'prəʊtiːn/ **(proteins)** NOUN **Protein** is a substance found in food and drink such as meat, eggs, and milk. You need **protein** in order to grow and be healthy. • *Fish is a major source of protein for us.*

relatively /'relətɪvli/ ADVERB **Relatively** means to a certain degree, especially when compared with other things of the same kind. • *I like to think I'm relatively easy to get along with.*

run /rʌn/ PHRASE If you talk about what will happen **in the long run**, you are saying what you think will happen over a long period of time in the future. • *Sometimes expensive drugs or other treatments can be economical in the long run.*

Passage 3

clay /kleɪ/ NOUN **Clay** is a kind of earth that is soft when it is wet and hard when it is dry. **Clay** is shaped and baked to make things such as pots and bricks. • *As the wheel turned, the potter shaped the lump of clay into a graceful shape.*

emit /ɪ'mɪt/ **(emits, emitting, emitted)** VERB If something **emits** heat, light, gas, or a smell, it produces it and sends it out by means of a physical or chemical process. [FORMAL] • *The new device emits a powerful circular column of light.*

endospore /'endəʊspɔː/ **(endospores)** NOUN An **endospore** is a spore which develops inside some bacteria cells. • *The DNA was protected in bacterial endospores that can survive in soil for thousands of years.*

extra-terrestrial /,ekstrətɪ'restriəl/ ADJECTIVE **Extra-terrestrial** means happening, existing, or coming from somewhere beyond the planet Earth. [FORMAL] • *NASA has started a 10-year search for extra-terrestrial intelligence.*

geomicrobiologist /,dʒiːəʊmaɪkrəʊbaɪ'ɒlədʒɪst/ **(geomicrobiologists)** NOUN A **geomicrobiologist** is someone who studies how geology and microbiology interact. • *A geomicrobiologist is one of the article's seven co-authors.*

hydrothermal vent /,haɪdrəʊθɜːməl'vent/ **(hydrothermal vents)** NOUN A **hydrothermal vent** is an opening on the floor of the sea which releases hot liquid rich in minerals. • *There were hydrothermal vents at the bottom of the ocean.*

inhospitable /,ɪnhɒ'spɪtəbəl/ ADJECTIVE An **inhospitable** place does not have favourable conditions to live in. • *These are some of the Earth's most inhospitable regions.*

longevity /lɒn'dʒevɪti/ NOUN **Longevity** is long life. [FORMAL] • *Human longevity runs in families.*

metabolism /mɪ'tæbəlɪzəm/ **(metabolisms)** NOUN Your **metabolism** is the way that chemical processes in your body cause food to be used in an efficient way, for example to make new cells and to give you energy. • *Cooling slows the metabolism and lowers the body's need for energy.*

puzzle /'pʌzəl/ **(puzzles)** NOUN You can describe a person or thing that is hard to understand as a **puzzle**. • *This data has presented astronomers with a puzzle about why our outermost planet exists.*

replicate /'replɪkeɪt/ **(replicates, replicating, replicated)** VERB If you **replicate** someone's experiment, work, or research, you do it yourself in exactly the same way. [FORMAL] • *He invited her to his laboratory to see if she could replicate the experiment.*

sustain /sə'steɪn/ **(sustains, sustaining, sustained)** VERB If something **sustains** someone or something, it supports them by providing necessities. • *The parameters within which life can be sustained on Earth are extraordinarily narrow.*

thrive /θraɪv/ **(thrives, thriving, thrived)** VERB If someone or something **thrives**, they do well and are successful, healthy, or strong. • *Lavender thrives in poor soil.*

uninhabitable /ˌʌnɪn'hæbɪtəbəl/ ADJECTIVE If a place is **uninhabitable**, it is impossible for people to live there, for example because it is dangerous or unhealthy. • *About 90 percent of the city's single-family homes are uninhabitable.*

TEST 2: LISTENING

Part 1

expand /ɪk'spænd/ **(expands, expanding, expanded)** VERB If something **expands**, it becomes larger. • *Engineers noticed that the pipes were not expanding as expected.*

line manager /'laɪnmænɪdʒə/ **(line managers)** NOUN Your **line manager** is the person at work who is in charge of your department, group, or project. [BRIT, BUSINESS] • *It is important that the HR manager and line managers work in tandem.*

settle /'setəl/ **(settles, settling, settled)** VERB If something **settles**, it sinks slowly down. • *Tap each one firmly on your work surface to settle the mixture.*

Part 2

pass /pɑːs , pæs/ **(passes)** NOUN A **pass** is a document that allows you to do something. • *I got myself a pass into the barracks.*

shuttle /'ʃʌtəl/ **(shuttles)** NOUN A **shuttle** is a plane, bus, or train which makes frequent journeys between two places. • *There are shuttle flights between London and Manchester.*

Part 3

deposit /dɪ'pɒzɪt/ **(deposits)** NOUN A **deposit** is a sum of money which is part of the full price of something, and which you pay when you agree to buy it. • *A £50 deposit is required when ordering, and the balance is due upon delivery.*

high-end /ˌhaɪ'end/ ADJECTIVE **High-end** products are the most expensive of their kind. • *They deal in high-end personal computers and computer workstations.*

Part 4

do-able /'duːəbəl/ ADJECTIVE If something is **do-able**, it is possible to do it. • *Is this project something that you think is do-able?*

fine-tune /ˌfaɪn'tjuːn/ **(fine-tunes, fine-tuning, fine-tuned)** VERB If you **fine-tune** something, you make very small and precise changes to it in order to make it as successful or effective as it possibly can be. • *We do not try to fine-tune the economy on the basis of short-term predictions.*

stiff /stɪf/ **(stiffer, stiffest)** ADJECTIVE **Stiff** can be used to mean difficult or severe. • *The film faces stiff competition for the Best Film nomination.*

worst-case scenario /ˌwɜːstkeɪssə'nɑːriəʊ/ **(worst-case scenarios)** NOUN If you describe a situation or event as the **worst-case** scenario, you mean that it is the worst possible thing that could happen. • *This would only be done in worst-case scenarios.*

TEST 2: READING

Passage 1

asteroid /'æstərɔɪd/ **(asteroids)** NOUN An **asteroid** is one of the very small planets that move around the sun, especially between Mars and Jupiter. • *It hopes to take water found frozen on the asteroids and turn it into fuel and oxygen.*

brick /brɪk/ **(bricks)** NOUN **Bricks** are rectangular blocks of baked clay used for building walls, which are usually red or brown. • *She built bookshelves out of bricks and planks.*

colonise /'kɒlənaɪz/ **(colonises, colonising, colonised)** VERB If people **colonise** somewhere, they go to live there and take control of it. • *The first British attempt to colonise Ireland was in the twelfth century.*

component /kəm'pəʊnənt/ **(components)** NOUN The **components** of something are the parts that it is made of. • *The management plan has four main components.*

constituent /kən'stɪtʃuənt/ ADJECTIVE The **constituent** parts of something are the things from which it is formed. [FORMAL] • *They had a plan to split the company into its constituent parts and sell them separately.*

cosmic radiation /ˌkɒzmɪkreɪdi'eɪʃən/ NOUN **Cosmic radiation** is made up of rays that reach Earth from outer space and consist of atomic nuclei. • *They are trying to find a way of using it in space to detect cosmic radiation there.*

crater /'kreɪtə/ **(craters)** NOUN A **crater** is a very large hole in the ground, which has been caused by something hitting it or by an explosion. • *Amateurs mostly observed bright objects, like the craters of the Moon.*

dome /dəʊm/ **(domes)** NOUN A **dome** is a round roof. • *Ahead us rose the dome of St Paul's Cathedral.*

electrolyse /ɪ'lektrəʊˌlaɪz/ **(electrolyses, electrolysing, electrolysed)** VERB To **electrolyse** a substance means to break it down by passing an electric current through it. [TECHNICAL] • *It uses wind power to electrolyse water.*

energy intensive /ˌenədʒiɪn'tensɪv/ ADJECTIVE If something is **energy intensive**, is uses a large amount of energy. • *The aluminium smelting process is very energy intensive.*

establish /ɪˈstæblɪʃ/ **(establishes, establishing, established)** VERB If someone **establishes** something, they create it. • *The school was established in 1989 by an Italian professor.*

fundamental /ˌfʌndəˈmentəl/ ADJECTIVE You use **fundamental** to describe things, activities, and principles that are very important or essential. They affect the basic nature of other things or are the most important element upon which other things depend. • *Our constitution embodies all the fundamental principles of democracy.*

harvest /ˈhɑːvɪst/ **(harvests, harvesting, harvested)** VERB If someone **harvests** something, they collect it. • *Millions of social media users have unknowingly had their personal data harvested.*

lava /ˈlɑːvə/ NOUN **Lava** is the very hot liquid rock that comes out of a volcano. • *Red hot lava was spewing metres up into the night-time sky.*

lead /liːd/ **(leads)** NOUN A **lead** is a piece of information or an idea which may help people to discover the facts in a situation where many facts are not known, for example in the investigation of a crime or in a scientific experiment. • *The inquiry team is also following up possible leads after receiving 400 calls from the public.*

logistical /ləˈdʒɪstɪkəl/ ADJECTIVE **Logistical** means relating to the organization of something complicated. • *Logistical problems may be causing the delay.*

lunar module /ˌluːnəˈmɒdjuː/ **(lunar modules)** NOUN A **lunar module** is a vehicle for travelling from a spacecraft to the surface of the moon and back to the spacecraft. • *With less than 30 seconds of fuel left, the lunar module landed in the Sea of Tranquility.*

magnetic field /mægˌnetɪkˈfiːld/ **(magnetic fields)** NOUN A **magnetic field** is an area around a magnet, or something functioning as a magnet, in which the magnet's power to attract things is felt. • *The overall magnetic field has a direction, just as Earth's north and south poles attract our compasses.*

mineral /ˈmɪnərəl/ **(minerals)** NOUN A **mineral** is a substance such as tin, salt, or sulphur that is formed naturally in rocks and in the earth. **Minerals** are also found in small quantities in food and drink. • *There were only about a dozen different minerals, including diamonds.*

processing plant /ˈprəʊsesɪŋplɑːnt, -plænt/ **(processing plants)** NOUN A **processing plant** is a factory where raw materials are treated or prepared by a special method. • *We'll need to have a small processing plant.*

prohibitive /prəˈhɪbɪtɪv , US prəʊ-/ ADJECTIVE If the cost of something is **prohibitive**, it is so high that many people cannot afford it. [FORMAL] • *The cost of private treatment can be prohibitive.*

simulation /ˌsɪmjʊˈleɪʃən/ **(simulations)** NOUN **Simulation** is the process of simulating something or the result of simulating it. • *Training includes realistic simulation of casualty procedures.*

source /sɔːs/ **(sources, sourcing, sourced)** VERB If something **is sourced**, a source for it is found. • *The materials are sourced globally.*

space agency /ˈspeɪseɪdʒənsi/ **(space agencies)** NOUN A **space agency** is an organization dedicated to space exploration. • *Canadian companies have a good working relationship with the space agency.*

sustain (see Test 1 Reading Passage 3)

touch down /ˌtʌtʃˈdaʊn/ **(touches down, touching down, touched down)** PHRASAL VERB When an aircraft **touches down**, it lands. • *When we touched down at Heathrow we were all relieved just to get home.*

transmit /trænzˈmɪt/ **(transmits, transmitting, transmitted)** VERB When computer data or other electronic messages **are transmitted**, they are sent from one place to another, using wires, radio waves, or satellites. • *This is currently the most efficient way to transmit certain types of data.*

underway /ˌʌndəˈweɪ/ ADJECTIVE If an activity is **underway**, it has already started. If an activity gets **underway**, it starts. • *An investigation is underway to find out how the disaster happened.*

Passage 2

access /ˈækses/ **(accesses, accessing, accessed)** VERB If you **access** something, you succeed in obtaining it. • *Organisations have criticised the lengthy process involved in accessing grants.*

algorithm /ˈælgərɪðəm/ **(algorithms)** NOUN An **algorithm** is a series of mathematical steps, especially in a computer program, which will give you the answer to a particular kind of problem or question. • *Computer algorithms can extract behaviours or patterns of movement.*

approve /əˈpruːv/ **(approves, approving, approved)** VERB If someone in a position of authority **approves** a plan or idea, they formally agree to it and say that it can happen. • *Parliament has approved a programme of radical economic reforms.*

assess /əˈses/ **(assesses, assessing, assessed)** VERB When you **assess** a person, thing, or situation, you consider them in order to make a judgment about them. • *Our correspondent has been assessing the impact of the sanctions.*

assign /əˈsaɪn/ **(assigns, assigning, assigned)** VERB If something is **assigned to** someone, it is for their use. • *Eight beautiful rooms had been assigned to her.*

backing /ˈbækɪŋ/ NOUN If someone has the **backing** of an organization, they receive support or money from that organization in order to do somethng. • *He said the president had the full backing of his government to negotiate a deal.*

bypass /ˈbaɪpɑːs, -pæs/ **(bypasses, bypassing, bypassed)** VERB If you **bypass** someone or something that you would normally have to get involved with, you ignore them, often because you want to achieve something more quickly. • *A growing number of employers are trying to bypass the rules altogether.*

credit rating /ˈkredɪtˌreɪtɪŋ/ NOUN Your **credit rating** is a judgment of how likely you are to pay money back if you borrow it or buy things on credit. • *The deals required the city to maintain a certain credit rating.*

crowdfunding /ˈkraʊdfʌndɪŋ/ NOUN **Crowdfunding** is when a large number of people each give an amount of money to pay for a project, especially by using a website to collect the money. • *The project was financed through crowdfunding.*

factor /ˈfæktə/ (**factors**) NOUN A **factor** is one of the things that affects an event, decision, or situation. • *Physical activity is an important factor in maintaining fitness.*

founder /ˈfaʊndə/ (**founders**) NOUN The **founder** of an institution, organization, or building is the person who got it started or caused it to be built, often by providing the necessary money. • *He was one of the founders of the university's medical faculty.*

generate /ˈdʒenəreɪt/ (**generates, generating, generated**) VERB To **generate** something means to cause it to begin and develop. • *The Employment Minister said the reforms would generate new jobs.*

invest /ɪnˈvest/ (**invests, investing, invested**) VERB If you **invest** a sum of money, you use your money in a way that you hope will increase its value, for example by paying it into a bank, or buying shares or property. • *When people buy houses they're investing a lot of money.*

investor /ɪnˈvestə/ (**investors**) NOUN An **investor** is a person or organization that buys stocks or shares, or pays money into a bank in order to receive a profit. • *The main investor is a French bank.*

peer /pɪə/ (**peers**) NOUN Your **peers** are the people who are the same age as you or who have the same status as you. • *His engaging personality made him popular with his peers.*

regulate /ˈreɡjʊleɪt/ (**regulates, regulating, regulated**) VERB To **regulate** an activity or process means to control it, especially by means of rules. • *Serious reform is needed to improve institutions that regulate competition.*

regulation /ˌreɡjʊˈleɪʃən/ (**regulations**) NOUN **Regulations** are rules made by a government or other authority in order to control the way something is done or the way people behave. • *Employers are now working to the new regulations.*

reserve /rɪˈzɜːv/ (**reserves**) NOUN A **reserve** is a supply of something that is available for use when it is needed. • *It is believed that the airline also has strong cash reserves.*

revenue /ˈrevənjuː/ (**revenues**) NOUN **Revenue** is money that a company, organization, or government receives from people. [BUSINESS] • *It was a boom year at the cinema, with record advertising revenue.*

safeguard /ˈseɪfɡɑːd/ (**safeguards**) NOUN A **safeguard** is a law, rule, or measure intended to prevent someone or something from being harmed. • *Many* people took second jobs as a safeguard against unemployment.

security /sɪˈkjʊərɪti/ (**securities**) NOUN If something is **security** for a loan, you promise to give that thing to the person who lends you money, if you fail to pay the money back. [BUSINESS] • *The central bank will provide special loans, and the banks will pledge the land as security.*

share /ʃeə/ (**shares**) NOUN A company's **shares** are the many equal parts into which its ownership is divided. **Shares** can be bought by people as an investment. [BUSINESS] • *This is why the chairman has been so keen to buy shares in the rival airline.*

significance /sɪɡˈnɪfɪkəns/ NOUN The **significance** of something is the importance that it has, usually because it will have an effect on a situation or shows something about a situation. • *Ideas about the social significance of religion have changed over time.*

transaction /trænˈzækʃən/ (**transactions**) NOUN A **transaction** is a piece of business, for example an act of buying or selling something. [FORMAL] • *The city or state levied a tax on every financial transaction.*

vehicle /ˈviːɪkəl/ (**vehicles**) NOUN You can use **vehicle** to refer to something that you use in order to achieve a particular purpose. • *Her art became a vehicle for her political beliefs.*

Passage 3

breeding ground /ˈbriːdɪŋɡraʊnd/ (**breeding grounds**) NOUN A **breeding ground** is a place where many animals or birds of a particular kind breed. • *Migrating birds need rest stops as they fly across the desert to reach their breeding grounds .*

deny /dɪˈnaɪ/ (**denies, denying, denied**) VERB If you **deny** someone something that they need or want, you refuse to let them have it. • *They would sometimes padlock the gates to deny us access.*

encounter /ɪnˈkaʊntə/ (**encounters, encountering, encountered**) VERB If you **encounter** problems or difficulties, you experience them. • *Every day of our lives we encounter stresses of one kind or another.*

endurance /ɪnˈdjʊərəns, US -dʊr-/ NOUN **Endurance** is the ability to continue with an unpleasant or difficult situation, experience, or activity over a long period of time. • *The exercise obviously will improve strength and endurance.*

geopositioning /ˌdʒiːəʊpəˈzɪʃənɪŋ/ NOUN **Geopositioning** is technology which is used to identify someone's current location. • *Geopositioning systems track goods in transit.*

hemisphere /ˈhemɪsfɪə/ (**hemispheres**) NOUN A **hemisphere** is one half of the earth. • *We live in the northern hemisphere.*

imprint /ɪmˈprɪnt/ (**imprints, imprinting, imprinted**) VERB If a young animal **imprints**, it learns very quickly to recognise things, such as other members of its own species. • *If nothing is moving or quacking at that* critical point, the ducklings don't become imprinted at all.

interpret /ɪnˈtɜːprɪt/ (**interprets, interpreting, interpreted**) VERB If you **interpret** something in a particular way, you decide that this is its meaning or significance. • *Both approaches agree on what is depicted in the poem, but not on how it should be interpreted.*

intuitively /ɪnˈtjuːɪtɪvli, US -tuː-/ ADVERB If you do something **intuitively**, you do it instinctively, without any prior knowledge or experience. • *He seemed to know intuitively that I must be missing my mother.*

magnetic current /mægˌnetɪkˈkʌrənt/ (**magnetic currents**) NOUN **Magnetic current** is a type of electric current. • *Experiments have shown that, within the substance of anti-ice, intensely strong magnetic currents flow.*

mate /meɪt/ (**mates, mating, mated**) VERB When animals **mate**, a male and a female have sex in order to produce young. • *It is easy to tell when a female is ready to mate.*

migration /maɪˈɡreɪʃən/ NOUN **Migration** is when birds, fish, or animals move at a particular season from one part of the world or from one part of a country to another, usually in order to breed or to find new feeding grounds. • *Visitors arrange whale-watching tours during migration in hopes of witnessing the massive mammal.*

navigator /ˈnævɪɡeɪtə/ (**navigators**) NOUN In the past, a **navigator** was an explorer who travelled by sea. • *These maps reflect the discoveries of early Portuguese navigators.*

overcast /ˈəʊvəkɑːst, -kæst/ ADJECTIVE If it is **overcast**, or if the sky or the day is **overcast**, the sky is completely covered with cloud and there is not much light. • *For three days it was overcast.*

planetarium /plænɪˈteəriəm/ (**planetariums**) NOUN A **planetarium** is a building where lights are shone on the ceiling to represent the planets and the stars and to show how they appear to move. • *It inspired generations of children, but now the planetarium is focusing on lesser stars.*

project /prəˈdʒekt/ (**projects, projecting, projected**) VERB If a film or picture **is projected** onto a screen or wall, it appears there. • *There is a list of words projected onto a wall and a neon sign.*

random /ˈrændəm/ ADJECTIVE If you describe events as **random**, you mean that they do not seem to follow a definite plan or pattern. • *Children's words and actions are often fairly random.*

rear /rɪə/ (**rears, rearing, reared**) VERB If a person or animal **rears** a young animal, they keep and look after it until it is old enough to look after itself. [MAINLY BRITISH] • *She spends a lot of time rearing animals.*

receptor /rɪˈseptə/ (**receptors**) NOUN **Receptors** are nerve endings in your body which react to changes and stimuli and make your body respond in a particular way. [TECHNICAL] • *The report mentioned the information receptors in our brain.*

seek /siːk/ (**seeks, seeking, sought**) VERB If you **seek** something, you try to find it. • *Drought has forced the animals to seek food and water in urban areas.*

stamina /ˈstæmɪnə/ NOUN **Stamina** is the physical or mental energy needed to do a tiring activity for a long time. • *You have to have a lot of stamina to be a top-class dancer.*

stopover /ˈstɒpəʊvə/ (**stopovers**) NOUN A **stopover** is a short stay in a place in between parts of a journey. • *The Sunday flights will make a stopover in Paris.*

trace /treɪs/ (**traces**) NOUN A **trace** of something is a very small amount of it. • *Wash them in cold water to remove all traces of sand.*

TEST 3: LISTENING

Part 2

dispose /dɪˈspəʊz/ (**disposes, disposing, disposed**) VERB If you **dispose of** something that you no longer want or need, you throw it away. • *Just fold up the nappy and dispose of it in the normal manner.*

dotted /ˈdɒtɪd/ ADJECTIVE If things are **dotted** around a place, they can be found in many different parts of that place. • *Many pieces of sculpture are dotted around the house.*

shed /ʃed/ (**sheds**) NOUN A **shed** is a small building that can be used for storing things. • *It is the smallest shed on the allotments.*

stroke /strəʊk/ (**strokes, stroking, stroked**) VERB If you **stroke** someone or something, you move your hand slowly and gently over them. • *Carla, curled up on the sofa, was stroking her cat.*

tempting /ˈtemptɪŋ/ ADJECTIVE If something is **tempting**, it makes you want to do it or have it. • *At first glance, it would be tempting to agree.*

Part 3

internship /ˈɪntɜːnʃɪp/ (**internships**) NOUN An **internship** is the position held by an intern, or the period of time when someone is an intern. • *He went to Atlanta for a month-long internship.*

placement /ˈpleɪsmənt/ (**placements**) NOUN If someone who is training gets a **placement**, they get a job for a period of time which is intended to give them experience in the work they are training for. • *He had a six-month work placement with the Japanese government.*

reflective /rɪˈflektɪv/ ADJECTIVE If something you do is **reflective**, you have thought deeply while doing it. [WRITTEN] • *There is a reflective silence before he goes on.*

stead /sted/ PHRASE If you say that something will **stand** someone **in good stead**, you mean that it will be very useful to them in the future. • *My years of teaching stood me in good stead.*

stick with /ˌstɪk'wɪð/ (sticks with, sticking with, stuck with) PHRASAL VERB If you **stick with** something, you do not change to something else. • *If you're in a job that keeps you busy, stick with it.*

Part 4

application /ˌæplɪ'keɪʃən/ (applications) NOUN The **application** of something is the use of it in a particular situation. • *Research and development on the application of nuclear energy to produce electricity began in the 1940s.*

brittle /'brɪtəl/ ADJECTIVE An object or substance that is **brittle** is easily broken. • *Pine is brittle and breaks.*

crosswire /'krɒswaɪə/ (crosswires) NOUN **Crosswires** are the lines or wires that cross each other in the sight of a gun and provide a point to focus on. • *I tried my best to keep the crosswires centred on the target.*

dread /dred/ (dreads, dreading, dreaded) VERB If you **dread** something which may happen, you feel very anxious and unhappy about it because you think it will be unpleasant or upsetting. • *I'm dreading Christmas this year.*

dress /dres/ (dresses, dressing, dressed) VERB When someone **dresses** a wound, they clean it and cover it. • *She never cried or protested when I was dressing her wounds.*

equation /ɪ'kweɪʒən/ PHRASE If you **take** something **out of the equation**, you no longer need to consider it with other factors. • *This takes the high upfront cost out of the equation.*

eradicate /ɪ'rædɪkeɪt/ (eradicates, eradicating, eradicated) VERB To **eradicate** something means to get rid of it completely. [FORMAL] • *They are already battling to eradicate illnesses such as malaria and tetanus.*

harvest (see Test 2 Reading Passage 1)

indigenous /ɪn'dɪdʒɪnəs/ ADJECTIVE **Indigenous** people or things belong to the country in which they are found, rather than coming there or being brought there from another country. [FORMAL] • *There was no consultation with the indigenous population.*

industrial scale /ɪnˌdʌstriəl'skeɪl/ PHRASE If something is produced **on an industrial scale**, you mean that a very large amount of it is made. • *Sulphur was being manufactured on an industrial scale.*

intricate /'ɪntrɪkət/ ADJECTIVE You use **intricate** to describe something that has many small parts or details. • *He has hand carved intricate patterns into the wooden stairways.*

liquid /'lɪkwɪd/ ADJECTIVE A **liquid** substance is in the form of a liquid rather than being solid or a gas. • *Wash in warm water with liquid detergent.*

misleading /mɪs'liːdɪŋ/ ADJECTIVE If you describe something as **misleading**, you mean that it gives you a wrong idea or impression. • *It would be misleading to say that we were friends.*

optical /'ɒptɪkəl/ ADJECTIVE **Optical** devices, processes, and effects involve or relate to vision, light, or images.

• *The microscope can be practically any high-end optical device.*

scaffold /'skæfəʊld/ (scaffolds) NOUN A **scaffold** is a temporary metal or wooden framework that is used for support during building work. • *Joiners and labourers set to work, building the scaffold.*

scuttle /'skʌtəl/ (scuttles, scuttling, scuttled) VERB When people or small animals **scuttle** somewhere, they run there with short quick steps. • *Crabs scuttle along the muddy bank.*

sight /saɪt/ (sights) NOUN The **sights** of a weapon such as a rifle are the part which helps you aim it more accurately. • *In this scene, everything is seen through the sights of a gun.*

solid /'sɒlɪd/ ADJECTIVE A **solid** substance or object stays the same shape whether it is in a container or not. • *He did not eat solid food for several weeks.*

spin /spɪn/ (spins, spinning, spun) VERB When people **spin**, they make thread by twisting together pieces of a fibre using a device or machine. • *Other festivities will include folk art demonstrations such as spinning and quilting.*

stiff /stɪf/ (stiffer, stiffest) ADJECTIVE Something that is **stiff** is firm or does not bend easily. • *His waterproof trousers were brand new and stiff.*

strand /strænd/ (strands) NOUN A **strand** of something such as hair, wire, or thread is a single thin piece of it. • *She tried to blow a grey strand of hair from her eyes.*

territorial /ˌterɪ'tɔːriəl/ ADJECTIVE If you describe an animal or its behaviour as **territorial**, you mean that it has an area which it regards as its own, and which it defends when other animals try to enter it. • *Two cats or more in one house will also exhibit territorial behaviour.*

withstand /wɪð'stænd/ (withstands, withstanding, withstood) VERB If something or someone **withstands** a force or action, they survive it or do not give in to it. [FORMAL] • *Exercise really can help you withstand stresses and strains more easily.*

TEST 3: READING

Passage 1

address /ə'dres, US 'ædres/ (addresses, addressing, addressed) VERB If you **address** a problem or task, you try to understand it or deal with it. • *The CEO sought to address those fears when he spoke at the meeting.*

adjust /ə'dʒʌst/ (adjusts, adjusting, adjusted) VERB When you **adjust** to a new situation, you get used to it by changing your behaviour or your ideas. • *I felt I had adjusted to the idea of being a mother very well.*

assimilate /ə'sɪmɪleɪt/ (assimilates, assimilating, assimilated) VERB If you **assimilate** new ideas, techniques, or information, you learn them or adopt them. • *I was speechless, still trying to assimilate the enormity of what he'd told me.*

basis /ˈbeɪsɪs/ (bases) NOUN The **basis** of something is its starting point or an important part of it from which it can be further developed. • *Both groups have broadly agreed that the plan is a possible basis for negotiation.*

concept /ˈkɒnsept/ (concepts) NOUN A **concept** is an idea or abstract principle. • *She added that this concept is misunderstood in the west.*

cope /kəʊp/ (copes, coping, coped) VERB If a machine or a system can **cope** with something, it is large enough or complex enough to deal with it satisfactorily. • *The banks were swamped by compensation claims and were unable to cope.*

crucial /ˈkruːʃəl/ ADJECTIVE If you describe something as **crucial**, you mean it is extremely important. • *Improved consumer confidence is crucial to an economic recovery.*

embrace /ɪmˈbreɪs/ (embraces, embracing, embraced) VERB If you **embrace** a change, political system, or idea, you accept it and start supporting it or believing in it. [FORMAL] • *The new rules have been embraced by government watchdog organizations.*

framework /ˈfreɪmwɜːk/ (frameworks) NOUN A **framework** is a particular set of rules, ideas, or beliefs which you use in order to deal with problems or to decide what to do. • *They acted within the framework of federal regulations.*

grief /griːf/ NOUN **Grief** is a feeling of extreme sadness. • *Their grief soon gave way to anger.*

inevitable /ɪnˈevɪtəbəl/ ADJECTIVE If something is **inevitable**, it is certain to happen and cannot be prevented or avoided. • *If the case succeeds, it is inevitable that other trials will follow.*

objection /əbˈdʒekʃən/ (objections) NOUN If you make or raise an **objection** to something, you say that you do not like or agree with it. • *Some managers have recently raised objections to the PFA handling these negotiations.*

patient /ˈpeɪʃənt/ (patients) NOUN A **patient** is a person who is receiving medical treatment from a doctor or hospital. A patient is also someone who is registered with a particular doctor. • *He specialized in treatment of cancer patients.*

propose /prəˈpəʊz/ (proposes, proposing, proposed) VERB If you **propose** a theory or an explanation, you state that it is possibly or probably true, because it fits in with the evidence that you have considered. [FORMAL] • *This highlights a problem faced by people proposing theories of ball lightning.*

resentment /rɪˈzentmənt/ NOUN **Resentment** is bitterness and anger that someone feels about something. • *She expressed resentment at being interviewed by a social worker.*

response /rɪˈspɒns/ (responses) NOUN Your **response** to an event or to something that is said is your reply or reaction to it. • *The meeting was called in response to a request from Venezuela.*

slip /slɪp/ (slips, slipping, slipped) VERB If something **slips** to a lower level or standard, it falls to that level or standard. • *Shares slipped to 117p.*

sphere /sfɪə/ (spheres) NOUN A **sphere** of activity or interest is a particular area of activity or interest. • *The decision affected nurses working in all spheres of the health service.*

status /ˈsteɪtəs/ NOUN Your **status** is your social or professional position. • *The fact that the burial involved an expensive coffin signifies that the person was of high status.*

status quo /ˌsteɪtəsˈkwəʊ/ NOUN The **status quo** is the state of affairs that exists at a particular time, especially in contrast to a different possible state of affairs. • *They have no wish for any change in the status quo.*

traumatic /trɔːˈmætɪk, US trɑʊ-/ ADJECTIVE A **traumatic** experience is very shocking and upsetting, and may cause psychological damage. • *I suffered a nervous breakdown. It was a traumatic experience.*

turmoil /ˈtɜːmɔɪl/ (turmoils) NOUN **Turmoil** is a state of confusion, disorder, uncertainty, or great anxiety. • *Her life was in turmoil.*

undermine /ˌʌndəˈmaɪn/ (undermines, undermining, undermined) VERB If you **undermine** someone's position or authority, you make their authority or position less secure, often by indirect methods. • *The conversations were designed to undermine her authority.*

Passage 2

accumulation /əˌkjuːmjʊˈleɪʃən/ NOUN **Accumulation** is the collecting together of things over a period of time. • *The rate of accumulation decreases with time.*

chain reaction /ˌtʃeɪnriˈækʃn/ (chain reactions) NOUN A **chain reaction** is a series of events, each of which causes the next. • *Whenever recession strikes, a chain reaction is set into motion.*

course /kɔːs/ NOUN The **course** of something is the route along which it is travelling. • *The pilot requested clearance to alter course to avoid the storm.*

debris /ˈdebriː, US ˈdeɪbriː/ NOUN **Debris** is pieces from something that has been destroyed or pieces of rubbish or unwanted material that are spread around. • *I watched the rescue workers sifting through the debris.*

dock /dɒk/ (docks, docked, docking) VERB When one spacecraft **docks** or **is docked** with another, the two crafts join together in space. • *The shuttle was docked at the International Space Station 220 miles above Earth.*

encounter /ɪnˈkaʊntə/ (encounters, encountering, encountered) VERB If someone or something **encounters** another person or thing, they meet them, usually unexpectedly. [FORMAL] • *Did you encounter anyone in the building?*

fire /faɪə/ (fires, firing, fired) VERB When the engine of a motor vehicle **fires**, or when you **fire** it, an electrical spark is produced which causes the fuel to burn and the engine to work. • *The engine fired and we moved off.*

fragment /ˈfrægmənt/ (fragments) NOUN A **fragment** of something is a small piece or part of it. • *The accident left fragments of metal in my shoulder.*

harpoon /hɑːˈpuːn/ (harpoons) NOUN A **harpoon** is a long pointed weapon with a long rope attached to it, which is usually fired or thrown by people hunting whales or large sea fish. • *They used eel skins to bind everything from sledges and clothing to spears and harpoons.*

impact /ˈɪmpækt/ (impacts) NOUN An **impact** is the action of one object hitting another, or the force with which one object hits another. • *The plane is destroyed, a complete wreck: the pilot must have died on impact.*

impose /ɪmˈpəʊz/ (imposes, imposing, imposed) VERB If you **impose** something on people, you use your authority to force them to accept it. • *Many companies have imposed a pay freeze.*

junk /dʒʌŋk/ NOUN **Junk** is old and used goods that have little value and that you do not want any more. • *What are you going to do with all that junk, Larry?*

launch /lɔːntʃ/ (launches, launching, launched) VERB To **launch** a rocket, missile, or satellite means to send it into the air or into space. • *The rocket was launched early this morning.*

legislation /ˌledʒɪˈsleɪʃən/ NOUN **Legislation** consists of a law or laws passed by a government. [FORMAL] • *They wrote a letter calling for legislation to protect women's rights.*

missile /ˈmɪsaɪl , US -səl/ (missiles) NOUN A **missile** is a tube-shaped weapon that travels long distances through the air and explodes when it reaches its target. • *Helicopters fired missiles at the camp.*

monitor /ˈmɒnɪtə/ (monitors, monitoring, monitored) VERB If you **monitor** something, you regularly check its development or progress, and sometimes comment on it. • *You need feedback to monitor progress.*

obsolete /ˈɒbsəliːt/ ADJECTIVE Something that is **obsolete** is no longer needed because something better has been invented. • *So much equipment becomes obsolete almost as soon as it's made.*

orbit /ˈɔːbɪt/ (orbits) NOUN An **orbit** is the curved path in space that is followed by an object going round and round a planet, moon, or star. • *The planet is probably in orbit around a small star.*

plot /plɒt/ (plots, plotting, plotted) VERB When someone **plots** the course of something, especially a plane or a ship, they mark it on a map using instruments to obtain accurate information. • *We were trying to plot the course of the submarine.*

refer /rɪˈfɜː/ (refers, referring, referred) VERB If you **refer to** someone or something as a particular thing, you use a particular word, expression, or name to

mention or describe them. • *Our economy is referred to as a free market.*

remnant /ˈremnənt/ (remnants) NOUN The **remnants** of something are small parts of it that are left over when the main part has disappeared or been destroyed. • *Beneath the present church were remnants of Roman flooring.*

stabilise /ˈsteɪbɪlaɪz/ (stabilises, stabilising, stabilised) VERB If something **stabilises**, it becomes stable. • *Officials hope the move will stabilize exchange rates.*

thruster /ˈθrʌstə/ (thrusters) NOUN A **thruster** is a small rocket engine on a spacecraft. • *Then the rocket's thrusters propel him into space.*

trash /træʃ/ NOUN **Trash** consists of unwanted things or waste material such as used paper, empty containers and bottles, and waste food. [US] • *The yards are overgrown and cluttered with trash.*

waste /weɪst/ (wastes) NOUN **Waste** is material which has been used and is no longer wanted, for example because the valuable or useful part of it has been taken out. • *Up to 10 million tonnes of toxic waste are produced every year in the U.K.*

wayward /ˈweɪwəd/ ADJECTIVE If you describe something as **wayward**, you mean that it is unpredictable and difficult to control. • *She was hit by a wayward ball while walking across the park.*

withstand (see Test 3 Listening Part 4)

Passage 3

alike /əˈlaɪk/ ADVERB You use **alike** after mentioning two or more people, groups, or things in order to emphasize that you are referring to both or all of them. • *The techniques are being applied almost everywhere by big and small firms alike.*

arid /ˈærɪd/ ADJECTIVE **Arid** land is so dry that very few plants can grow on it. • *Scientists were developing new strains of crops that can withstand arid conditions.*

baboon /bæˈbuːn/ (baboons) NOUN A **baboon** is a large monkey that lives in Africa. • *A study found baboons are capable of recognizing patterns of letters.*

bushbaby /ˈbʊʃˌbeɪbɪ/ (bushbabies) NOUN A **bushbaby** is a monkey with large eyes and ears and a long tail that lives in Africa. **Bushbabies** are nocturnal animals. • *You can spend your time walking through forests filled with bushbabies .*

crevice /ˈkrevɪs/ (crevices) NOUN A **crevice** is a narrow crack or gap, especially in a rock. • *He pointed out a huge boulder with rare ferns growing in every crevice.*

disintegrate /dɪsˈɪntɪgreɪt/ (disintegrates, disintegrating, disintegrated) VERB If an object or substance **disintegrates**, it breaks into many small pieces or parts and is destroyed. • *At 420 mph the windscreen disintegrated.*

distinctive /dɪˈstɪŋktɪv/ ADJECTIVE Something that is **distinctive** has a special quality or feature which makes it easily recognizable and different from other things of the same type. • *His voice was very distinctive.*

ecosystem /ˈiːkəʊsɪstəm, US ekə-/ **(ecosystems)** NOUN An **ecosystem** is all the plants and animals that live in a particular area together with the complex relationship that exists between them and their environment. [TECHNICAL] • *Madagascar's ecosystems range from rainforest to semi-desert.*

faint /feɪnt/ **(fainter, faintest)** ADJECTIVE A **faint** sound, colour, mark, feeling, or quality has very little strength or intensity. • *He became aware of the soft, faint sounds of water dripping.*

fever /ˈfiːvə/ **(fevers)** NOUN If you have a **fever** when you are ill, your body temperature is higher than usual and your heart beats faster. • *My Uncle Jim had a high fever.*

fibre /ˈfaɪbə/ **(fibres)** NOUN A **fibre** is a thin thread of a natural or artificial substance. • *If you look at the paper under a microscope you will see the fibres.*

fuse /fjuːz/ **(fuses, fusing, fused)** VERB When things **fuse** together or **are fused** together, they join together physically or chemically, usually to become one thing. • *The flakes seem to fuse together and produce ice crystals.*

harsh /hɑːʃ/ **(harsher, harshest)** ADJECTIVE **Harsh** climates or conditions are very difficult for people, animals, and plants to live in. • *The weather grew harsh, chilly and unpredictable.*

hemisphere (see Test 2 Reading Passage 3)

hollow out /ˌhɒləʊˈaʊt/ **(hollows out, hollowing out, hollowed out)** PHRASAL VERB If something is **hollowed out**, the inside part of it is removed. • *Someone had hollowed out a large block of stone.*

iconic /aɪˈkɒnɪk/ ADJECTIVE An **iconic** image or thing is important or impressive because it seems to be a symbol of something. [FORMAL] • *The ads helped the brand to achieve iconic status.*

impressive /ɪmˈpresɪv/ ADJECTIVE Something that is **impressive** impresses you, for example because it is great in size or degree, or is done with a great deal of skill. • *It is an impressive achievement.*

mammal /ˈmæməl/ **(mammals)** NOUN **Mammals** are animals such as humans, dogs, lions, and whales. In general, female mammals give birth to babies rather than laying eggs, and feed their young with milk. • *Unlike most marine mammals, otters have no blubber to insulate them.*

naturalist /ˈnætʃərəlɪst/ **(naturalists)** NOUN A **naturalist** is a person who studies plants, animals, insects, and other living things. • *As early as 1643, naturalists began compiling detailed catalogues of the flora.*

nectar /ˈnektə/ NOUN **Nectar** is a sweet liquid produced by flowers, which bees and other insects collect. • *The marica sunbird feeds on nectar from long-throated flowers.*

observe /əbˈzɜːv/ **(observes, observing, observed)** VERB If you **observe** a person or thing, you watch them carefully, especially in order to learn something about them. • *Stern also studies and observes the behaviour of babies.*

percussion /pəˈkʌʃən/ NOUN **Percussion** instruments are musical instruments that you hit, such as drums. • *A one-man act, he played all the instruments, including keyboard, drums and percussion.*

pierce /pɪəs/ **(pierces, piercing, pierced)** VERB If a sharp object **pierces** something, or if you **pierce** something with a sharp object, the object goes into it and makes a hole in it. • *Pierce the skin of the potato with a fork.*

pod /pɒd/ **(pods)** NOUN A **pod** is a seed container that grows on plants such as peas or beans. • *My favourite is fresh peas in the pod.*

pollinate /ˈpɒlɪneɪt/ **(pollinates, pollinating, pollinated)** VERB To **pollinate** a plant or tree means to fertilize it with pollen. This is often done by insects. • *Many of the indigenous insects are needed to pollinate the local plants.*

radiocarbon /ˌreɪdiəʊˈkɑːbən/ NOUN **Radiocarbon** is a type of carbon which is radioactive, and which therefore breaks up slowly at a regular rate. Its presence in an object can be measured in order to find out how old the object is. • *The most frequently used method is radiocarbon dating.*

sapling /ˈsæplɪŋ/ **(saplings)** NOUN A **sapling** is a young tree. • *The newly planted saplings were swaying gently in the spring breeze.*

scent /sent/ **(scents)** NOUN The **scent** of something is the smell that it has, especially if the smell is pleasant. • *Flowers are chosen for their scent as well as their look.*

stem /stem/ **(stems)** NOUN The **stem** of a plant is the thin, upright part on which the flowers and leaves grow. • *He stooped down, cut the stem for her with his knife and handed her the flower.*

sub-Saharan Africa /ˌsʌbsəˌhɑːrənˈæfrɪkə/ NOUN **Sub-Saharan Africa** is the region of Africa to the south of the Sahara desert. • *The museum's focus turned to the traditional visual arts of sub-Saharan Africa.*

trunk /trʌŋk/ **(trunks)** NOUN The **trunk** of a tree is the large main stem from which the branches grow. • *He leant against the gnarled trunk of a birch tree.*

TEST 4: LISTENING

Part 2

alleviate /əˈliːvieɪt/ **(alleviates, alleviating, alleviated)** VERB If you **alleviate** pain, suffering, or an unpleasant condition, you make it less intense or severe. [FORMAL] • *Nowadays, a great deal can be done to alleviate back pain.*

blind /blaɪnd/ **(blinds)** NOUN A **blind** is a roll of cloth or paper which you can pull down over a window as a covering. • *Every morning I tweaked the blinds in the bedroom upon waking.*

brim /brɪm/ (brims) NOUN The **brim** of a hat is the wide part that sticks outwards at the bottom. • *Rain dripped from the brim of his baseball cap.*

dehydrate /diːhaɪˈdreɪt/ (dehydrates, dehydrating, dehydrated) VERB If you **dehydrate** or if something **dehydrates** you, you lose too much water from your body so that you feel weak or ill. • *People can dehydrate in weather like this.*

face wipe /ˈfeɪswaɪp/ (face wipes) NOUN A **face wipe** is a small moist cloth for cleaning your face and is designed to be used only once. • *No camping trip would be complete without face wipes.*

hydrated /haɪˈdreɪtɪd/ ADJECTIVE If you are **hydrated**, you have enough water or other liquid in your body. • *Volunteers will be distributing water sachets to keep runners hydrated.*

ill effects /ɪlɪˈfekts/ PLURAL NOUN If something has **ill effects**, it causes problems or damage. • *Some people are still suffering ill effects from the contamination of their water.*

linen /ˈlɪnɪn/ (linens) NOUN **Linen** is a kind of cloth that is made from a plant called flax. It is used for making clothes and things such as tablecloths and sheets. • *I was wearing a white linen suit.*

mineral (see Test 2 Reading Passage 1)

vulnerable /ˈvʌlnərəbəl/ ADJECTIVE Someone who is **vulnerable** is weak and without protection, with the result that they are easily hurt physically or emotionally. • *Old people are often particularly vulnerable members of our society.*

Part 3

assessor /əˈsesə/ (assessors) NOUN An **assessor** is a person who judges the performance of someone else, for example in an exam. • *They relied on external assessors for the exam results.*

biased /ˈbaɪəst/ ADJECTIVE If something is **biased**, it has a tendency to prefer one person or thing to another, and to favour that person or thing. • *Even the politically biased newspapers are having to applaud what he is doing.*

online portal /ˌɒnlaɪnˈpɔːtl/ (online portals) NOUN An **online portal** is a site that consists of links to other websites. [COMPUTING] • *The foundation hopes to set up an online portal next year.*

relevant /ˈreləvənt/ ADJECTIVE Something that is **relevant** to a situation or person is important or significant in that situation or to that person. • *We have passed all relevant information on to the police.*

Part 4

boost /buːst/ (boosts, boosting, boosted) VERB If one thing **boosts** another, it causes it to increase or improve. • *It wants the government to take action to boost the economy.*

counteract /ˌkaʊntərˈækt/ (counteracts, counteracting, counteracted) VERB To **counteract** something means to reduce its effect by doing something that produces an opposite effect. • *My husband has to take several pills to counteract high blood pressure.*

dominant /ˈdɒmɪnənt/ ADJECTIVE Something that is **dominant** is more powerful, successful, or noticeable than another similar thing. • *You should plant your dominant foot forward, then shift your weight back and forth to keep the hoop moving.*

flexible /ˈfleksɪbəl/ ADJECTIVE If someone is **flexible**, they can bend parts of their body easily. • *There is a myth that yoga is only for people who are very flexible.*

grazed /ɡreɪzd/ ADJECTIVE If part of your body is **grazed**, your skin is injured because you have scraped against something. • *He was hit by the bonnet and wing mirror and suffered a grazed elbow.*

hormone /ˈhɔːməʊn/ (hormones) NOUN A **hormone** is a chemical, usually occurring naturally in your body, that makes an organ of your body do something. • *They showed no increase in cortisol levels, a hormone that measures stress level increases.*

imbalance /ɪmˈbæləns/ (imbalances) NOUN If there is an **imbalance** in a situation, the things involved are not the same size, or are not the right size in proportion to each other. • *The crowd gathered on one side of the boat to pose for a photo, creating an imbalance.*

joint /dʒɔɪnt/ (joints) NOUN A **joint** is a part of your body such as your elbow or knee where two bones meet and are able to move together. • *Her joints ache if she exercises.*

ligament /ˈlɪɡəmənt/ (ligaments) NOUN A **ligament** is a band of strong tissue in a person's body which connects bones. • *He suffered torn ligaments in his knee.*

posture /ˈpɒstʃə/ (postures) NOUN Your **posture** is the position in which you stand or sit. • *Exercise, fresh air, and good posture are all helpful.*

regime /reɪˈʒiːm/ (regimes) NOUN A **regime** is a set of rules about food, exercise, or beauty that some people follow in order to stay healthy or attractive. • *He has a new fitness regime to strengthen his back.*

repetitive /rɪˈpetɪtɪv/ ADJECTIVE **Repetitive** movements or sounds are repeated many times. • *These problems can occur as the result of repetitive movements.*

stamina /ˈstæmɪnə/ NOUN **Stamina** is the physical or mental energy needed to do a tiring activity for a long time. • *You have to have a lot of stamina to be a top-class dancer.*

sustain /səˈsteɪn/ (sustains, sustaining, sustained) VERB If you **sustain** something such as a defeat, loss, or injury, it happens to you. [FORMAL] • *Every aircraft in there has sustained some damage.*

tailor-made /ˌteɪləˈmeɪd/ ADJECTIVE If something is **tailor-made**, it has been specially designed for a particular person or purpose. • *Each client's programme is tailor-made.*

TEST 4: READING

Passage 1

absorb /əbˈzɔːrb/ (absorbs, absorbing, absorbed) VERB If something **absorbs** light, heat, or another form of energy, it takes it in. • *The dark material absorbs light and warms up.*

attribute /əˈtrɪbjuːt/ (attributes, attributing, attributed) VERB If you **attribute** something to an event or situation, you think that it was caused by that event or situation. • *The striker attributes the team's success to a positive ethos at the club.*

cliff /klɪf/ (cliffs) NOUN A **cliff** is a high area of land with a very steep side, especially one next to the sea. • *The car rolled over the edge of a cliff.*

combat /ˈkɒmbæt/ (combats, combatting, combatted) VERB If someone or something **combats** something, they try to stop it happening. • *Congress has criticised new government measures to combat crime.*

deflect /dɪˈflekt/ (deflects, deflecting, deflected) VERB If someone or something **deflects** something that is moving, they make it go in a slightly different direction, for example by hitting or blocking it. • *On a putting green, weeds deflect the ball and frustrate even the most talented golfer.*

deposit (see Test 2 Reading Passage 2)

destruction /dɪˈstrʌkʃən/ NOUN **Destruction** is the act of destroying something, or the state of being destroyed. • *They were working towards an international agreement aimed at halting the destruction of the ozone layer.*

dune /djuːn, US duːn/ (dunes) NOUN A **dune** is a hill of sand near the sea or in a desert. • *In northwestern Oklahoma, you can race buggies on the vast dunes.*

erosion /ɪˈrəʊʒən/ NOUN **Erosion** is the gradual destruction and removal of rock or soil in a particular area by rivers, the sea, or the weather. • *As their roots are strong and penetrating, they prevent erosion.*

extend /ɪkˈstend/ (extends, extending, extended) VERB If you **extend** something, you make it longer or bigger. • *This year they have introduced three new products to extend their range.*

groyne /grɔɪn/ (groynes) NOUN A **groyne** is a wooden or stone wall that extends from the shore into the sea and is built in order to protect a harbour or beach from the force of the waves. • *The piers would act as groynes, reducing the rate of erosion of the coastline.*

habitat /ˈhæbɪtæt/ (habitats) NOUN The **habitat** of an animal or plant is the natural environment in which it normally lives or grows. • *In its natural habitat, the hibiscus will grow up to 25ft.*

longshore drift /ˌlɒŋʃɔːˈdrɪft/ (longshore drifts) NOUN **Longshore drift** is the movement of beach material such as sand and small stones along the shore as a result of waves coming onto the the shore at an angle. • *Longshore drift is especially active on long, straight coastlines.*

marsh /mɑːʃ/ (marshes) NOUN A **marsh** is a wet, muddy area of land. • *A pair of sandhill cranes land in the marsh behind the house.*

mound /maʊnd/ (mounds) NOUN A **mound** of something is a large rounded pile of it. • *The bulldozers piled up huge mounds of dirt.*

mud flat /ˈmʌdflæt/ (mud flats) NOUN A **mud flat** is a piece of level muddy land that is uncovered at low tide and flooded at high tide. • *The scene is of mud flats, pebbles and a misty sea.*

nourishment /ˈnʌrɪʃmənt, US ˈnɜːr-/ NOUN If something provides a person, animal, or plant with **nourishment**, it provides them with the food that is necessary for life, growth, and good health. • *The mother provides the embryo with nourishment and a place to grow.*

phenomenon /fɪˈnɒmɪnən, US -nɑːn/ (phenomena) NOUN A **phenomenon** is something that is observed to happen or exist. [FORMAL] • *This phenomenon occurs only when the atmospheric conditions are right during a full moon.*

pressing /ˈpresɪŋ/ ADJECTIVE A **pressing** problem, need, or issue has to be dealt with immediately. • *It is one of the most pressing problems facing this country.*

reef /riːf/ (reefs) NOUN A **reef** is a long line of rocks or sand, the top of which is just above or just below the surface of the sea. • *An unspoilt coral reef encloses the bay.*

reinforced concrete /ˌriːɪnfɔːstˈkɒŋkriːt/ NOUN **Reinforced concrete** is concrete that is made with pieces of metal inside it to make it stronger. • *The prison was made of reinforced concrete.*

retreat /rɪˈtriːt/ NOUN **Retreat** is the action of moving away from something or someone. • *After a retreat of about 50 yards, Kevin turned to face his assailant.*

shore /ʃɔː/ (shores) NOUN The **shores** or the **shore** of a sea, lake, or wide river is the land along the edge of it. • *They walked down to the shore.*

undermine /ˌʌndəˈmaɪn/ (undermines, undermining, undermined) VERB If someone or something **undermines** something, they make it less strong or less secure than it was before. • *Residents complained of bird droppings and the nest's twigs undermining the building's façade.*

Passage 2

collaboration /kəˌlæbəˈreɪʃən/ NOUN **Collaboration** is the act of working together to produce a piece of work, especially a book or some research. • *There is substantial collaboration with neighbouring departments.*

critical thinking /ˌkrɪtɪklˈθɪŋkɪŋ/ NOUN **Critical thinking** is the ability to think clearly and rationally, and understand the connection between ideas. • *Today's kids employ logical reasoning and critical thinking.*

diverse /daɪˈvɜːs, US dɪ-/ ADJECTIVE If a group or range of things is **diverse**, it is made up of a wide variety of things. • *Society is now much more diverse than ever before.*

emerge /ɪ'mɜːdʒ/ **(emerges, emerging, emerged)** VERB If something **emerges** from a period of thought, discussion, or investigation, it becomes known as a result of it. • *They can't ignore the growing corruption that has emerged in the past few years.*

evidence /'evɪdəns/ NOUN **Evidence** is anything that you see, experience, read, or are told that causes you to believe that something is true or has really happened. • *Ganley said he'd seen no evidence of widespread fraud.*

exclude /ɪk'skluːd/ **(excludes, excluding, excluded)** VERB If you **exclude** something that has some connection with what you are doing, you deliberately do not use it or consider it. • *They eat only plant foods, and exclude animal products from other areas of their lives.*

hierarchy /'haɪərɑːki/ **(hierarchies)** NOUN A **hierarchy** is a system of organizing people into different ranks or levels of importance, for example in society or in a company. • *Even in the desert there was a kind of social hierarchy.*

interaction /ˌɪntər'ækʃən/ **(interactions)** NOUN When there is **interaction** between two things, the two things affect each other's behaviour. • *There are studies into the interaction between physical and emotional illness.*

interpersonal /ˌɪntə'pɜːsənəl/ ADJECTIVE **Interpersonal** means relating to relationships between people. • *Training in interpersonal skills is essential.*

prize /praɪz/ **(prizes, prizing, prized)** VERB Something that **is prized** is wanted and admired because it is considered to be very valuable or very good quality. • *Military figures made out of lead are prized by collectors.*

promotion /prə'məʊʃən/ **(promotions)** NOUN If you are given a **promotion**, you are given a more important job or rank in the organization that you work for. • *Consider changing jobs or trying for promotion.*

soft skills /'sɒftskɪlz/ PLURAL NOUN **Soft skills** are interpersonal skills such as the ability to communicate well with other people and to work in a team. • *There's a new emphasis on soft skills such as communication and interaction.*

stability /stə'bɪlɪti/ NOUN **Stability** means that something is not likely to change or come to an end suddenly. • *It was a time of political stability and progress.*

staged /steɪdʒd/ ADJECTIVE Something that is **staged** occurs or is planned to occur in stages. • *Foetal development is a staged process.*

stagnation /stæg'neɪʃən/ NOUN **Stagnation** is when something such as a business or society stops changing or progressing. • *Economic stagnation followed the sharp increase in oil prices.*

stream /striːm/ **(streams, streaming, streamed)** VERB If you stream music, films, or television programmes, you play them directly from the internet. • *You can stream music to your stereo system from your mobile phone.*

swiftly /'swɪftli/ ADVERB If something happens **swiftly**, it happens very quickly or without delay. • *They have acted swiftly and decisively to protect their industries.*

territorial /ˌterɪ'tɔːriəl/ ADJECTIVE If you describe a person or a group of people as **territorial**, you mean that they have something that they regard as their own, and which they do not want to share. • *A key problem is that cats are solitary and territorial animals.*

willingness /'wɪlɪŋnəs/ NOUN If someone shows a **willingness** to do something, they are fairly happy about doing it and will do it if they are asked or required to do it. • *Persistence, enthusiasm and a willingness to take anything thrown his way led to more work.*

Passage 3
algorithm (see Test 2 Reading Passage 2)

browse /braʊz/ **(browses, browsing, browsed)** VERB If you **browse** on a computer, you search for information in computer files or on the internet. [COMPUTING] • *Try browsing around in the network bulletin boards.*

conversely /'kɒnvɜːsli, kən'vɜːsli/ ADVERB You say **conversely** to indicate that the situation you are about to describe is the opposite or reverse of the one you have just described. [FORMAL] • *In real life, nobody was all bad, nor, conversely, all good.*

curation /kjʊ'reɪʃn/ NOUN **Curation** is the process of carefully choosing, arranging, and presenting different items in order to get a particular effect. • *He was confident that readers would always demand the intelligent curation of news.*

determine /dɪ'tɜːmɪn/ **(determines, determining, determined)** VERB If you **determine** something, you decide it or settle it. • *My aim was first of all to determine what I should do next.*

disconnected /ˌdɪskə'nektɪd/ ADJECTIVE **Disconnected** things are not linked in any way. • *His ability to absorb bits of disconnected information was astonishing.*

distinguish /dɪ'stɪŋgwɪʃ/ **(distinguishes, distinguishing, distinguished)** VERB If you can **distinguish** between two things, you can see or understand how they are different. • *Research suggests that babies learn to see by distinguishing between areas of light and dark.*

end user /ˌend'juːzə/ **(end users)** NOUN The **end user** of a product or service is the person that it has been designed for, rather than the person who installs or maintains it. • *You have to be able to describe things in a form that the end user can understand.*

engagement /ɪn'geɪdʒmənt/ NOUN **Engagement** with something or with a group of people is your involvement with that thing or group and the feeling that you are connected with it or have real contact with it. • *She suffers from a lack of critical engagement with the literary texts.*

filter /'fɪltə/ **(filters, filtering, filtered)** VERB To **filter** something means to sort it so that certain things are removed from it. • *Advances in computer technology mean we can filter data much faster.*

gather /ˈɡæðə/ (gathers, gathering, gathered) VERB
If you **gather** information or evidence, you collect it, especially over a period of time and after a lot of hard work. • *The private detective was using a hidden recording device to gather information.*

generate (see Test 2 Reading Passage 2)

interpret /ɪnˈtɜːprɪt/ (interprets, interpreting, interpreted) VERB If you **interpret** data, you study it to find out its meaning or significance. • *The software is used to scan and interpret data on documents such as invoices.*

intervene /ˌɪntəˈviːn/ (intervenes, intervening, intervened) VERB If you **intervene**, you become involved in a situation and try to change it. • *She has asked the ministers of agriculture and of environmental affairs to intervene.*

messy /ˈmesi/ (messier, messiest) ADJECTIVE If you describe something as **messy**, you are emphasizing that it is confused or complicated. • *The couple had a messy break-up earlier this year.*

misleading /ˌmɪsˈliːdɪŋ/ ADJECTIVE If you describe something as **misleading**, you mean that it gives you a wrong idea or impression. • *The article contains several misleading statements.*

moderate /ˈmɒdəreɪt/ (moderates, moderating, moderated) VERB If you **moderate** something or if it **moderates**, it becomes less extreme or violent and easier to deal with or accept. • *They are hoping that once in office he can be persuaded to moderate his views.*

questionnaire /ˌkwestʃəˈneə/ (questionnaires) NOUN A **questionnaire** is a written list of questions which are answered by a lot of people in order to provide information for a report or a survey. • *Headteachers will be asked to fill in a questionnaire.*

revenue (see Test 2 Reading Passage 2)

rival /ˈraɪvəl/ (rivals) NOUN Your **rival** is a person, business, or organization who you are competing or fighting against in the same area or for the same things. • *In Europe, rival companies send one another their catalogues.*

sensational /senˈseɪʃənəl/ ADJECTIVE You can describe stories or reports as **sensational** if you disapprove of them because they present facts in a way that is intended to cause feelings of shock, anger, or excitement. • *It has been a summer of sensational headlines.*

GENERAL TRAINING TEST A: READING

Section 1

fumes /fjuːmz/ PLURAL NOUN **Fumes** are the unpleasant and often unhealthy smoke and gases that are produced by fires or by things such as chemicals, fuel, or cooking. • *They have been protesting about fumes from a chlorine factory.*

odour /ˈəʊdə/ (odours) NOUN An **odour** is a particular and distinctive smell. • *The whole herb has a characteristic taste and odour.*

stacks /stæks/ PLURAL NOUN If you say that there is **stacks** of something, you mean that there is a lot of it. [INFORMAL] • *If the job's that good, you'll have stacks of money.*

Section 2

deteriorate /dɪˈtɪəriəreɪt/ (deteriorates, deteriorating, deteriorated) VERB If something **deteriorates**, it becomes worse in some way. • *The weather conditions are deteriorating.*

disrupt /dɪsˈrʌpt/ (disrupts, disrupting, disrupted) VERB If someone or something **disrupts** an event, system, or process, they cause difficulties that prevent it from continuing or operating in a normal way. • *The drought has severely disrupted agricultural production.*

enhance /ɪnˈhɑːns, -ˈhæns/ (enhances, enhancing, enhanced) VERB To **enhance** something means to improve its value, quality, or attractiveness. • *They'll be keen to enhance their reputation abroad.*

Section 3

estuary /ˈestʃʊri, US ˈestʃueri/ (estuaries) NOUN An **estuary** is the wide part of a river where it joins the sea. • *They were carrying out naval manoeuvres in the Clyde estuary.*

larva /ˈlɑːvə/ (larvae) NOUN A **larva** is an insect at the stage of its life after it has developed from an egg and before it changes into its adult form. • *The eggs quickly hatch into larvae.*

nocturnal /nɒkˈtɜːnəl/ ADJECTIVE **Nocturnal** creatures are active mainly at night. • *When there is a full moon, this nocturnal rodent is careful to stay in its burrow.*

pesticide /ˈpestɪsaɪd/ (pesticides) NOUN **Pesticides** are chemicals which farmers put on their crops to kill harmful insects. • *The pesticides led to a dramatic decline of bumblebee queens.*

slug /slʌɡ/ (slugs) NOUN A **slug** is a small slow-moving creature with a long soft body and no legs, like a snail without a shell. • *The plant lures slugs into the interior of its tube-shaped leaves.*

spawn /spɔːn/ (spawns, spawning, spawned) VERB When fish or animals such as frogs **spawn**, they lay their eggs. • *Salmon and trout go upstream, spawn and then die.*

vulnerable /ˈvʌlnərəbəl/ ADJECTIVE Something that is **vulnerable** can be easily harmed or affected by something bad. • *Proper measures to protect the most vulnerable species of sharks must be put in place.*

weir /wɪə/ (weirs) NOUN A **weir** is a low barrier which is built across a river in order to control or direct the flow of water. • *The waterfall is really an elegantly curved weir across a 70-mile-long river.*

GENERAL TRAINING TEST B: READING

Section 1

access /'ækses/ (accesses, accessing, accessed) VERB
If you **access** a building or other place, you are able or allowed to go into it. • *If you are accessing the campus by car, there's only one route in.*

comply /kəm'plaɪ/ (complies, complying, complied) VERB If someone or something **complies** with an order or set of rules, they are in accordance with what is required or expected. • *Some beaches had failed to comply with European directives on bathing water.*

forthcoming /ˌfɔːθ'kʌmɪŋ/ ADJECTIVE A **forthcoming** event is planned to happen soon. • *He addressed the remark to his opponents in the forthcoming elections.*

goggles /'gɒgəlz/ PLURAL NOUN **Goggles** are large glasses that fit closely to your face around your eyes to protect them from such things as water, wind, or dust. • *Visitors have been advised to wear plastic safety goggles.*

hazard /'hæzəd/ (hazards) NOUN A **hazard** is something which could be dangerous to you or your health or safety. • *A new report suggests that chewing-gum may be a health hazard.*

maintenance /'meɪntɪnəns/ NOUN The **maintenance** of a building, vehicle, road, or machine is the process of keeping it in good condition by regularly checking it and repairing it when necessary. • *The window had been replaced last week during routine maintenance.*

mask /mɑːsk, mæsk/ (masks) NOUN A **mask** is a piece of cloth or other material that you wear over all or part of your face to protect you from germs or harmful substances. • *You must wear goggles and a mask that will protect you against the fumes.*

regulation (see Test 2 Reading Passage 2)

upgrade /ˌʌp'greɪd/ (upgrades, upgrading, upgraded) VERB If buildings, equipment, or services **are upgraded**, they are improved or made more efficient. • *Helicopters have been upgraded and modernized.*

ventilation system /ˌventɪ'leɪʃnsɪstəm/ (ventilation systems) NOUN The **ventilation system** is the equipment in a building that provides a supply of fresh air. • *All they still had to do was install a proper ventilation system.*

Section 2

accessible /æk'sesɪbəl/ ADJECTIVE If you describe a book, painting, or other work of art as **accessible**, you think it is good because it is simple enough for people to understand and appreciate easily. • *Many literary books are accessible to a general audience.*

assess (see Test 2 Reading Passage 2)

asset /'æset/ (assets) NOUN The **assets** of a company or a person are all the things that they own. [BUSINESS] • *By the end of 1989 the group had assets of 3.5 billion dollars.*

awareness /ə'weənəs/ If you have an **awareness** of something, you know about it. • *Candidates must demonstrate an awareness of diversity issues within the workplace.*

compelling /kəm'pelɪŋ/ ADJECTIVE If you describe something such as a film or book as **compelling**, you mean you want to keep watching it or reading it because you find it so interesting. • *It makes for a compelling and provocative film.*

connectivity /kɒˌnek'tɪvəti/ NOUN **Connectivity** is the ability of a computing device to connect to other computers or to the internet. [COMPUTING] • *I've now got a new phone with faster mobile internet connectivity.*

dismiss /dɪs'mɪs/ (dismisses, dismissing, dismissed) VERB If you **dismiss** something, you decide or say that it is not important enough for you to think about or consider. • *The spokesman dismissed any suggestion that his leader had cancelled the meeting at the last minute.*

downtime /'daʊntaɪm/ NOUN In computing, **downtime** is time when a computer is not working. • *However, the cost of network downtime is not the only concern.*

flash /flæʃ/ (flashes, flashing, flashed) VERB If a picture or message **flashes** up on a screen, or if you **flash** it onto a screen, it is displayed there briefly or suddenly, and often repeatedly. • *The words 'Good Luck' were flashing on the screen.*

inconvenience /ˌɪnkən'viːnɪəns/ (inconveniences, inconveniencing, inconvenienced) VERB If someone or something **inconveniences** you, they cause problems or difficulties for you. • *He promised to be quick so as not to inconvenience them any further.*

interpret (see Test 2 Reading Passage 3)

kale /keɪl/ NOUN **Kale** is a vegetable that is similar to a cabbage. • *Add the kale and bring to the boil.*

land /lænd/ (lands, landing, landed) VERB If you **land** something that is difficult to get and that many people want, you are successful in getting it. [INFORMAL] • *He landed a place on the graduate training scheme.*

liability /ˌlaɪə'bɪlɪti/ (liabilities) NOUN A company's or organization's **liabilities** are the sums of money which it owes. [BUSINESS] • *The company had assets of $138 million and liabilities of $120.5 million.*

notification /ˌnəʊtɪfɪ'keɪʃən/ (notifications) NOUN A **notification** is a message, sound, or symbol on your phone or computer telling you that someone has sent you a message or put something new for you to look at on a website. • *The thought of logging back on and sifting through a huge number of notifications was tiring.*

outage /'aʊtɪdʒ/ (outages) NOUN An **outage** is a period of time when the electricity supply to a building or area is interrupted, for example because of damage to the cables. [MAINLY US] • *A windstorm in Washington is causing power outages throughout the region.*

periodically /ˌpɪəri'ɒdɪkli/ ADVERB If something happens **periodically**, it happens occasionally, at fairly regular intervals. • *Treatment is to periodically remove blood.*

phenomenon (see Test 4 Reading Passage 1)

productivity /ˌprɒdʊkˈtɪvɪti/ NOUN **Productivity** is the rate at which goods are produced. • *The third-quarter results reflect continued improvements in productivity.*

revenue (see Test 2 Reading Passage 2)

scheduled /ˈʃedjuːld/ ADJECTIVE If something is **scheduled**, it has been arranged or planned according to a programme or timetable. • *The Foreign Minister paid a scheduled visit to the White House.*

suspension /səˈspenʃən/ NOUN The **suspension** of something is the act of delaying or stopping it for a while or until a decision is made about it. • *A strike by ground staff has led to the suspension of flights between London and Manchester.*

upgrade (see General Training Test B Reading Section 1)

Section 3

aggressiveness /əˈɡresɪvnəs/ NOUN If a person or animal shows **aggressiveness**, they have a quality of anger and determination that makes them ready to attack other people. • *Her aggressiveness made it difficult for him to explain his own feelings.*

competent /ˈkɒmpɪtənt/ ADJECTIVE Someone or something that is **competent** is efficient and effective. • *He was a loyal, distinguished and very competent civil servant.*

desire /dɪˈzaɪə/ (desires) NOUN A **desire** is a strong wish to do or have something. • *They seem to have lost their desire for life.*

fallacy /ˈfæləsi/ (fallacies) NOUN A **fallacy** is an idea which many people believe to be true, but which is in fact false because it is based on incorrect information or reasoning. • *It's a fallacy that the affluent give relatively more to charity than the less prosperous.*

gamble /ˈɡæmbəl/ (gambles, gambling, gambled) VERB If you **gamble** an amount of money, you bet it in a game such as cards or on the result of a race or competition. • *Most people visit Las Vegas to gamble their hard-earned money.*

gut instinct /ɡʌtˈɪnstɪŋkt/ (gut instincts) NOUN **Gut instinct** is an instinctive feeling, rather than an opinion or idea based on facts. • *Sometimes your gut instinct is the right one.*

influence /ˈɪnfluəns/ (influences, influencing, influenced) VERB If someone or something **influences** a person or situation, they have an effect on that person's behaviour or that situation. • *We became the best of friends and he influenced me deeply.*

instinctively /ɪnˈstɪŋktɪvli/ ADVERB If you do something **instinctively**, you do it without thinking or reasoning. • *Jane instinctively knew all was not well with her 10-month-old son.*

likability /ˌlaɪkəˈbɪləti/ NOUN Someone's **likability** is the fact that they are pleasant and easy to like. • *Students rated each other for trustworthiness and likability.*

millisecond /ˈmɪlisekənd/ (milliseconds) NOUN A **millisecond** is a unit of time equal to one thousandth of a second.• *The lights flicker, dim, go out for a millisecond, then go on again.*

rational /ˈræʃənəl/ ADJECTIVE **Rational** decisions and thoughts are based on reason rather than on emotion. • *He's asking you to look at both sides of the case and come to a rational decision.*

snap /snæp/ ADJECTIVE A **snap** decision or action is one that is taken suddenly, often without careful thought. • *I think this is too important for a snap decision.*

stick with (see Test 3 Listening Part 3)

tempt /tempt/ (tempts, tempting, tempted) VERB If you **tempt** someone, you offer them something they want in order to encourage them to do what you want them to do. • *A million dollar marketing campaign was launched to tempt American tourists back to Britain.*

valid /ˈvælɪd/ ADJECTIVE A **valid** argument, comment, or idea is based on sensible reasoning. • *They put forward many valid reasons for not exporting.*

validation /ˌvælɪˈdeɪʃən/ (validations) NOUN **Validation** of a person, state, or system means proving or confirming that they are valuable or worthwhile. • *I think the film is a validation of our lifestyle.*

Audio script

Track 01

TEST 1　　LISTENING PART 1

Teresa:	Well, Michael, have you had any thoughts about what we can get Dad for his birthday?
Michael:	Yes, lots, but I haven't come up with anything I think he'd like. He's so difficult to buy for! And there are so many big days this year: Mum's fiftieth in September, their thirtieth anniversary at the end of the year, then there's December …
Teresa:	Well, I've come up with an idea for Dad's sixtieth. I've got it here on the laptop. It's a weekend break learning painting techniques. There's a workshop at that posh country house in Swansfield. It'd be ideal for Dad. It's aimed at amateur artists who want to improve their painting technique. It's a bit expensive but we'll share the cost and after all, it's a big birthday, isn't it? He deserves something special.
Michael:	That would be perfect for him. He's really got the painting bug lately, hasn't he? So, what's it like?
Teresa:	It takes place over two and a half days, from Friday to Sunday evening so Dad would spend two nights there. There's a workshop on the Friday evening and a guest speaker on Saturday night. On Saturday and Sunday, they spend the day painting in these gorgeous surroundings. It's so picturesque around there and they'll have some great scenes to paint.
Michael:	That sounds fantastic.
Teresa:	Apparently, the food is excellent, and it's full board so meals are provided, and they've got a special offer at the moment. It's usually £380 for the weekend but I've got a discount code so we can get it for £330.
Michael:	OK, let's go for it. Can we book online?
Teresa:	Yes, look, I've got the booking form open here.
Michael:	Pass me the laptop and I'll pay with my credit card. You can pay me back your share later. Name, John Meacher. Address, 56 Spring Road, Blandfield. Postcode … What's the postcode? I can never remember it.
Teresa:	Nor can I, but hang on. I've got it here on my phone. Let's see … it's B07 6QT.
Michael:	OK. So, that's his details. Now there are some options. They have four different courses here: watercolour, mixed media – whatever that is, oil painting and pen and ink. What do you think Dad would like best?
Teresa:	Watercolour. Yes, definitely watercolour. Mum says he's been doing a lot of that lately and he really enjoys it.
Michael:	They've got a list of dates here. We need the August dates, don't we? The 14th to the 16th, then the 17th of July to the 19th – that's too soon, and also the 11th of September to the 13th – that's too late.
Teresa:	Yes, it'll have to be August. That's the weekend closest to his birthday and besides, there's too much going on later in the year.
Michael:	There's a question here: 'How would you describe your level?' I wouldn't describe Dad as a beginner, would you? Shall we say intermediate?
Teresa:	Yes, put that. Mum says he's been painting for months now and some of his stuff's quite good. Hopefully, he'll be advanced after this course! Is that everything?
Michael:	Just one more thing. There's a bit here on dietary requirements. I know he and Mum have been experimenting with going vegetarian but I think Mum's keener than he is, so he might appreciate some meat on his plate, don't you think?
Teresa:	Yes, good idea. But remember, he's not fond of fish so if there's a place to put that on the form …
Michael:	Done that. Now, you said you had a discount code. What is it?
Teresa:	Yes, it's CYP20.
Michael:	Great, that's it. I'll add my details and pay. I think this'll make a great present.
Teresa:	I'm sure it will.

Track 02

TEST 1　　LISTENING PART 2

Presenter:	So, now on to local news, and first up, something that's been causing quite a stir ever since it was announced. Yes, I'm talking about the planned re-routing of traffic around the shopping centre on the High Street. Judging by some of the emails we've received, there seems to be a great deal of confusion as well as controversy about what's actually going to happen so let me start with an explanation.
	The aim of the project is to tackle traffic congestion along the High Street, which, as we all know, can be terrible during rush hour. The project will run over two stages. To begin with, there'll be a trial period, a pilot project, if you like. If the changes prove to be successful, stage two will be rolled out, and this will

probably involve making any necessary adjustments and ironing out any problems. The first stage will run from the 1st of June through to the 31st of July, with the second stage continuing on through to the 30th of September. This will allow two months for the council to reflect on feedback from local residents and shopkeepers before stage two begins. The council are inviting you the public to email them with your feedback. I had a look at the council's website before the show and there doesn't seem to be a dedicated telephone number for those of you without internet access, but we'll keep you posted if this changes.

There's a view that the traffic problem is partly caused by vehicles entering the High Street from side roads and that if access to the High Street was limited, there would be a lot less interference with the flow of traffic. This is going to mean making some roads one-way only, and one or two other roads will be restricted to pedestrians so cars and lorries will no longer be able to use them. Another major cause of congestion, according to the council, is the parking of cars and delivery vehicles outside shops. In order to maintain the flow of traffic, parking will be banned along the High Street.

This all means that access to the High Street from certain side roads will be blocked. At the north end by the railway station, drivers will be able to join the High Street from Malvern Road, which will remain unchanged, with two-way traffic. Lincoln Road will be made one-way and be open only to emergency services, which require access to the hospital. Motorists will no longer be able to use Hazelhurst Road, which will be pedestrianised, though delivery drivers will be given access to the cafés and restaurants. Elmdon Avenue, which is currently two-way, will be made one-way, and vehicles will be able to use it to join the High Street. There was talk of closing Botteville Road completely and making it for pedestrians only but this idea has been shelved until feedback has been received.

As I mentioned earlier, the plan to re-route traffic hasn't gone down well with all members of the community. Parents have been concerned about cars speeding along back streets for some time and welcome the idea of keeping vehicles on the High Street and off the side roads. Cyclists, on the other hand, are concerned that cycle lanes don't appear on any of the new plans and are worried that those lanes that currently exist will be scrapped. There have also been questions raised by the emergency services as to whether their vehicles would be affected by these changes but they're generally very supportive of the proposals. However, local shopkeepers along the High Street are far from happy about the changes. As we've discussed on previous programmes, those on streets planned for pedestrianisation are looking forward to the changes. Those on the High Street are wondering how they'll get supplies and goods delivered if delivery vehicles can't park outside their premises. In fact, there seems to be a feeling amongst local residents that there's been far too little consultation about these changes. Hopefully, your feedback will inform the plans for stage two.

Track 03

TEST 1   LISTENING PART 3

Counsellor: Hiya, Stephen. It's been a while since I last saw you. How are you getting on?

Stephen: Not too bad. Thanks for your help last time. I managed to speak to my tutor as you suggested and solved the problem with timetable clashes. And I also went to see the accommodation officer. She was great and she helped me a lot with the problems I was having with our landlord.

Counsellor: That's good to hear. Well done you for getting things sorted out. So, why did you need to see me?

Stephen: Well, I need some advice to help me manage my time better. I've been here for six months now and my friends are having no problem getting down to work and finishing assignments. But I always seem to leave things to the last minute. I try not to do that but it's the same every time. I end up only just being able to get essays in on time. It's really stressing me out.

Counsellor: Well, that *is* a problem, but don't be too hard on yourself. A lot of the students I see struggle with time in the same way. Especially students who've come straight from school and are used to having everything organised for them by their teachers. Now, why don't you tell me about a typical day? Maybe we'll be able to identify any habits you have that aren't helping. Then we can see how you can change those habits.

Stephen: Well, during the first few weeks at uni, I was going out every night till late, getting to know people and making new friends. But I'm not doing that too often now. I don't want to spend all my money – that would be another problem! Apart from one or two evenings a week, I tend to be on my own in my room so it's not as if I don't have enough time to study and do my work. But I find it difficult to prioritise and I end up doing nothing at all. That's why it's always a bit of a panic with assignment deadlines. I leave things till the last minute and it's always a rush. And lately, the books and materials I need are never in the library because they've all been taken by other students.

Counsellor: OK, well, look. We've got lots of help sheets here to deal with issues like this. Personally, I think it's best to deal with problems one step at a time rather than setting too many challenges. Let's focus on time management. Do you have one of those big wall calendars? You know, the huge poster calendars with all the days, months, etc. on them?

Stephen:	No, but I've seen them on sale in the student shop so I should be able to get one.
Counsellor:	Good. While you're there, buy yourself a diary as well, a big one, so you have plenty of space to write in it.
Stephen:	OK, so what do I do when I have them?
Counsellor:	Well, you tell me. How do you think the calendar might come in useful?
Stephen:	I could use that to put in term dates, assignment deadlines, the dates of any presentations I've got to give, that kind of thing.
Counsellor:	That's it. A calendar is perfect for giving you an overview of the year ahead so you won't forget key dates and what you might need to be thinking about longer term. Now, what about the diary?
Stephen:	I don't know, really. I could put in things I have to do each day. If it's one page per day, I could write down how I'm feeling. That kind of thing.
Counsellor:	I think it's best to use it to structure the week. Sit down with it on a Sunday evening and start with all the things you have to do that week. For example, you might write: 'Wednesday, lecture, nine to eleven; Thursday, seminar, twelve o'clock; Friday, first draft of essay'. Do you see what I mean? That'll give you an overview of the week ahead.
Stephen:	Yes, I can see how that would help. I tend to keep information like that in my head so it's not surprising things get forgotten.
Counsellor:	OK, but you should also write a to-do list. Before you go to bed every night, have a look through the diary for the rest of the week and write a list of things you could try to do the next day to help you with some of those tasks. Don't be over-ambitious and try to do too much. Prioritise what's important and think about what can wait until the following day or later in the week.
Stephen:	Yes, I like that idea. It'll be a good reminder. I just need to decide what things are more important than others.
Counsellor:	Well, you'll get better with practice, and doing this will also give you the sense that you're in control of your life and your studies.
Stephen:	OK, so let me make sure I've got this. I start with the big picture, the calendar for what's ahead over the weeks and months, then plan my week with the diary, and finally decide what I need to do each day.
Counsellor:	Exactly. Do you think you can manage that?
Stephen:	Hopefully, yes. It seems pretty straightforward. Thanks for your help.

Track 04

TEST 1   LISTENING PART 4

Lecturer:	Good morning, everyone. Today we're going to look at a topic that you'll no doubt have read about on your favourite self-help or psychology blogs and websites, and that topic is neuroplasticity. It's an issue that's caught the attention of psychologists as it opens up the possibility of treating patients in ways that we might once have thought were impossible.

Neuroplasticity refers to the way the brain is able to adapt over the course of our lives as a result of our experiences and interactions with our environment. The opinion held years ago was that the brain was an organ that grew and developed until adulthood, at which point it stopped generating new cells, and the way it worked or operated became fixed. So, for example, if someone suffered a brain injury of some kind, scientists believed the damage was permanent and the most anyone could hope for was to limit the damage to the brain and prevent more damage from taking place.

However, more recently scientists have proved that our brains aren't hard-wired like a computer at adulthood, and that the neurons – the cells in our brain – can re-organise. For example, if we learn a new skill like playing the guitar, new connections are created between neurons. As we go through life, we're effectively re-wiring our brains.

People who can see receive information about the world from their eyes. This information is sent via the optic nerve to the part of the brain called the visual cortex. In blind people, the visual cortex doesn't get any information from the eyes, but one scientist, Paul Bach-y-Rita, thought the brains of blind people might be able to get this information from another part of their body, their skin. In a number of experiments, he used various techniques to stimulate the skin on their backs. Amazingly, the blind people began to say they experienced 'seeing'. Later, brain scans showed that the information the brain was getting from the skin was being processed in the visual cortex. It seems their brains had formed new connections between neurons in a way nobody would have believed possible in the past.

Another example that's often quoted is a study carried out on cabbies – the drivers of London's famous black taxis. To pass the tests to become a London cabbie, people must spend years learning all the roads and possible routes around the city. Scientists discovered that the area of the brain responsible for memorising all this actually became larger. Interestingly, it became larger than that of London bus drivers, who don't have to memorise the same information but simply follow the same route.

It seems that certain activities can promote neuroplasticity. When we travel, our brains are stimulated by new experiences, and new connections between neurons are triggered. Connectivity can also be enhanced through memory training activities, which can certainly help people as they get older. And whether you are left- or right-handed, doing exercises using the other hand can, over time, have a similar effect. Even the simple act of reading fiction is said to be beneficial.

It's not surprising to learn that the phenomenon of neuroplasticity is regarded as having the potential for miracle cures for people who are struggling with physical and mental problems. It's natural that our hopes are raised when we hear of people recovering from serious brain injuries or stories about how we can alter undesirable personality traits. The idea that negative thinkers can develop a more positive outlook, that we can change our personalities as a consequence of our 'plastic brain' and do or be whatever we want to is very appealing.

However, there are several reasons why we should be cautious and maintain a realistic view of what's possible. As psychologists, we need to question some of the claims being made about neuroplasticity. Such changes as have been observed don't come about without a great deal of effort. For example, people who have lost the use of an arm following a brain injury would need to do specific physical exercises thousands of times for the brain to make new neural connections, and even then, there's no guarantee of success. And research showing that activities like learning a second language have an effect on neural connections is very interesting. But I don't think this supports the idea that the phenomenon of neuroplasticity can be used in a wonder treatment for people with physical or mental ailments. I'd argue that just like the patient learning to regain the use of an arm, such achievements require a tremendous amount of effort. They aren't something that can be achieved overnight. Neither can we ignore the effect of age. What's possible for a younger person might not be achievable for an older one. And then there's the effect of our genes and how these might limit the degree of plasticity our brains are capable of. Nevertheless, this is a fascinating area of science for anyone interested in psychology and one that I'm sure you'll hear a lot more about during your studies and later on in your professional lives.

Track 05

TEST 1   SPEAKING PART 1

In this first part of the exam, I'd like to ask you some questions about yourself. Let's talk about your daily routines.
What time do you usually get up?
What do you like to eat for breakfast?
Would you say the morning is your favourite part of the day?
If you could change anything about your daily routine, what would it be?
Let's move on to talk about celebrations. Do you enjoy going to parties?
What do people like to celebrate in your country?
What's your favourite celebration?
Would you say it's more fun celebrating with friends or relations?

Track 06

TEST 1   SPEAKING PART 2

I'm going to give you a topic and I'd like you to talk about it for one or two minutes. Before you talk, you have one minute to think about what you are going to say. You can make some notes if you wish. Here is your topic. ... [one-minute pause] All right? Remember you have one or two minutes for this, so don't worry if I stop you. I'll tell you when the time is up. Can you start speaking now, please?

Track 07

TEST 1   SPEAKING PART 3

We've been talking about the subject of shops and shopping. I'd like to discuss this subject with you with some more general questions relating to this topic.
First, do you think people often buy things they don't really need?
What are the advantages of shopping on the high street rather than online?
How important is good customer service?
Do you think shops should be required to close on certain days?
What are the benefits of going shopping with a friend?
In which ways do adverts persuade us to buy a particular product?

Track 08

TEST 2   LISTENING PART 1

Sarah:	Good afternoon. You're through to Rightway Furnishings. My name's Sarah. How can I help you?
Thomas:	Yes, good afternoon. I'm phoning to complain about the condition of some items I ordered from you.
Sarah:	Oh, I'm sorry to hear you've had problems. Let's see if I can help. Could you give me the order reference number?
Thomas:	Certainly. It's 96678.
Sarah:	Thanks. And could you confirm your name, please?
Thomas:	It's Thomas Horton. That's H-O-R-T-O-N.
Sarah:	That's great, thanks. I have your order details here so how can I help you?
Thomas:	Well, as you'll see, I had a delivery of some furniture from you on the 20th of July, a few days ago. I ordered it on the 13th of July to benefit from the free delivery you were offering at the time. The items arrived but there's a problem with every single one.
Sarah:	I'm very sorry to hear that. Let's go through the items, then, and I'll see what I can do.
Thomas:	Well, take the sofa for starters.
Sarah:	I see here that you ordered the Hamilton three-seater sofa. Is that right?
Thomas:	Yes, that's the one. It was wrapped in plastic when it arrived – to protect it, I imagine, but when we took this off, we noticed that one end of the sofa was damp, which wasn't a good start. We decided at that point to send it back but inspected it first for signs of any other damage. We then noticed that one of the wooden legs was badly scratched. It's very noticeable. I'm surprised it wasn't picked up by anyone at your warehouse.
Sarah:	Thanks. I've made a note of that. We'll certainly collect the faulty one but it'll probably be a few weeks before we can send a replacement. That's a very popular design and there might not be one in stock immediately. Would you like to wait or would you prefer a refund?
Thomas:	As long as that? I think in that case, I'll have the refund and I'll look elsewhere.
Sarah:	You also ordered a rug from us, the Regent rug. Was that all right?
Thomas:	Yes, the three- by two-metre Regent. There are two issues with this. The colour isn't the same as appears in the photo on your website. It's clearly black and white in the photo but the one we had delivered is dark blue rather than black. We could live with that but the problem is that it isn't the size advertised. I've measured it and the dimensions are three metres by one ninety.
Sarah:	Actually, you may find that the rug will settle as it gets walked on. The difference may very well be due to the fact that it's been rolled up for some time. It will slowly expand with use. Can I suggest you give it a few days and call back next week if there's no improvement?
Thomas:	OK, I'll leave that one for now and see what happens. But then there's the coffee table. This is the self-assembly Morrison table. I'm not particularly talented when it comes to DIY and I appreciate having clear instructions with things like this. It didn't help when I discovered the instructions sent out were for a different table. Luckily, I found the correct ones on your website and downloaded them. When I checked to see if all the bits were included in the pack, I couldn't find four plastic discs. They're the ones that go on the bottom of the legs to protect the floor. According to the instructions, they were supposed to be included. I had to go out and buy some myself.
Sarah:	Oh dear. Again, I do apologise. Just to confirm: would you like to return this item or is this feedback?
Thomas:	No, I've put it all together now. I don't want to go through that again. I just thought it's something you need to report to your quality control people.
Sarah:	Of course, Mr Horton. Well, I must apologise once more for all this. We pride ourselves on the quality of our products and customer service and you seem to have caught us on a bad day. I'll certainly pass on your complaints to my line manager, who will no doubt get back to you to offer her own apologies. But in the meantime, please accept a gift voucher from us by way of an apology. I'll email this to you immediately.
Thomas:	Yes, OK. I look forward to hearing from you.

Track 09

TEST 2   LISTENING PART 2

Interviewer:	Now, here's something that I'm very much looking forward to. Hagley Food Festival takes place this weekend and we're lucky to have Julie Smart with us in the studio today to tell us all about it. Welcome to the show, Julie. Another year and another great festival to look forward to.
Julie:	Good morning, Tim. Yes, the festival has been such a huge success with the public that it's hard to believe it was first held just four years ago. In fact, there have been three events; this year's will be number four. Sadly, we had to cancel last year due to the terrible weather that weekend. But everything's looking good for this one. In fact, I'm really excited about this year's event. We've been fortunate enough to attract two new members to the organising committee, one of whom has a wide

range of experience in running festivals, and the other has lots of industry contacts. Judging by the interest we've had, this year looks like being the busiest so far. We're expecting record crowds and we've planned loads of additional activities. So, if your listeners are interested in coming, we'd suggest getting there nice and early to get the most from their visit.

Interviewer: That's good to know. Planning such a large festival must involve a lot of work and a lot of people.

Julie: Yes, it does, but we're lucky to have a brilliant team of volunteers. We couldn't manage without them.

Interviewer: So, when can we look forward to attending?

Julie: Well, we can only start to get the site ready a day before the festival opens so our volunteers will be working all day on Thursday. That means the site will be closed to visitors until the next day, Friday the 30th, and then we'll be there right the way through until Sunday. We open at 12.00 p.m. on Friday and stay open until 10.00 p.m. every evening. We'd have liked an eleven o'clock closing time but public transport stops running at ten thirty. We're encouraging people to use buses and trains to reduce traffic in the area, which is why we're stopping early enough for people to get away in time. We've also tried to keep costs down and this year, for the first time, we've introduced a weekend pass for £15 per person and £10 for children under the age of 16. Of course, you can pay by the day if you prefer: that's £10 for adults and £6 for children. The entrance fee covers things like the children's entertainment and access to all the cooking demonstrations, which we think are worth the entrance fee on their own. Oh, and before I forget, I've been asked to point out that we're offering free parking on site and visitors are asked to use this rather than the streets in or near residential areas as we don't want to upset local people. For those travelling to the festival by train, we're running a shuttle service – that's a double-decker bus – every half hour from the station to the site. This is also available to take people back to the station.

Interviewer: Wonderful! So, what kind of things will be taking place?

Julie: Well, based on feedback from previous events, we've made a few changes this year. A significant development is that we've partnered with a local organisation, Food for the Homeless, and there'll be several fundraising activities during the weekend that visitors can support. We've got some very famous chefs you'll recognise from TV giving demonstrations and some of them will be signing copies of their latest book if you're interested in buying one. There will, of course, be a large number of stalls selling a huge variety of food from around the world. There's a slight change to the advertised programme as the Vietnamese stall won't be with us this year. One new idea we're trying out is a second-hand book stall. Pop along and pick up a bargain, or even better, donate some of your old books. What else? Oh yes, we all know there's growing demand for organic food and visitors will be able to purchase a variety of fruit and vegetables from our organic stall holders. Finally, in our children's area, there'll be lots of child-friendly activities, including colouring worksheets to encourage them to learn how to cook.

Interviewer: That all sounds brilliant, Julie. I can't wait for the weekend!

Track 10

TEST 2   LISTENING PART 3

Susan: Hiya, Lee. I saw you coming out of the accommodation office earlier. Have you found anywhere yet? I've had no luck at all so far.

Lee: Yes, they're really helpful in there. They talked me through what's available on campus and what I'd expect to have to pay.

Susan: Really? Then I guess I'll pay them a visit as well. So, have you found somewhere?

Lee: I haven't made a decision yet, to be honest. I'll be going into my final year after the summer so I'm guaranteed a place on campus in any one of the university halls. Did you know they give priority to first and final year students?

Susan: Yes, I know. That's why I'm having trouble finding somewhere. I've still got two years to go on my course so it's impossible for me to get a place. So, what are you going to do?

Lee: I'm not sure I want to live on campus, actually. Broomfield Hall is where all the high-end, so-called luxury rooms are. Really nicely decorated, your own shower and toilet. You have to share a kitchen, but they're huge. You could hold a party in there. They're not cheap, though. There's no way I could afford to live in one.

Susan: What about Crifield – that block near the sports hall? I've got a friend who lives there and the rooms seem OK.

Lee: Yes, we talked about them. They're not quite so expensive. There used to be a great view of the fields by the back of the university from there until they built that new conference centre. I'm not that keen on living there.

Susan: But you might not have any choice unless you're prepared to find somewhere off campus.

Lee: I hadn't considered living in town again but then the accommodation officer showed me a couple of places that looked interesting. They're both three-bedroom town houses. One's on the High Street and there's a lot of passing traffic so it could be a bit noisy. There are two students living there and they're looking for someone to take the third bedroom, but I think I'd prefer to live with people I know.

Susan:	Still, it could work out OK for you. Hopefully you'd get on with the people who live there.
Lee:	Well, that's the thing. The other house the accommodation officer told me about doesn't have any tenants yet. It's another three-bedroom place. No garden, like the other one, but it's fully furnished. It's in a residential area, there's not much traffic outside and there's a living room that everyone can use.
Susan:	Sounds promising.
Lee:	It's also down the road from the train station, and the bus onto campus stops just around the corner.
Susan:	You'd have to find people to share with. Have you got anyone in mind?
Lee:	Well, what about you? If you got in quick, you'd be able to take one of the two large bedrooms. The third one's not tiny but one of the other two would suit you. And you haven't found anywhere yet, have you?
Susan:	I've been asked if I'm interested in sharing with a couple of people on my course, but I'm not sure I want to live with them and I haven't agreed to anything yet. So, yes, I'd be interested in having a look. What do we have to do?
Lee:	Well, the first thing is to book an appointment to see it. Are you free this week?
Susan:	Our lectures have come to an end so it should be OK. I did have an appointment to see my tutor but she hasn't confirmed yet so any time after Wednesday. I've got my assignment deadline then.
Lee:	OK. I'll book a date to see it and pick up any forms that need to be completed from the accommodation office. The problem is we'll have to pay a deposit. And that would be for the whole house, all three rooms. Unless we pay that ourselves, we'll need to find someone else soon.
Susan:	That shouldn't be difficult. Some of our friends have already found places but there are a few like us still having problems finding somewhere. But let's have a look at it first, just in case it's not suitable.
Lee:	But if you see anyone today who might be interested, try to get them to join us when we have a look.
Susan:	All right. I'll do that. And when you go to the accommodation office, ask them if we can pay something towards the deposit just to reserve it. Then maybe they can take it off the system for 48 hours so nobody else can view it.
Lee:	OK, I'll let you know later how I get on.

Track 11

TEST 2   LISTENING PART 4

Lecturer: Good morning, everyone. In last week's lecture we looked at managing your costs as a business. If you missed the lecture, the video is available online. Now, this week I'd like to talk to you about an area that often gets ignored or, at best, isn't given sufficient attention by new businesses: market research.

The entrepreneurs amongst you will all know the feeling: you're lying in bed one night when suddenly you get this idea for a fantastic product. You're sure there's a huge market for it and that it will sell well. You start planning what it will look like in your head – you've even got ideas for the website and how you're going to make those sales. And for a lot of small businesses and inexperienced entrepreneurs, the next step is creating that product or service and getting it out there as quickly as possible.

But unless they're incredibly lucky or have a business instinct that most of us lack, this is a huge mistake that could cost a lot of money or even see the business fail. The missing piece of the jigsaw is market research. Why does this get missed out? Often, it's because the business owner is blinded by their idea. It's so innovative that it's bound to be successful. The entrepreneur thinks they know what the customer wants, perhaps thinks that the customer doesn't even realise they want it. Sometimes it's the concern that the research will be complicated and cost a lot of money and time, and for a start-up without any income, that can be a real concern. More often than not, however, it's because the person concerned doesn't want to get negative feedback or be shown that in fact, there's no market for their idea.

But well thought-out market research carried out before production and launch can avoid expensive mistakes, help the business fine-tune its offer or, in the worse-case scenario, accept that the idea is weak, allowing it to come up with another idea that stands a better chance of success without wasting a lot of valuable time and money.

The first step is to clearly define your market. Entrepreneurs often make the mistake of failing to distinguish between a global market and a smaller, more niche market. It doesn't matter whether you're dreaming of opening a café on the local high street or hope to sell goods or services online. Even if you think you have a potential market of millions of customers, how will you market your product or service? If you try to appeal to everyone, your offering will lack focus. That's not to say it can't be done, but appealing to as wide a market as possible requires facing stiff competition, will probably make excessive demands on your marketing budget, and ultimately may fail as you won't be able to appeal to individual tastes or requirements.

Next, research the competition. Remember: if there's a lot of competition, that at least indicates there's a market for your idea. What is the competition, and are you prepared to compete against them on price or quality of product or service? Why should customers decide to buy from you rather than them? Alternatively, perhaps you see a gap in the market, something that nobody else is offering. Researching the competition is crucial, whether it's serving a local, national or an international market.

The next step is something that often gets ignored. You should be prepared to ask your potential customers what they think. Research like this provides invaluable feedback and is particularly do-able when you plan to sell online or have an online following. Start by looking at the most popular posts on your social media page or blog: what do they tell you about your visitors' interests? Links to a questionnaire can be used to dig down further to find out more about your visitors' needs. You could create a free sample of your product and ask if visitors to your social media or blog page would be prepared to buy more. You can ask whether there's anything about the sample they'd like to see changed before they'd consider buying it. Ask them how much they'd be prepared to pay. The important thing is to ask the questions and listen to what your potential customers have to say. You might not like to hear that you have to go back to the drawing board or come up with a completely different idea, but these results will help you steer your business towards a successful launch rather than an expensive failure.

Track 12

TEST 2   SPEAKING PART 1

In this first part of the exam, I'd like to ask you some questions about yourself. Let's talk about the weather.
Tell me about the weather in your country.
What kind of weather do you like best?
What kind of weather do you like when you go on holiday?
Would you prefer to live in a country with a hot or cold climate?
Let's move on to talk about exercise. Do you like to keep fit?
Which sports are popular in your country?
Did you do any sports when you were younger that you don't do now?
Is there a sport you'd like to do that you've never done before?

Track 13

TEST 2   SPEAKING PART 2

I'm going to give you a topic and I'd like you to talk about it for one or two minutes. Before you talk, you have one minute to think about what you are going to say. You can make some notes if you wish. Here is your topic. ... [one-minute pause] All right? Remember you have one or two minutes for this, so don't worry if I stop you. I'll tell you when the time is up. Can you start speaking now, please?

Track 14

TEST 2   SPEAKING PART 3

We've been talking about the subject of food. I'd like to discuss this subject with you with some more general questions relating to this topic.
First, what is the appeal of eating out in a restaurant?
What do you think makes a good dinner host?
Fast food is often criticised by food experts so why is it so popular with people?
Do you think it's always best to eat food with ingredients that have been produced locally?
Is it important to eat together at the dinner table rather than in front of the TV, for example?
How can we best encourage people to eat a healthy diet?

Track 15

TEST 3   LISTENING PART 1

Matthew:	Good morning, Tessa. Welcome to Jamieson's. I'm Matthew Reed. Thanks for your interest in working with us. Please take a seat.
Tessa:	Thank you.
Matthew:	So, we advertised three jobs on our website and I can see from your CV that you might be a suitable candidate for all of them. Would you be interested in telephone helpline work? Or we're still looking for a delivery person.

Tessa:	Well, I've had experience of telephone sales but I'd prefer to have face-to-face contact with customers. I'm afraid I don't have a driving licence so the position of delivery person isn't possible. But I'd be keen to apply for the retail assistant post that was advertised.
Matthew:	OK, that's fine. I see from your CV you're currently at university.
Tessa:	Yes. I'm in my second year at the moment. It's a four-year degree course and I spend the third year abroad. I'm planning on going to France.
Matthew:	Yes, I see you did French, English and Maths for your A levels, and now you're studying French. Is that right?
Tessa:	Yes. I love learning languages and Welworth offers a joint degree in English and French so I decided to do that. I didn't fancy the idea of Maths at university.
Matthew:	No, I can understand that. Now, you've had some work experience. That's excellent. A couple of jobs last year? Tell me about them.
Tessa:	Yes, I worked as a sales assistant in Stacey's – that's a small boutique in town – at the weekend from January to May, Saturdays and Sundays. I was responsible for serving customers and occasionally helping the person who ran the shop with window displays. I really enjoyed that job. I got plenty of practice in dealing with money, customer service skills, that kind of thing.
Matthew:	That must have been a busy time for you, what with your studies as well. You clearly aren't put off by a bit of hard work!
Tessa:	No, I like to keep myself occupied and, as I said, I enjoyed the job and it made a change from studying. Then from June to August last year, I took a job at a summer school. I was offered the role of social organiser for students from abroad who were studying English. I planned trips and evening events like quizzes.
Matthew:	Did you enjoy that?
Tessa:	Yes, it was great fun. I really appreciated the opportunity to work in a team and to practise my language skills as there were several French students on the course.
Matthew:	And what do you like to do in your spare time? Have you got any hobbies or interests?
Tessa:	I'm a big reader, especially science fiction. I've recently started dance classes – I think that's a more enjoyable way of keeping fit than going to the gym.
Matthew:	OK. So, tell me about your availability. You're mainly interested in work over the summer period, is that right?
Tessa:	Yes. I'd certainly be keen to join you when I finish my studies in May. I start my third year in September so I'd be free in June, July and August. I finish on the 25th of May. I have one week holiday booked but I'm back on the 6th of June and I'd be ready to start on the 7th of June.
Matthew:	That would fit in nicely with our busy summer schedule. What about hours? We actually need someone who's available for five days a week and some of the days are likely to be weekends. Are you pretty flexible in terms of when you can work?
Tessa:	I think so. Saturdays and Sundays are no problem. I'm taking driving lessons at the moment and they tend to be on a Wednesday but I could always re-arrange them. I'd like to keep Tuesdays free, though, as I volunteer at my local community centre then.
Matthew:	OK, Tessa. That all seems great. Let me just confirm your contact details and we'll be in touch with you later in the week with our decision.

Track 16

TEST 3   LISTENING PART 2

Speaker:	Hello everyone, and welcome to Marston Country Farm. We always look forward to group visits from local schools and I'm sure you'll all have a fantastic time while you're here. I'd just like to take a couple of minutes to explain what we have here at the farm and point out a few health and safety issues you need to be aware of.

Let's start with a tour of the farm. I can see you all have a copy of the plan we sent out so let me just go through it with you. You'll see we're here in the Visitors Centre, just by the entrance. This is a useful place to head for if you get lost or want to meet up with friends later. The farm covers quite a large area so we've made sure there are toilets nearby should you need them, wherever you are. There are toilets on the left of the entrance as you come in, just behind the Visitors Centre. There are also some in the café. You'll find this if you walk round the duck pond, go over the bridge and turn to your right, past the picnic area. You'll see the café in front of you. In front of us we have the duck pond. It's very tempting to feed the ducks and other water birds with bread from your sandwich box but actually, bread isn't very good for them so please can we ask you not to feed them. Now, to our left, next to the toilets, you'll see a long building. This is the goat shed, and just past that there's a pair of double gates. This is the entrance to the donkey rides. I'm afraid these are only suitable for younger children than yourselves and you won't be allowed to ride one. But you're welcome to stroke the donkeys that nobody's riding and we've even supplied a large sack full of apples so that you can feed them if you think they look hungry. Now, directly opposite us, on the other side of the pond, is the rabbit house. This is always extremely popular and very busy. You might have to queue for a while to get in. But if this is the case, pop over the bridge and pay the insect house a visit – it's immediately on your left. For some strange reason, this doesn't tend to be quite as popular as the rabbits. And just over here, closer to us, on the right side of the entrance, you'll find our gift shop if you want to buy something to remember your visit or a gift for someone special.

So, that's the farm. Now before you go, there are a few things I'd like to point out to ensure you remain safe and healthy during and after your visit. Please take care walking around the duck pond. Don't worry, it's not deep. If you did fall in, the water would only come up to your knees. But the bank around it is very muddy after all the rain we've had and visitors are likely to spoil their footwear. There are hand wash stations dotted around the site. Don't forget to use these to wash your hands after touching or handling any of our animals, and especially before eating. Oh yes, can we ask you please to help us keep these stations tidy and dispose of the paper towels in the bins provided? Last but not least, do remember that this is a working farm. At certain times of the day, there will be vehicles entering the farm from the main gate here. Please remain alert and pay attention when you're in this area. We have fully trained first aiders on a nearby site, and in the unlikely event you have an accident or feel ill, simply come into the Visitors Centre and the receptionist will call them. Your teachers have been given our health and safety leaflets and they'll be able to answer some of your questions during your visit.

Track 17

TEST 3   LISTENING PART 3

Lecturer: Good morning, everyone. As promised, I've invited Kelly from the university Careers Service to come along and talk to you about your work experience year. Thanks for coming, Kelly.

Kelly: Thanks for inviting me. Hello everyone. As you'll all be aware, the third year of your degree course is spent working in industry. This is an extremely valuable part of your education. You'll gain a deeper understanding of the area of work you're interested in, apply some of the things you've learned in the workplace, and perhaps even get a full-time job at the end of your degree. You'll be on what we term a 'work experience year', not to be confused with an internship.

Lecturer: What's the difference between the two?

Kelly: Internships are placements students tend to organise themselves, during the summer holidays or after they've graduated. We're happy to offer some advice but we don't organise them on your behalf. Your work experience programme is a compulsory part of your degree and as a result, you're supported by the university in finding a suitable placement.

Student 1: I've been told we'll get paid for the work experience. Is this true?

Kelly: Short-term placements, like summer internships, may or may not be paid. Again, that's something you'd need to discuss with the employer. But the year-long work experience placements we organise for you will be paid posts. The salary varies but will reflect the responsibilities you'll have.

Student 2: Can we choose the company we want to work with?

Kelly: We've got a database of companies we've worked with in the past and in most cases, we'll be able to offer you two or three options for placements. However, it's a very competitive process and students all want to work for the more well-known companies so you may not get your first choice.

Lecturer: I understand students will often be asked to attend interviews. Is this the case?

Kelly: Yes, students will be required to attend an interview of some kind. Companies don't want to take on someone they haven't had the chance to meet and have a chat with. How formal the interview is will depend on the company. If there is an interview, I'd strongly recommend putting in some work beforehand to make sure you're ready for it.

Lecturer: You offer support for that kind of thing, don't you?

Kelly: Yes, it's a whole package of support, really. We'll start by helping you identify a company that's a good fit for both you and them. We want to keep the employers happy in order to maintain a good relationship. At one time we used to offer interview practice with members of staff but we now direct you to our training videos online to help you with this.

Student 1: What if we have problems working with the company? Who do we speak to?

Kelly: It's rare that we have problems like this. If you're lucky, you'll find yourself doing the perfect job, but bearing in mind how difficult it is to find a place, we always advise students to stick with it. We do have a contact in each company who we can talk with on your behalf if there are any serious issues, but as I said, that's not often the case.

Student 2: I've heard students will be assessed on their work placement. Is that true?

Kelly: There'll be some kind of assessment, yes, but you'll be told about that by your tutor and they'll be the one to talk to you about any specific issues. If the assessment involves anything to do with work-based skills, you'll also usually be supported by someone at the company. We can help you with things like keeping a reflective journal. This is a really useful exercise even if you're not required to keep one as it will provide you with a record of what you did each day at work, the things you learned on the job as well as any difficulties you've had. It will help you keep track of issues or topics that you need to read up on and act as one of the resources you can use when you come to write your end-of-year report – if that's something the course tutor needs. Again, you'll have to discuss that with the course tutor. We don't get involved with academic work as this is something your tutors will help you with.

Lecturer: Thanks for that, Kelly. That was really useful.

Kelly: My pleasure. Some students get a little stressed at the thought of joining the workforce but you'll look back on it as a really useful exercise. You might discover that it is indeed the perfect career choice and love what you do. Alternatively, it might be that it helps you to reconsider the area of work you want to get into. If you make a good impression during the year, you may find yourself being offered a job at the end of your degree, and at the very least, you'll develop skills and experience that will stand you in good stead when you start job hunting. You may also make a few contacts with people in the industry who might be able to help you with your career.

Track 18

TEST 3   LISTENING PART 4

Lecturer: If you dread being taken by surprise by a spider when you're relaxing in front of the TV, you'll no doubt be one of the millions of people who find spiders terrifying. But hopefully, this morning I can change your perception of these creatures. You might continue to find them scary but you might also see them in a slightly different light.

I'd like to focus specifically on the silk that spiders make. The substance they use to make their intricate webs is stored in the form of a liquid protein inside their body and it only turns solid when it's exposed to the air. The common garden spider of the UK can create up to five different types of silk. Some of these silks are responsible for allowing the web to stretch while others make the web less brittle.

It's often claimed that spider silk is stronger than steel but this is misleading. A material can be strong in different ways: for example, it can be stiff, which means it resists bending, and silk is much less stiff than steel. But spider silk does have some incredible characteristics. It can stretch by up to 30 per cent without breaking before returning to its original size. It can even withstand sub-zero temperatures without becoming brittle.

People have used spider silk in many practical applications for centuries. The ancient Greeks used cobwebs to dress wounds and to help stop the flow of blood. Spider silk was used by Indigenous Australians to make fishing lines, and in the Solomon Islands people use spider webs to catch fish. In the 1900s it was used in optical devices, such as in the crosswires in a rifle sight.

If spider silk could be produced on an industrial scale, it could have a wide range of applications. In a recent experiment, scientists used it to help grow human skin in order to treat burn victims. Some companies have even shown an interest in using spider silk to make airbags in cars. They believe it could absorb more of the impact and so limit the impact of the airbag on the body itself. Spider silk has even been considered as an ideal material to use in biodegradable bottles.

However, there's one significant problem. It isn't possible to obtain the amount of silk needed for applications like these from spiders. It would take ages to collect the material from their natural habitat, and farming spiders isn't possible as they are aggressive, territorial creatures who will attack and eat each other. Furthermore, because the silk goes hard when it's exposed to air, it's difficult to work with.

Scientists have tried to overcome some of these problems by taking the spider itself out of the equation. One team of scientists extracted the silk genes from two species of spiders and inserted them into cells from a cow. The cells were grown in the laboratory and produced the silk proteins that the scientists were able to harvest. The proteins were then spun into silky strands and the fibres produced were stronger than Kevlar, a material used to make bulletproof vests, but they were lighter than Kevlar and nearly as elastic as nylon. Scientists have also genetically engineered living goats that carry spider silk genes. The first two goat kids produced in this manner were called Webster and Pete. The hope is that milk from goats like these will contain significant amounts of usable spider silk proteins.

Another approach is to use silkworms. The silk from silkworms can be farmed in ways that spider silk can't and so researchers have looked at making genetic changes to the silkworm. The silk that's produced in this way is a mixture of silkworm silk and spider silk. Initial attempts created silk that was stretchy but not as strong as spider silk. However, researchers subsequently managed to increase the amount of spider silk by a factor of seven. One of the advantages of obtaining spider silk in this way is that the silk is ready for use as soon as it's spun by the insect.

A group of researchers at the University of Nottingham have developed artificial spider silk made of proteins that are similar to those in naturally produced spider silk. This man-made silk can be used in a variety of medical applications. It was shown to act as a scaffold or support for the growth of new tissue. The researchers were also able to coat it with an antibiotic, and their experiments showed that the antibacterial properties of the silk lasted for several days. So, thanks to its ability to release antibiotics in a controlled way, the silk could be used in the manufacture of dressings to treat wounds that take a while to heal.

We may only be a few years away from being able to see some of those applications in use. If the outcome of this research is that we'll be able to create materials with properties similar to those of spider silk, we might also be one step towards eradicating the production of synthetic materials that can have negative effects on the environment.

I hope this has given you an insight into the amazing spider. Next time you see one scuttling across the floor, stop to marvel at what it can achieve rather than jump on the sofa to escape.

Track 19

TEST 3   SPEAKING PART 1

In this first part of the exam, I'd like to ask you some questions about yourself. Let's talk about friends.
How often do you see your friends?
What do you like to do when you meet up with friends?
Do you still have friends from when you were young?
What qualities do you think make a good friend?
Let's move on to talk about the future. Do you think you will always live in the same town or city you live in now?
Do you think your local area will change much over the next few years?
How do you think your life might be different in 10 years' time?
Are you optimistic that we will solve the environmental problems we face today?

Track 20

TEST 3   SPEAKING PART 2

I'm going to give you a topic and I'd like you to talk about it for one or two minutes. Before you talk, you have one minute to think about what you are going to say. You can make some notes if you wish. Here is your topic. ... [one-minute pause] All right? Remember you have one or two minutes for this, so don't worry if I stop you. I'll tell you when the time is up. Can you start speaking now, please?

Track 21

TEST 3   SPEAKING PART 3

We've been talking about the subject of buildings. I'd like to discuss this subject with you with some more general questions relating to this topic.
First, do you think it's important to save old historic buildings?
Are modern buildings as impressive as those built in the past?
What kind of buildings are most memorable?
To what extent do the buildings in a city give it its character?
Why do tourists tend to spend so much time visiting important buildings?
What makes a house a home?

Track 22

TEST 4   LISTENING PART 1

Natalie: Thanks for agreeing to help out, Matti. It'll be much quicker with two of us. These training days take such a lot of organising. There are so many things to think about and you know how stressed I get when things don't go according to plan. If we can sort out the catering now, it'll be one less thing to think about.

Matti: No problem. I'm happy to help. I know what a nightmare these events can be. Where will everybody be eating?

Natalie: At first, I thought about having the food in the training room itself. That would be the least amount of trouble for everyone. Trouble is, it'd have to be hidden from them or they'll start snacking as soon as they arrive. We could use the main meeting room, I suppose. That would give them the chance to get outside the training room for a little while. As long as they don't go back to the office during lunch. I'd like them to mix and chat about the training. And there's more room for a large table there. Yes, let's do that.

Matti: Yes, I think that'll work. When do you want the food for: breakfast, lunch or both?

Natalie:	I thought it'd be nice to start the day with breakfast so they can eat before they start and it would give people a chance to chat before the training gets underway. We haven't got the budget for two lots of food, though, so Finance agreed to settle for lunch. We can supply teas and coffees ourselves in the morning when they arrive and again at about half past ten.
Matti:	Yes, that's a good idea. Maybe we could serve some biscuits too. So, who's attending the event? Who do we need to include?
Natalie:	It'll be all the sales team, of course. Then there's the office staff, three of them. Oh, and we need to feed the trainer as well.
Matti:	What about the manager? Is he going to be there?
Natalie:	I know he wanted to come but I don't think he'll be able to join us. His secretary just told me he has an important meeting that morning.
Matti:	OK. I've printed the order form off. Let's fill it in now and I can transfer the information online later. What's the date of the event?
Natalie:	We usually run training days during the first week of October but this year that proved difficult to timetable so we had to move it to the 13th of November. That's two weeks from today.
Matti:	And what time do we want the food delivered?
Natalie:	As early as possible, really. I don't want it arriving after we've started. The first session begins at nine so let's ask for eight. That'll give me time to sort it out before the trainer arrives at half past eight.
Matti:	So, how many people will we need the buffet for? The caterers will only deliver for a minimum of 10 people.
Natalie:	There'll be 15 altogether.
Matti:	Right. Now we have some options here, depending on how much we have to spend. There's the Standard Buffet package. That's £3.25 per person. All you get for that are sandwiches, crisps, hot and cold drinks. If I remember correctly, there were complaints from staff the last time we had a training event. Do you remember? They weren't happy with the sandwiches on offer – or something like that.
Natalie:	Yes, I vaguely remember. Well, what else do they offer?
Matti:	There's the Premium package. That's £5.50 per person and you get some additional snacks. There's a salad bowl and something for dessert, like fruit and cakes. I reckon it'll be more appreciated by staff than the first option, don't you?
Natalie:	Well, that's an easy one. We've got a budget of £6 per person so let's go for the Premium package.
Matti:	Do we know if there's anything anyone can't eat? Any vegetarians or vegans, for example? Or people with allergies?
Natalie:	I've emailed everyone who's attending. You'd think there'd be one or two vegetarians, but no. They're all meat eaters. There's one person who has to have dairy free food, though, and no one's said anything about allergies.
Matti:	Right. That's about it. The caterers need a contact person. I'll put you down, shall I?
Natalie:	No, not me. Put down Carol in Finance. She asked to be the contact person as she'll be sorting out payment. It's Carol Beecham. B-E-E-C-H-A-M.
Matti:	And what's her telephone number in Finance?
Natalie:	It's our number, 455 2298, Extension 523.
Matti:	That's done. One less job for you to worry about. I'll get back on their website and fill in these details.
Natalie:	Thanks, Matti! I owe you one!

Track 23

TEST 4   LISTENING PART 2

Speaker:	Thanks for giving me the chance to come along today to talk to you about the steps you can take to alleviate the ill effects of living through a heatwave. We certainly seem to have experienced a lot more of these recently, and with climate change an ongoing issue, things aren't likely to change in the near future. Extreme heat can be very uncomfortable for the fit and healthy and it can be quite dangerous for the more vulnerable. So, I'd like to give you some tips on how to remain as comfortable as possible during these challenging periods.
	OK, let's start by looking at what you can do inside the house. During the day, do what you can to keep direct sunlight out of rooms. If you have curtains or blinds, pull them shut. Having dark heavy curtains doesn't really help much in a heatwave as the material will trap the heat and transmit it into the room, so consider investing in lighter colours that don't absorb as much heat. And on the subject of windows, if it's safe to do so, keep windows open at night as this will allow the cooler air to circulate around the rooms. If you're one of the lucky people to have air conditioning in your home, you'll certainly appreciate being able to sit in a cool room but it's important to keep an eye on your energy usage. A simple alternative for those without air conditioning is to use a fan and place a bowl of ice in front of

it. Buy yourself a little spray bottle, you know, one of those cheap plastic bottles we use to spray water on plants in the garden, and spray cold water on your face. And treat yourself to a cool shower every so often. A packet of face wipes can also serve a similar purpose and help you cool down. Remember where your body's cooling points are, namely your wrists and the back of your neck. Put some cloths in the freezer and place them on these areas when you're feeling particularly hot.

Even if you do all of these things, you're still likely to be affected by the very high temperatures, and there are other things you should bear in mind. Pay close attention to your diet as this will help you to deal with the heat. It's really important to eat healthily in order to replace the vitamins and minerals you'll lose through sweating. Remember to drink lots of water, at least two litres a day. It's easy to forget to do this so keep a bottle of water by your side. But avoid drinking too much coffee as this can have the opposite effect and dehydrate you.

It's sometimes very tempting to pop outside and enjoy the sunny weather but during a heatwave it's best to leave the house only when necessary. Avoid going out between 11 a.m. and 3 p.m., when temperatures are at their highest. Try to stay in the shade when you're walking around and wear a hat with a wide brim to keep the sun off your face. You could even take an umbrella with you to give you some protection. Wear loose-fitting, light-coloured clothes. Anything made with cotton or linen is particularly suitable for hot weather. Of course, it's essential that you put lots of sun cream on whenever you go out. If you like to get some physical exercise on a daily basis and insist on going out for your daily run or whatever your favourite activity is, you should be prepared to reduce the effort you'd normally put into it. And remember to stay hydrated.

Finally, it's really important to consider how others might be affected by extreme heat. Certainly, don't leave your pets in a car with the windows closed. And remember to check on your neighbour if they happen to be old or have health issues. The elderly are particularly affected during a heatwave and will definitely benefit from you keeping an eye on their well-being. Just knock on their door each day to see if they're all right. And if they can't get out, why not help them out with some shopping?

Track 24

TEST 4   LISTENING PART 3

Student: Thanks for making time to see me, Mr Gregson. I really appreciate it. I've got an assignment due in for Professor Collins next Monday and I'm having a few problems with it. I was hoping you could help me with a few questions.

Tutor: Well, not with the topic itself, of course. It's not my area.

Student: No, I understand that. It's more about the writing process.

Tutor: OK, how far have you got?

Student: I haven't actually started yet. Professor Collins is away until next week and I thought I'd speak to you in the meantime. It took me a few days to get an appointment. The deadline's the end of next week so I need to get started as soon as possible.

Tutor: I hope you aren't going to use me as an excuse if you don't finish in time. Tutors usually set essays some time in advance of the deadline to give you the chance to read the required literature. If you leave it till the last minute, the books are often all out on loan. I presume you've got the reading list?

Student: Yes, there are lots of sources on there and I've managed to get hold of some of the main ones. I wanted to speak with you to get some more advice on essay writing. You know, just some general tips on what makes a good essay. I don't feel confident writing an academic piece of work but that lesson you gave everyone on planning essays was really useful.

Tutor: Pleased to hear it. You should always start by focusing on the question. Do you remember my advice? It's really important to underline any key words and make sure you check whether there's more than one part to the question. You'd be surprised how many students fail to do this and only provide a partial answer.

Student: Yes, I remember you telling us that. What confuses me are all the different words you see in a question, like 'analyse', 'discuss', 'evaluate', and so on. I'm never quite sure what the difference is between them.

Tutor: Well, that often depends on the context of the question. In your subject area, History, you're expected to be able to show you understand why certain events took place and to be able to evaluate various points of view. One historian will have a different opinion from that of another, and a good response to the question will show an understanding of the arguments put forward by different people. When you're asked to analyse or discuss or evaluate different views, it's often a similar exercise.

Student: Yes, I think I see what you mean. The essay for Professor Collins is on whether there would have been a revolution in Russia without Lenin, and yes, it's basically all about presenting different points of view.

Tutor: That's it. Now, I'm planning on holding a session on research and referencing with your year soon. You say you've managed to get some of the sources on the reading list?

Student:	Yes, there were a couple of books in the library that I managed to get. And there are journals we can use on the online portal.
Tutor:	Yes, that's very useful. The information in the journals will be up to date and a great addition to the books.
Student:	Is it best to avoid using blogs, wikis, that kind of thing?
Tutor:	Yes, definitely. Students who rely on internet sources like those tend to be marked down by assessors. You just can't trust the accuracy of the information and it's likely to be politically biased and often promotes a particular point of view.
Student:	But isn't that the case with the books we're recommended as well? The authors all have a particular opinion.
Tutor:	That's true. The books on the reading list will often have a wide range of opinions but they'll have been critically reviewed by other academics and will be respected by the academic community. The authors will have researched their subject thoroughly and basically met certain academic standards.
Student:	OK, I'll remember that. Thanks for your help.
Tutor:	No problem. The other thing to remember is to proofread your work carefully before you submit it.
Student:	Yes, I do tend to make some basic spelling mistakes.
Tutor:	Well, it's partly about that, yes, but you need to do a bit more than just check for spelling mistakes. Read your work through first to make sure your arguments are clear. Are the paragraphs well constructed and in a logical order?
Student:	Yes, that's where planning comes in, doesn't it?
Tutor:	Yes, and remember what I said earlier. Check you've answered the question fully and make sure everything you've written is relevant. Some students think it's all about hitting the word count and fill their essay with information that doesn't answer the question.
Student:	Yes, I think I might have been guilty of that in the past.
Tutor:	Once you've read through the main content, check your use of language. Make sure you haven't used any informal language. This is an academic piece of work so you don't want to be using slang words or idiomatic language. Watch out for any typing mistakes as well as incorrect spelling. And don't forget to check your grammar: your sentence structures need to be correct. Finally, punctuation can make a huge difference to how effective a piece of work is so give that some attention as well.
Student:	OK, I will do. Many thanks for all your help.

Track 25

TEST 4 LISTENING PART 4

Lecturer: Good morning, everyone, and welcome to week five in our sports coaching module. In this lecture we're going to look at the importance of strength training for amateur and professional athletes. One thing you'll often hear from people participating in a sport like running, cycling or swimming, and especially those who do it for fun rather than competitively, is how little, if any, strength training they do. They'll all tell you that they know it's good for them and worth doing but it's not their 'thing'. They like running, cycling or swimming, not lifting weights or doing pull-ups and press-ups.

Unfortunately for those with this attitude, without regular strength training, it's unlikely they'll achieve their full potential. They may also suffer long periods of inactivity through injury, and professional athletes may even find they have to retire from their sport too early. It may be something that doesn't come naturally but encouraging people to look outside of their chosen sport will benefit them in various ways. And it doesn't have to require a visit to their local gym or the use of special equipment.

It's unfortunately the case that people who do a sport are more likely to injure themselves than people who don't. Virtually all athletes will have an accident at some point or other. The accident could be something as minor as falling during a run and result in nothing more than grazed knees, but accidents can also lead to pulled muscles, torn ligaments or broken bones. These injuries are unpredictable and need to be dealt with as and when they occur. Sadly, there's not much a strength training regime can do to avoid injuries sustained this way.

However, much of the time an athlete spends injured is probably due to those accidents that could have been avoided with correct strength training. Each sport involves repetitive movements that over time put excessive pressure on joints and muscles, or that can lead to the body becoming out of balance. Think how much stronger a tennis player's dominant arm must be over the non-dominant one. This kind of imbalance can be avoided to some extent by cross-training, that is by doing more than one sport, such as running and cycling, which spreads the pressure on the body more evenly. However, nothing beats following a tailor-made strength training routine. Doing exercises that counteract repetitive movements and imbalances helps to create more all-round body strength. You'll become more flexible and you'll strengthen those muscles that are under-used, all of which will help avoid injury.

A training programme shouldn't just be focused on strengthening an athlete's muscles. It should be developed to suit their particular sport and also improve their flexibility, which, in turn, will affect their overall performance. No matter how strong you might be, if you can't touch your toes, that stiffness will work against you when you work out. Including flexibility exercises will help with muscle and joint movement, improve your posture and allow you to deal with the aches and pains of everyday life.

For older athletes or for those who wish to continue doing sport into their old age, strength training helps counteract the natural process of muscle loss. As the body gets older, it gradually loses the ability to convert the food we eat into muscle because it produces less of the hormones that are necessary to burn fat and build muscle. Weight training can boost the production of these hormones.

Strength training is important for other reasons as well. Let's not forget that it can also benefit a person's mental health. In the winter months, when the opportunities to participate in an athlete's chosen sport are few and far between, or during periods of injury, strength training can fill the gap and help the person feel they're still making progress. It's still possible to set goals and see improvements in strength or stamina and so it helps promote a positive attitude. Lengthy periods without exercise can seriously affect people used to working their bodies so a programme like this can help keep them motivated.

So, including a strength training programme for athletes, both amateur and professional, young and old, can help avoid injury, develop posture, increase strength and flexibility and maintain mental health.

Track 26

TEST 4   SPEAKING PART 1

In this first part of the exam, I'd like to ask you some questions about yourself. Let's talk about books and films.
What kind of books or films do you like?
Do you prefer reading digital or traditional books?
How often do you go to the cinema?
Would you prefer to spend an evening reading a book or going to the cinema?
Let's move on to talk about travelling. What form of transport do you use most often?
Is there any type of transport that you don't like?
What's the public transport system like in your country?
Is there anything about travelling around your local area that you would change?

Track 27

TEST 4   SPEAKING PART 2

I'm going to give you a topic and I'd like you to talk about it for one or two minutes. Before you talk, you have one minute to think about what you are going to say. You can make some notes if you wish. Here is your topic. ... [one-minute pause] All right? Remember you have one or two minutes for this, so don't worry if I stop you. I'll tell you when the time is up. Can you start speaking now, please?

Track 28

TEST 4   SPEAKING PART 3

We've been talking about the subject of presents. I'd like to discuss this subject with you with some more general questions relating to this topic.
First, do you think it's better to give rather than receive?
What type of gifts are particularly special for the person receiving them?
Is giving someone money for a birthday present more thoughtful than buying a gift?
Is it important how much we spend on a gift?
Are certain ages easier to buy presents for than others?
Why might it be good for a company to give a customer a free gift?

Sample answer sheet: Listening

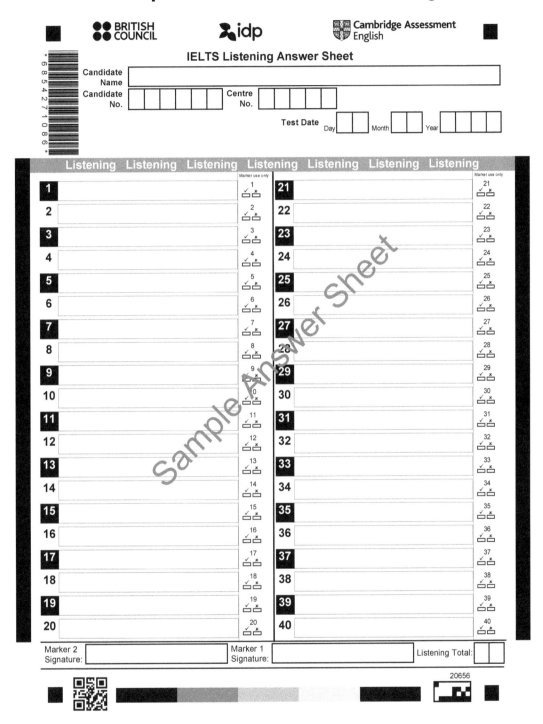

Sample answer sheet: Reading

BRITISH COUNCIL   **idp**   **Cambridge Assessment English**

IELTS Reading Answer Sheet

Candidate Name

Candidate No.   Centre No.

Test Module   ☐ Academic   ☐ General Training   Test Date   Day ☐☐   Month ☐☐   Year ☐☐☐☐

Reading   Reading   Reading   Reading   Reading   Reading   Reading

	Marker use only			Marker use only
1	1 ✓ ✗	**21**	21 ✓ ✗
2	2 ✓ ✗	22	22 ✓ ✗
3	3 ✓ ✗	**23**	23 ✓ ✗
4	4 ✓ ✗	24	24 ✓ ✗
5	5 ✓ ✗	**25**	25 ✓ ✗
6	6 ✓ ✗	26	26 ✓ ✗
7	7 ✓ ✗	**27**	27 ✓ ✗
8	8 ✓ ✗	28	28 ✓ ✗
9	9 ✓ ✗	**29**	29 ✓ ✗
10	10 ✓ ✗	30	30 ✓ ✗
11	11 ✓ ✗	**31**	31 ✓ ✗
12	12 ✓ ✗	32	32 ✓ ✗
13	13 ✓ ✗	**33**	33 ✓ ✗
14	14 ✓ ✗	34	34 ✓ ✗
15	15 ✓ ✗	**35**	35 ✓ ✗
16	16 ✓ ✗	36	36 ✓ ✗
17	17 ✓ ✗	**37**	37 ✓ ✗
18	18 ✓ ✗	38	38 ✓ ✗
19	19 ✓ ✗	**39**	39 ✓ ✗
20	20 ✓ ✗	40	40 ✓ ✗

Sample Answer Sheet

Marker 2 Signature: Marker 1 Signature: Reading Total:

61788

IELTS Reading Answer Sheet reproduced with permission of Cambridge Assessment English © UCLES 2021

Sample answer sheet: Writing

This is just one page of a longer booklet.

BRITISH COUNCIL   **idp**   **Cambridge Assessment English**

IELTS Writing Answer Sheet - TASK 1

Candidate Name

Candidate No.   Centre No.

Test Module ☐ Academic ☐ General Training   Test Date Day Month Year

If you need more space to write your answer, use an additional sheet and write in the space provided to indicate how many sheets you are using: Sheet ☐ of ☐

Writing   Task 1   Writing   Task 1   Writing   Task 1   Writing   Task 1

Sample Answer Sheet

Do not write below this line

Do not write in this area. Please continue your answer on the other side of this sheet.

23505

IELTS Writing Answer Sheet reproduced with permission of Cambridge Assessment English © UCLES 2021

Listening and Reading answer key

TEST 1   Listening

Part 1   Questions 1–10
1 A
2 B
3 B
4 56 Spring Road
5 B07 6QT
6 mixed media
7 14–16
8 intermediate
9 fish
10 CYP20

Part 2   Questions 11–20
11 rush hour
12 1st June / 1 June
13 email
14 limited
15 Parking
16 & 17 IN ANY ORDER
A
E
18–20 IN ANY ORDER
B
C
F

Part 3   Questions 21–30
21 B
22 A
23–25
B
D
G
26 overview
27 one page
28 structure
29 Sunday evening
30 in control

Part 4   Questions 31–40
31 C
32 B
33 A
34 B
35 travel
36 memory
37 hand
38–40 IN ANY ORDER
B
E
G

TEST 1   Reading

Passage 1   Questions 1–14
1 D
2 B
3 E
4 A
5 C
6 pressure
7 traps
8 organic waste
9 drain out
10 sterilises
11 TRUE
12 TRUE
13 FALSE
14 NOT GIVEN

Passage 2   Questions 15–28
15 D
16 C
17 B
18 B
19 A
20 B
21 stable
22 cool
23 hot
24 release
25 B
26 C
27 E
28 F

Passage 3   Questions 29–40
29 B
30 D
31 C
32 TRUE
33 TRUE
34 NOT GIVEN
35 FALSE
36 TRUE
37 FALSE
38 lifespan
39 replicate
40 energy

TEST 2   Listening

Part 1   Questions 1–10
1 96678
2 Horton
3 13th July
4 damp
5 refund
6 colour
7 next week
8 plastic discs
9 quality control
10 gift voucher

Part 2   Questions 11–20
11 A
12 B
13 A
14 10 p.m.
15 weekend pass
16 residential areas / the street
17 half hour / 30 minutes
18–20 IN ANY ORDER
A
C
E

Part 3   Questions 21–30
21 B
22 A
23 C
24 C
25 & 26 IN ANY ORDER
B
E
27 A
28 C
29 C
30 B

Part 4   Questions 31–40
31 A
32–34 IN ANY ORDER
B
D
F
35 A
36 C
37 online
38 interests / needs
39 questionnaire
40 free sample

TEST 2   Reading

Passage 1   Questions 1–14
1 NOT GIVEN
2 TRUE
3 NOT GIVEN
4 TRUE
5 FALSE
6 D
7 B
8 G
9 E
10 reflected

11 fuel
12 solar panels

13 (lunar / Moon's) poles
14 B

TEST 3   Reading

Passage 2   Questions 15–26

15 E
16 A
17 B
18 applies
19 credit rating
20 client
21 paying back

22 fee
23 & 24 IN ANY ORDER
   A
   D
25 & 26 IN ANY ORDER
   B
   C

Passage 3   Questions 27–40

27 vii
28 ii
29 iii
30 vi
31 viii
32 planetarium
33 sky map

34 retinas
35 light
36 different
37 beak(s)
38 chemicals
39 efficient
40 visual access

TEST 3   Listening

Part 1   Questions 1–10

1 website
2 retail assistant
3 English and French
4 sales assistant
5 window displays
6 June to August /
   June–August

7 planned trips
8 dance classes
9 7th June / 7 June
10 Tuesdays

Part 2   Questions 11–20

11 Toilets
12 Goat shed
13 Donkey rides
14 Rabbit house
15 Insect house

16 Picnic area
17 Gift shop
18 A
19 C
20 B

Part 3   Questions 21–30

21 B
22 B
23 C
24 B
25 & 26 IN ANY ORDER
   B
   D

27 career
28 reconsider
29 impression
30 contacts

Part 4   Questions 31–40

31 A
32 C
33 ancient Greeks
34 fishing lines
35 burn victims

36 impact
37 D
38 A
39 C
40 B

TEST 3   Reading

Passage 1   Questions 1–14

1 B
2 C
3 A
4 C
5 B
6 A
7 D
8 D

9 FALSE
10 TRUE
11 NOT GIVEN
12 FALSE
13 & 14 IN ANY ORDER
   C
   D

Passage 2   Questions 15–29

15 D
16 E
17 A
18 G
19 B
20 B
21 C
22 C

23 A
24 re-enter
25 penalties
26 stabilise
27 size
28 harpoons or nets
29 satellite service station

Passage 3   Questions 30–40

30 branches
31 shelter
32 disintegrates
33 cone
34 growth
35 broadens out

36 D
37 E
38 C
39 A
40 B

TEST 4   Listening

Part 1   Questions 1–10

1 C
2 C
3 C
4 13th November /
   13 November
5 8.00 / 8 a.m. / eight

6 15 / fifteen
7 £3.25
8 dairy-free / dairy free
9 Beecham
10 523

Part 2   Questions 11–20

11 direct sunlight
12 energy usage
13 cool shower
14 cooling points
15 sweating
16 11 to 3 / 11 a.m. to
   3 p.m. / eleven to three

17 umbrella
18 cotton or linen
19 physical exercise
20 health issues

Part 3   Questions 21–30

21 C
22 C
23 B
24 A
25 C

26 well constructed
27 relevant
28 typing mistakes
29 sentence structures
30 punctuation

Part 4   Questions 31–40

31 & 32 IN ANY ORDER
B
C
33 A
34 C
35 B

36 A
37 C
38 winter months
39 positive attitude
40 motivated

TEST 4   Reading

Passage 1   Questions 1–14

1 C
2 F
3 I
4 B
5 G
6 action
7 angle

8 re-form
9 undermined
10 crashing
11 absorbing
12 lifespan
13 D
14 B

Passage 2   Questions 15–29

15 hierarchy
16 emerge
17 cooperation
18 norms
19 performance
20 & 21 IN ANY ORDER
B
E

22 & 23 IN ANY ORDER
D
E
24 NOT GIVEN
25 TRUE
26 FALSE
27 NOT GIVEN
28 TRUE
29 TRUE

Passage 3   Questions 30–40

30 confusion
31 patterns
32 interpret
33 & 34 IN ANY ORDER
A
B
35 & 36 IN ANY ORDER

B
C
37 basis
38 fine-tunes
39 deletes
40 curation

GENERAL TRAINING TEST A
Reading

Section 1   Questions 1–14

1 iii
2 vii
3 v
4 viii
5 vi
6 D
7 C

8 A
9 E
10 C
11 D
12 B
13 F
14 D

Section 2   Questions 15–28

15 B
16 A
17 C
18 F
19 D
20 E
21 G

22 NOT GIVEN
23 FALSE
24 TRUE
25 FALSE
26 NOT GIVEN
27 TRUE
28 TRUE

Section 3   Questions 29–40

29 D
30 D
31 transparent
32 estuaries
33 colour
34 undersides

35 stomach(s)
36 London
37 glass eel
38 acidic waters
39 ocean currents
40 man-made

GENERAL TRAINING TEST B
Reading

Section 1   Questions 1–13

1 B
2 C
3 D
4 A
5 C
6 D
7 C

8 NOT GIVEN
9 TRUE
10 FALSE
11 TRUE
12 FALSE
13 NOT GIVEN

Section 2   Questions 14–28

14 TRUE
15 NOT GIVEN
16 FALSE
17 NOT GIVEN
18 FALSE
19 TRUE
20 NOT GIVEN
21 TRUE

22 TRUE
23 confusion
24 downtime
25 home
26 repeating
27 old-fashioned
28 pop-up

Section 3   Questions 29–40

29 iii
30 iv
31 v
32 i
33 ix
34 vi

35 A
36 C
37 E
38 D
39 B
40 F

Writing: model answers

Test 1 Task 1

This chart estimates the growth in freight transport around the world by air, road, rail and sea between 2010 and 2050, and the impact of this on carbon dioxide emissions.

All four means of transport show huge growth over this forty-year period. The largest percentage increase is in air freight transport, rising from 191 billion tons per kilometre in 2010 to 1,111 billion tons in 2050, a 482% increase. Sea transport is estimated to grow by 327%, from 60,053 billion tons per kilometre in 2010 to 256,433 billion in 2050. Road transport is expected to increase by 384% to 30,945 billion tons and rail by 349% to 19,126 billion tons.

Percentage growth in carbon dioxide emissions is greatest with air travel, from 150,000,000 tons in 2010 to 767,000,000 in 2050, a 411% increase. This compares to a 238% increase in sea transport, 304% for road and 250% for rail transport.

Overall, freight transport is expected to increase from 70,894 billion tons per kilometre in 2010 to 307,615 billion tons in 2050, which would lead to a 286% increase in carbon dioxide emissions.

Test 1 Task 2

It goes without saying that technology has had a huge impact on our reading habits and for many, the emergence of the e-book offers significant advantages over its hardback or paperback alternatives. However, there are many who would argue it would be wrong to predict the end of the traditional book.

The e-book offers several advantages that make it a popular choice. To begin with, the ordering process is far more convenient and the reader can download and be reading the book in seconds. Then, of course, there is the convenience of being able to store thousands of books in a hand-held gadget that we can take with us on our journey to work, on holiday or wherever else our lives take us. Finally, for younger people accustomed to using technology for various purposes, the use of an e-reader comes naturally and is, perhaps, more appealing.

It is difficult to argue against such a list of advantages, and what the traditional book offers the reader in comparison is not so easy to explain. Its supporters might argue that compared to the light emitted from screens, reading from paper is far better for our eyes. However, the true benefits are more intangible, such as the pleasure of holding a book in your hands, of enjoying the artwork on the cover, of feeling the pages pass through your fingers and the smell of a new book. Finally, seeing your favourite titles arranged neatly on a bookcase is a pleasure for many.

In conclusion, the advantages of the e-book far outweigh those of the traditional book. However, I feel both forms will be used by people in the foreseeable future.

Test 2 Task 1

These two graphs compare part-time and full-time employment patterns of both mothers and fathers of 3–4-year-old children between 1997 and 2017.

The line graph focuses on mothers and shows that women featured more in part-time than full-time employment. The percentage of those in part-time work remained relatively steady over the period covered, ranging from 35% to 40%. However, the number of women entering full-time employment increased over the same period, from 17% in 1997 to approximately 25% in 2017.

The bar chart looks at the equivalent figures for fathers, the vast majority of whom were in full-time employment. Figures in this category remained steady, ranging from just below to just over 90%. There was a slight increase in the percentage of fathers entering part-time employment, which peaked in 2016 at approximately 8%.

The two graphs suggest that despite slight changes in employment patterns, women were more likely to be responsible for childcare during this period of time than men.

Test 2 Task 2

The problem of loneliness and isolation amongst the older generation and the impact of this on mental health is a major concern in many countries around the world. What can lead to a person feeling isolated, and is there anything that can be done to avoid this?

Possibly one of the major reasons is retirement, which can have an enormous impact as busy working lives are replaced by days that can feel aimless. In addition, the death of a partner can result in someone living alone for the first time and can also lead to a growing sense of loneliness. In previous years, children would be around to keep in contact with elderly relatives. However, social and economic changes have meant that sons and daughters are more likely to live far away from parents, making regular contact difficult. In some countries, the situation is made worse by a decline in the sense of community that existed years ago.

Nevertheless, there are steps older people can take to avoid suffering from loneliness. There are always opportunities to get involved in the local community. Clubs and societies of all kinds exist to suit a wide range of interests. For those keen on volunteering, giving up a few hours a week to help out at a local organisation can replace the loss felt through retirement. For people who are less able to leave the house, inviting friends round for a coffee morning can be something to look forward to. And if the person is able to use technology, there are lots of opportunities to meet up with people online.

To sum up, an active social life is key to avoiding loneliness, and older people should be encouraged to see their diary as their best friend, filling it with enjoyable activities for the days and weeks ahead.

Test 3 Task 1

This line graph shows the changing demographics in Scotland between the years 1940 and 2020, looking at birth and death rates and overall population growth.

The birth rate peaked in 1940 at 2.5% but then dropped significantly in the five following years. There was a steep fall of 0.5% between 1940 and 1945 and then a marked decrease again between 1950 and 1960 of almost 1%. Since then, with one or two exceptions, the rate has continued to fall, reaching just 0.6% in 2020.

There was a noticeable fall in the death rate between 1940 and 1956 from 1.5% to 0.5% but this then remained relatively steady at between 0.5% to 0.3% in 2007. Since then there has been a steady increase and it is projected to reach around 0.8% in 2023.

The decline in the birth rate is reflected in the figures for overall population growth. Whilst this peaked more sharply around 1954, the rate of decline matched that of the birth rate until 1990, when overall growth continued to fall until going into negative growth in 2005.

Test 3 Task 2

It is a widely held belief that the domestic skills our grandparents may have had are lacking in the younger generation and few people would argue against encouraging the development of these skills today. However, the view that a change in the school curriculum could bring this about and reverse the trend is questionable.

In the past, people would enjoy nutritious meals that were home-cooked and only have an occasional treat in a restaurant on special occasions. In contrast, the virtually universal availability of takeaways and the large number of fast food outlets mean that today most younger people frequently rely on unhealthy processed food for their diet. What is more, this development has led to a decline in culinary skills and an increase in health conditions such as obesity. It is clearly a concern that most young people leaving home would find it a challenge to prepare and cook healthy meals throughout the week.

However, whether a change in the school curriculum would be sufficient on its own to improve matters is doubtful. Most people are aware of the unhealthy nature of fast food and lessons at school would probably not in themselves have a significant effect on behaviour. It would probably require a wider cultural change for this to happen. That said, there is a resurgence of interest in cooking as can be seen from the many cookery programmes that feature on TV. People are also taking a greater interest in animal welfare along with an increased interest in eating healthy ingredients. A wider exposure to this kind of information in the media as well as lessons in domestic science might eventually lead to the positive changes we would all like to see.

Test 4 Task 1

This flow-chart outlines the steps that should be taken by an organisation when deciding to take on a new employee to fill a role.

Once a company has decided that a position needs to be filled, it is necessary to get approval. This might have to come from the Human Resources team or the person in charge of the area of work, such as the Head of Department. If the request to take on a new member of staff is declined, a discussion should be had with the Head of Department to decide what should be done to resolve the situation. If the request is approved, a job description or advertisement can be drawn up and given to the Human Resources team.

Following the placement of the advertisement, the applications that are received are assessed. Applications that are not suitable can be discarded. Qualified candidates should be added to a shortlist and called for an interview. Finally, if someone is suitable for the role, they can be offered the position.

Test 4 Task 2

Our widespread participation in social media in recent years has led to the emergence of what is termed 'social media influencers'. These online entrepreneurs are people who have created a positive reputation amongst their followers for providing knowledge or expertise on a particular subject. As a result, brands have seen them as a means of promoting their product or service to thousands and sometimes millions of people and therefore form a business partnership with them.

Because of the relationship they develop with their fans, the opinions of social media influencers can be very persuasive. People tend to trust information and opinions from people they can identify with. Consequently, if the influencer is seen to use a particular product or has positive things to say about one, their audience is likely to trust their recommendation. If this recommendation is authentic, it can benefit all concerned. The influencer will maintain their trusted relationship with their followers, their audience will be able to make an informed purchasing decision, and the company concerned might sell more products or services.

However, if the promotion lacks authenticity, there can be problems. If an influencer does not make it clear that a company has paid them to promote a particular product, the positive relationship between them and their audience can be undermined if the fact becomes known. Followers are likely to accept paid promotions if these are made apparent but not if a promotion is presented as anything other than an advertisement.

To sum up, just as online reviews now serve a worthwhile purpose in helping us decide whether to pay for something or not, social media influencers can be equally helpful but only if what they say is authentic and based on trust.

General Training Test A Task 1

Dear Martin,

Great to hear from you! I'm so pleased you're still able to visit me for that weekend in October – the dates you suggested are fine, by the way.

You said you were travelling down by train – it's easy to get to my house from the station. As you leave the exit, there's a bus stop immediately in front of you – you need the number 4. It's about a ten-minute journey. Ask the driver to tell you when you've reached the library. If you call me when you're on the way, I'll meet you there.

I know you're into music and there's a great band playing at a local venue on Saturday so I thought we could go and see that. But feel free to tell me if you'd like to do something else. I should warn you it's getting a little cold now so you'd better bring some warm clothes to wear and something to stay dry in case it rains.

Looking forward to seeing you soon!

Best wishes,
Tom

General Training Test A Task 2

Learning a second language is a huge challenge: it takes a great deal of time and effort, and language students are understandably keen to make progress as quickly as possible. This gives rise to the question of whether it is better to study in a country where the language is spoken or to try to achieve proficiency while staying at home.

For most language students, studying the language in their own country is the only option. It is certainly cheaper than travelling and living abroad and is less disruptive to family or work life. Students can have lessons at a local school at a time that is convenient. In addition to formal classes, there are lots of opportunities to get further practice online, whether that involves listening to podcasts and videos, reading newspapers and online magazines, or taking part in speaking practice through the various video conferencing technologies available.

However, it is obviously the case that spending a period of time abroad would be very beneficial. Being immersed in the target language throughout the day means a student is able to pick it up more quickly, and their listening and speaking skills in particular could improve significantly. Moreover, they also have the chance to experience the culture of the country concerned, which can be educational in itself.

Clearly, if the student concerned does not have any work or family commitments and has the necessary financial resources, a long period of time abroad would be beneficial. For most people, however, perhaps the best solution is a compromise. For example, if the person concerned is sitting an exam, a week or two spent in the target country could improve their fluency and listening skills.

General Training Test B Task 1

Dear Sir or Madam,

I am writing with regards to a recent visit my wife and I paid to your restaurant and some of the problems we faced.

Despite the fact that I had previously phoned your restaurant to book a table for two at 7.00 p.m. on 11th August, when we arrived, I was surprised to be told there was no reservation in our name. Fortunately, there was one table free and although this was right by the door, we accepted it as the only option. We were each given menus but were told that several of the dishes were unavailable. The few that were left were not meals that we would normally order, but as we had no choice in the matter, we chose from the limited dishes remaining.

We then had to wait for almost one hour for our meals to be served. We pointed this out to the waiter, who informed us that there was a new chef on duty, that things were a little slower than normal, and that we should be patient. When our meals arrived, they were both very disappointing. My steak was incredibly tough and the chicken my wife had ordered was over-cooked. To make matters worse, after we complained, the waiter simply said his shift was over and we would need to speak to someone else.

As you can imagine, this was not the kind of evening we had planned. Given the poor service and food, I am requesting a full refund of the costs of our meals. I would also suggest you speak to your staff and instruct them to be more sympathetic to your customers and try to be more helpful in future.

Yours faithfully,
Edward Collins

General Training Test B Task 2

In many countries around the world, a larger number of people are choosing to become self-employed than ever before. In some cases, this may have been forced on them through company restructuring and redundancies; in other cases, it is a deliberate career move. What are the advantages of this form of employment, and are there any drawbacks?

One of the major advantages of working for yourself is being able to make your own decisions. These might be creative choices, such as deciding what you want to sell or provide to customers as well as the hours you want to work. In addition, seeing your own business grow and become successful can be very satisfying, knowing that it is the result of your own hard work. Finally, being self-employed and working from home means there is no morning or evening commute, leaving more time for family life.

There are significant disadvantages, however. A self-employed person will often not have access to the same benefits an employed person would have, such as sick pay and holiday entitlement. Working for yourself can involve very long hours, especially at the beginning, when you are trying to build a customer base. Furthermore, your income can be unpredictable, and knowing you are the only person responsible for earning money to pay the bills can be very stressful. Last but not least, working for yourself can be quite isolating and some people will miss the company of other colleagues.

All in all, self-employment can be immensely rewarding for those who follow this path but it requires hard work, dedication and nerves of steel to make it a success. For those people with the necessary qualities, it can be an exciting career move.

Speaking: model answers

Track 29

Test 1 Part 1

In this first part of the exam, I'd like to ask you some questions about yourself.
Let's talk about your daily routines. What time do you usually get up?
It depends which day of the week it is. Monday to Friday, I have to get up early to go to college, so about seven thirty. But at weekends, if I haven't got anything to do, I like to stay in bed until around nine.

What do you like to eat for breakfast?
It's usually something light, like some toast or cereal. I prefer to wait until lunchtime to have a larger meal. What I really like to have as soon as I get up is a strong coffee.

Would you say the morning is your favourite part of the day?
Well, at weekends I enjoy a slow, relaxing start to the day and so yes, I like the mornings on Saturdays and Sundays. But mornings during the week are a bit too busy so I prefer the evenings.

If you could change anything about your daily routine, what would it be?
I wish I could be more organised in the morning. I'd like to do keep fit exercises before breakfast. I've tried a few times but I never seem to have enough time and haven't been able to make it a habit.

Let's move on to talk about celebrations. Do you enjoy going to parties?
To be honest, not as much as I used to. I enjoy family get-togethers as they're quite relaxed. But I'm not a fan of late-night parties with friends as I find them quite tiring.

What do people like to celebrate in your country?
Most people celebrate family events like birthdays, weddings, that kind of thing. Of course, there are also cultural and religious celebrations that people take part in. And there's always a huge celebration in places where a local football team has won a competition.

What's your favourite celebration?
That's a tricky question. I love it when it's something the community enjoys, like a big cultural event, but if I think about it, the celebrations I remember most of all are the parties that I go to with my family.

Would you say it's more fun celebrating with friends or relations?
I have to say that the ones I like best are with my family. I enjoy getting together with my friends and we have a lovely time when we go out for a meal or have a party, but it's nice to be surrounded by family members, especially uncles and aunts I haven't seen for a while.

Test 1 Part 2

I'm going to give you a topic and I'd like you to talk about it for one or two minutes. Before you talk, you have one minute to think about what you are going to say. You can make some notes if you wish. Here is your topic. ... All right? Remember you have one or two minutes for this, so don't worry if I stop you. I'll tell you when the time is up. Can you start speaking now, please?
OK, well, the shop I like visiting most is a small place in my town called 'Misty'. It's a tiny independent store that sells things for the home. It hasn't been open long but it's become really popular. Everything in there is beautiful, whether you're looking for an item of furniture for the living room, an ornament or something nice for the garden. I'd imagine the shop appeals more to women than men; certainly, when I go, there are often more women inside looking around while their husbands or partners stand outside waiting for them to come back out. I think people who

like to be surrounded by beautiful things enjoy going there. It's also a great place to go if you want to buy someone a present. If I had the chance, I'd buy everything on sale. The thing I like most about the shop is that the things it sells are different to what you find in the chain stores. They're handmade and produced by small local businesses and so you know you're buying something that nobody else has. It also sells a lot of things that have been recycled. For example, you'll often find an old cupboard or wardrobe that's been sanded down and painted in lovely patterns that make it look very bright and modern. Yes, that's definitely my favourite shop.

Test 1 Part 3

We've been talking about the subject of shops and shopping. I'd like to discuss this subject with you with some more general questions relating to this topic. First, do you think people often buy things they don't really need?
Well, I definitely have. It's very easy to fall in love with an item of clothing or a gadget of some kind and then change our mind when we get home. I think most people have lots of things in their homes that they've bought and never used, or used once and then forgotten about.

What are the advantages of shopping on the high street rather than online?
For me, the most important thing about the high street is that it's a place where you can walk around, window shop and actually examine the thing you might want to buy. Also, if it's a local high street, you might bump into friends you haven't seen for a while and that's always good.

How important is good customer service?
In my opinion, being treated well by shop assistants is really important. For example, I think it's nice to be left alone when you walk into a shop so that you can look around without feeling under pressure to buy. But if you have a question, it's always good to have someone who's knowledgeable to help you.

Do you think shops should be required to close on certain days?
I know that in my country in the past, shops used to be closed on Sundays. On the one hand, that was good because it gave everyone a day to relax and spend time with their families. But on the other hand, days can be quite boring if the shops are closed and you don't have anywhere else to go.

What are the benefits of going shopping with a friend?
Well, apart from having company, I think one advantage is that your friend can give you their opinion when you buy something. I mentioned earlier about buying things you don't need. Perhaps you are less likely to do this if you have someone with you to make you think before you spend your money.

In which ways do adverts persuade us to buy a particular product?
I think they try to make us feel our lives will be better or that we'll be happier if we buy the product. For example, if we drink their brand of coffee, we'll be surrounded by friends, or if we buy this meal for our family, we'll all sit around the table laughing and having fun.

Track 30

Test 2 Part 1

In this first part of the exam, I'd like to ask you some questions about yourself.
Let's talk about the weather. Tell me about the weather in your country.
In general, we have quite a mild climate. But perhaps because of global warming, it can get quite hot in the summer. We've also had a lot of flooding in parts of the country, which have also increased in recent years.*

What kind of weather do you like best?
I don't like extreme weather conditions. Snowy weather or really hot sunny days don't appeal to me at all. I prefer the weather during spring. It's not too hot and the days also get longer.

What kind of weather do you like when you go on holiday?
We usually spend our holidays walking in the countryside so I prefer dry weather. It's not very enjoyable walking in heavy rain. And not too sunny either as it's easy to get sunburned if you're outside a lot of the day.

Would you prefer to live in a country with a hot or cold climate?
Actually, I don't really like extreme weather conditions. The climate is quite mild in my country and it never really gets uncomfortable. I'm really not at all keen on cold weather so I wouldn't like to live anywhere where it snows a lot.

Let's move on to talk about exercise. Do you like to keep fit?
Yes, I take part in a lot of different sports. I play football for my college and go swimming once or twice a week. Having said that, I'm not fond of going to the gym. I find that a bit boring.

Which sports are popular in your country?
Football, probably. It's certainly the one that most people talk about and watch on TV even if they don't play it. However, I read once that fishing is also very popular and possibly the activity that most people take part in.

Did you do any sports when you were younger that you don't do now?
I used to play basketball when I was at school but I wasn't very good at it and didn't continue with it when I left. We used to do gymnastics as well and I enjoyed that. But again, I didn't do that once I finished school.

Is there a sport you'd like to do that you've never done before?
I can't swim but I'd love to learn. I've had lessons in the past, but I found it quite difficult. I'm always disappointed when I go on holiday with my friends and can't join them in the swimming pool or in the sea.

Test 2 Part 2

I'm going to give you a topic and I'd like you to talk about it for one or two minutes. Before you talk, you have one minute to think about what you are going to say. You can make some notes if you wish. Here is your topic. ... All right? Remember you have one or two minutes for this, so don't worry if I stop you. I'll tell you when the time is up. Can you start speaking now, please?
Food plays an important part in my life so this is a good question. It's really hard to choose just one meal as there are several things I enjoy eating. But if I had to choose one, it would be a curry, perhaps one with chicken, from a restaurant near where I live. We eat a lot of foreign food at home, for example Chinese, Italian and Indian. Usually my friends and I will take it in turns to cook and we have curry at least once a week. Our cooking is OK most of the time but we have a takeaway on Friday evening as a treat. It's always difficult trying to decide what to have but I try to persuade them to order Indian food. In the area where I live, there are lots of Indian restaurants and I've probably tried them all, but there's one in particular that makes really nice curries. There are so many different kinds and it depends on your taste which one you'd like best. What makes Indian food special for me is all the spices used. I usually order a hot curry, a dish with extra chilli in it. The first few mouthfuls burn a bit, of course, but you slowly get used to the heat. The food is always beautifully cooked and they often give you something free, like small side dishes.

Test 2 Part 3

We've been talking about the subject of food. I'd like to discuss this subject with you with some more general questions relating to this topic. First, what is the appeal of eating out in a restaurant?
I think one reason is that others do all the work: cooking the food, serving it and washing up afterwards. But also, it's exciting to eat out, especially if it's a nice restaurant with high quality food.

What do you think makes a good dinner host?
They should be able to cook. It wouldn't be a very nice evening if the meal wasn't tasty. I think it's important that a host makes you feel comfortable as well. And they should also be good at keeping the conversation going to encourage everyone to have a good time.

Fast food is often criticised by food experts so why is it so popular with people?
Probably because it's quick and convenient. If you've had a busy day at work or have been studying all day long, you might not want to spend time cooking. In some places you can just drive in, order your food, pay and drive home so it's very easy.

Do you think it's always best to eat food with ingredients that have been produced locally?
I think it's good for the environment. It means food isn't being transported around the country or even around the world. It's obviously also good for the local economy if food is bought from farmers and other food producers in the area.

Is it important to eat together at the dinner table rather than in front of the TV, for example?
My parents always made me and my sister eat at the table at mealtimes. We weren't allowed to have our mobile phones with us when we were eating. In my opinion, this was a good idea as it meant we were able to talk to each other and find out what was going on in our lives at the time.

How can we best encourage people to eat a healthy diet?
To be honest, I think you need to start by educating children so that they get into good habits. It's a good idea to encourage them to help prepare food. I think there's more chance they'll eat things they normally wouldn't like if they are involved more in cooking.

Track 31

Test 3 Part 1

In this first part of the exam, I'd like to ask you some questions about yourself.
Let's talk about your friends. How often do your see your friends?
I have two different groups of friends. The people I know from college I see most days, when we're studying and sometimes at weekends. I have some good friends from my dance class as well. We meet up for classes and often go to each other's houses.

What do you like to do when you meet up with friends?
We love to chat about what's happening in our lives. And we often go into town together and walk around the shops. We spend ages trying on clothes and giving each other our opinion about whether something suits us.

Do you still have friends from when you were young?
Not really. I don't see the friends I had when I was very young as we all went to different schools. I still keep in touch with the ones I met at secondary school, though. One of them is my closest friend.

What qualities do you think make a good friend?
In my opinion, you should be able to trust a good friend. If you have a problem, it's always important to be able to talk about it with someone. Even if they can't offer any help, a good friend should be willing to listen. That's what I like best about my closest friend, anyway.

Let's move on to talk about the future. Do you think you will always live in the same town or city you live in now?
That's a good question. On the one hand, I'd like to stay here as this is where my family all live and I'd hate to be apart from them. But on the other hand, I might have to move away for my job, so I imagine it's possible I could live somewhere else.

Do you think your local area will change much over the next few years?
Probably yes. We have a local shopping centre which has suffered a lot because people are buying things online or travelling into the city centre. Apparently, they're planning to convert the empty shops into accommodation so that will be a big difference.

How do you think your life might be different in 10 years' time?
Well, I'm engaged to my girlfriend so I expect I'll be married by then and have children. I hope I'll be working as an accountant because that's the course I'm doing at the moment.

Are you optimistic that we will solve the environmental problems we face today?
I think so, yes. People realise how serious the situation is and in the past few years our government has started to take more steps to deal with some of the problems in our country.

Test 3 Part 2

I'm going to give you a topic and I'd like you to talk about it for one or two minutes. Before you talk, you have one minute to think about what you are going to say. You can make some notes if you wish. Here is your topic. ... All right? Remember you have one or two minutes for this, so don't worry if I stop you. I'll tell you when the time is up. Can you start speaking now, please?
A few years ago I visited Barcelona with some friends. We had a long list of things we wanted to do and places we wanted to see but the most important one for all of us was La Sagrada Familia. If you've never heard of it, it's a large church or cathedral, I'm not sure which. It was designed by the famous architect Gaudí. We'd read so much about it in our tourist guides before we arrived and the photos of it were spectacular so we decided we had to see it. There were lots of other things we planned to do so in the end we decided to go there on the last day of our holiday. We took the subway from our hotel and when we arrived and came out of the train station, we couldn't believe our eyes. In front of us on the other side of the road was this enormous building. It was absolutely stunning. The stained-glass windows, the columns that rise up in the sky and the stone work are unbelievable. The building is still under construction, but this didn't spoil the experience at all. Unfortunately, there were also hundreds, maybe even thousands, of people who all wanted to get inside to see the interior and we decided not to queue to get in.

Test 3 Part 3

We've been talking about the subject of buildings. I'd like to discuss this subject with you with some more general questions relating to this topic. First, do you think it's important to save old historic buildings?
Yes, I do. There are lots of beautiful old buildings where I live that were built over a hundred years ago. They include lots of public buildings that have closed down and are no longer used. Quite often these get knocked down and replaced with modern office buildings or car parks. I think it would be better to try to save them if possible.

Are modern buildings as impressive as those built in the past?
I think a lot of them are. The older buildings are usually built with bricks, with lots of carvings on the outside, whereas modern buildings tend to be made with glass or more modern materials. That's the fashion today and in the future I think people will think they look as impressive as older buildings look now.

What kind of buildings are most memorable?
Huge buildings, like cathedrals or very tall skyscrapers always have a big impact on people. I think cathedrals in particular, or other religious buildings, are always very impressive because the architect spent a lot of time making them look beautiful, inside and outside.

To what extent do the buildings in a city give it its character?
I don't know, really. I haven't travelled a lot but I've seen photos and videos of cities around the world. Some cities seem very modern because they have lots of new shiny buildings. However, other cities like London or Paris have far more older buildings that make them feel more historic. So yes, I suppose buildings are important in that way.

Why do tourists tend to spend so much time visiting important buildings?
When you visit a new city, especially in a different country, it's our chance to see famous places. Some people go because it's something they feel they have to do. It's like a list of things they have to see. But other people will visit a building because it's something they've really looked forward to seeing with their own eyes.

What makes a house a home?
I don't think it's the building that makes a house a home. Some people live in very small apartments and others in large houses but they are all homes. It's what people do inside that's important. If it's warm and cosy with photographs of the people we love, I think a place will feel like home.

Track 32

Test 4 Part 1

In this first part of the exam, I'd like to ask you some questions about yourself.
Let's talk about books and films. What kind of books or films do you like?
I enjoy reading and don't really have a favourite genre but lately I've been reading a lot of science fiction. As far as films are concerned, I really like crime thrillers.

Do you prefer reading digital or traditional books?
It depends, really. If I'm travelling to college or on holiday, I like to read e-books as they're on my tablet and then I don't have to carry a book with me. But if I'm at home, I prefer a real book.

How often do you go to the cinema?
I don't go as often as I'd like. There isn't a cinema near my house and I have to go into town if I want to see a film. So, I probably go once a month or even once every two months.

Would you prefer to spend an evening reading a book or going to the cinema?
I really enjoy going to the cinema and I try to see a film every month or two. But actually, I also like lying on the sofa and reading a good book. It's much more relaxing than catching a train or a bus into town to go to the cinema.

Let's move on to talk about travelling. What form of transport do you use most often?
I go to college every day on the bus from my house so that's the one I use most often. The journey takes about half an hour and I have to catch two buses.

Is there any type of transport that you don't like?
I'm not fond of flying or of travelling on a ship. Being on a plane makes me feel quite anxious, especially when you take off and land. And I've only been on a ship once but I got quite seasick.

What's the public transport system like in your country?
In my city it's very good. The buses are reliable and the trains always run on time. People don't mind leaving their cars at home to go to work as the service is always good.

Is there anything about travelling around your local area that you would change?
I think they should create more cycle lanes. More people would probably travel to work or to their college or university if the roads were safer for cyclists. At the moment, if you ride a bike, you have to share the road with cars and lorries, which isn't very nice.

Test 4 Part 2

I'm going to give you a topic and I'd like you to talk about it for one or two minutes. Before you talk, you have one minute to think about what you are going to say. You can make some notes if you wish. Here is your topic. ... All right? Remember you have one or two minutes for this, so don't worry if I stop you. I'll tell you when the time is up. Can you start speaking now, please?
Well, I've received lots of nice gifts in the past from my friends and family but I think the one that comes to mind most of all is something my sister gave me last year for my birthday. She always gives people something thoughtful and for my birthday she made a photo album of my running achievements. On the inside page was a photo of the first race I'd done. I think it was a five-kilometre run. My sister had also done this run so the photo was of both of us

at the end of the race, holding our medals. She used each page for a different event or a big achievement and under each photo she wrote a nice message. Some of the messages were really funny. The pages are thick black paper and she used white ink to write the messages, which makes the whole thing look lovely. It was one of the nicest presents I've ever received. It shows how my running has become better over the past few years and the photos are memories of some happy occasions. The album was only about half full when she gave it to me so there are lots of pages left for future runs. Each time I do a special one, I add a photo and my sister writes a message next to it. There are lots of pages in the album and I think I'll be adding photos to it for many more years. It was a really thoughtful gift and I'm sure I'll save it forever.

Test 4 Part 3

We've been talking about the subject of presents. I'd like to discuss this subject with you with some more general questions relating to this topic. First, do you think it's better to give rather than receive?
It's always lovely to receive a present from someone, but I think it's better to give. It's a great feeling to give someone something they really value.

What type of gifts are particularly special for the person receiving them?
I think it's always nice when someone gives something that the person has mentioned in the past. For example, if a friend or a relative is chatting with someone and you hear them say there's something they were thinking of buying or have always wanted, getting them that means you've listened to them and shows it's a thoughtful present.

Is giving someone money for a birthday present more thoughtful than buying a gift?
Sometimes it might be. There might be something they're saving up for and giving them some money towards it could be better than buying them something they might not really want.

Is it important how much we spend on a gift?
Not at all. I learned an expression in English, 'It's the thought that counts', and I think this is true. Anyway, lots of people don't have enough money to spend a lot on a present but they can still get something that's valued.

Are certain ages easier to buy presents for than others?
Definitely yes. I have young nephews and nieces and it's always easy to choose something for them. But I find it quite difficult thinking of what to buy my older relatives as they usually have the things they want.

Why might it be good for a company to give a customer a free gift?
I think it's important that a company show customers they're appreciated. If they've been buying products or services from a company for a long time, giving the person a free gift shows them the company values their custom.

---

* In Track 30 on page 187, the test taker uses the incorrect form of the verb 'have'. It should be '... which has also increased in recent years.'